מסורה / ArtScroll Series®

Rabbi Nosson Scherman / Rabbi Meir Zlotowitz
General Editors

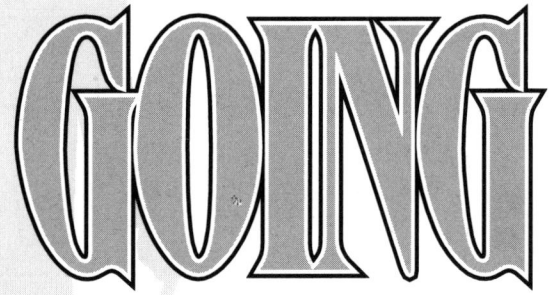

GOING

Published by
Mesorah Publications, ltd

FORWARD

A True Story of Courage, Hope and Perseverance

by
Peska Friedman
with **Fayge Silverman**

FIRST EDITION
First Impression . . . October 1994

Published and Distributed by
MESORAH PUBLICATIONS, Ltd.
4401 Second Avenue
Brooklyn, New York 11232

Distributed in Europe by
J. LEHMANN HEBREW BOOKSELLERS
20 Cambridge Terrace
Gateshead, Tyne and Wear
England NE8 1RP

Distributed in Israel by
SIFRIATI / A. GITLER — BOOKS
4 Bilu Street
P.O.B. 14075
Tel Aviv 61140

Distributed in Australia & New Zealand by
GOLD'S BOOK & GIFT CO.
36 William Street
Balaclava 3183, Vic., Australia

Distributed in South Africa by
KOLLEL BOOKSHOP
22 Muller Street
Yeoville 2198, Johannesburg, South Africa

THE ARTSCROLL SERIES®
GOING FORWARD

© Copyright 1994, by MESORAH PUBLICATIONS, Ltd. and Peska Friedman
4401 Second Avenue / Brooklyn, N.Y. 11232 / (718) 921-9000

ALL RIGHTS RESERVED.

This text, prefatory and associated textual contents and introductions,
including the typographic layout, cover artwork, charts and maps
have been designed, edited and revised as to content, form and style.

No part of this book may be reproduced
in any form without **written** permission from the copyright holder,
except by a reviewer who wishes to quote brief passages in connection with a review
written for inclusion in magazines or newspapers.

THE RIGHTS OF THE COPYRIGHT HOLDER WILL BE STRICTLY ENFORCED.

ISBN
0-89906-615-1 (hard cover)
0-89906-616-X (paperback)

Typography by Compuscribe at ArtScroll Studios, Ltd.

Printed in the United States of America by Noble Book Press Corp.
Bound by Sefercraft, Quality Bookbinders, Ltd. Brooklyn, N.Y.

*This book is dedicated
to my mother, a"h.
Thanks to her wisdom
and good judgment,
I went forward to life.*

Acknowledgments

There are a few people who deserve abundant thanks for helping me bring this project to completion. The first is Mr. Yosef Friedenson, my dear friend from the Warsaw ghetto, who helped me with names and dates, and who enhanced the manuscript with his incisive comments. His professional knowledge and advice provided the book with a great measure of historical authenticity.

I would like to thank my dear sister, Devorah Landau, for her constant encouragement. She urged me to persist in the project even when its realization seemed most remote, and she also provided me with valuable articles and pictures from our shared past.

To Rebbetzin Leah Brown I owe a special debt of gratitude for helping me formulate my memories. In our stimulating interview sessions, she helped me bring out my recollections with the proper flavor, and her continual reassurance gave me the courage to follow the book through to the end.

Finally, I would like to thank Fayge Silverman, my wonderful writer. Through our fruitful collaboration and friendship, we were able to create the book I have dreamt of for many years.

Before closing, I would like to mention that my intentions in writing the book were purely for the sake of fulfulling my mother's charge. In the process, I hope that I have done justice to the portrayal of all the dear family members and friends who are mentioned in the narrative.

Peska Friedman

Foreword

The holy Belzer Rebbe, Rabbi Aharon Rokeach זצ״ל — who himself was saved from Hitler's clutches only through a series of miracles — is said to have declared, "Every Jew who was in the hands of the wicked ones and managed to emerge alive could have done so only if two or three angels were escorting and protecting him. Otherwise his survival is incomprehensible."

Everyone who was there — in the ghettos, the concentration camps, or even concealed in a forest with partisans — can vouch for the truth of his comment.

The sadistic Nazi enemy was determined to kill us all. Hitler had pronounced a death sentence on every Jewish man, woman, and child. Doom lurked constantly at every footstep. With every movement we were surrounded by the danger of death, often the most horrible and painful kind.

Consequently, every survivor has his own remarkable and dramatic rescue story, which deserves to be recorded for posterity; although they may often seem a bit similar, they are still not the same. It is quite understandable, therefore, that many who lived through that hell feel an inner compulsion to share their story, to say in their own way "Blessed is Hashem Who did not present us as prey for their teeth " (*Psalms* 124:6).

But among all the stories of rescue and survival, there are some that are especially extraordinary, interesting, and even unique. Surely one of them is the memoir of Peska Friedman, member of a well-known and distinguished rabbinic family, whose father, the Partzever Rebbe, was the leader of a large chassidic community and whose mother — also the descendant of prominent chassidic leaders — was famed as a wise and righteous woman. After the liberation, Peska became the wife of the late Wolf Friedman, a prominent leader of the *She'aris Hapleitah* community. Together they established a home that was worthy of their glorious legacy.

What makes her memoir particularly unique is that it is not limited to the Holocaust period. She brings us into the joyous years of her youth in Warsaw and shares with us memories of her parents' home and the family's background in the chassidic *shtetl* of Sziedlice, of the Jewish metropolis of Warsaw, and of the many Torah personalities who frequented her mother's guest house on Warsaw's famous Gensha Street. Sadly, there are few still among us who can portray that vanished epoch and describe its inner beauty.

Of great historic value are her memories of the German bombardment and occupation of Warsaw, of life in the Warsaw ghetto, and, of course, her account of the bitter years of annihilation and the series of miracles that led to her salvation from a long string of dangers. Mrs. Friedman adds a poignant and inspiring chapter about the inadequately reported phenomenon of the survivors' longing and striving to create their own families, build on the ruins, and renew the Jewish life that refused to succumb to destruction. This, too, is a significant and inspiring lesson.

Her book captivates the reader. For all its pathos and tragedy, it is an uplifting, optimistic story. Its title conveys its message: Going Forward. Mrs. Friedman always looked ahead — and draws us along with her.

Joseph Friedenson

Introduction

I was twenty years old when my mother sent me out of the ruins of the Warsaw ghetto, the last of the eight children she lost either to death or separation. She knew that she would never see me again. As I stood on the bottom step of the staircase in the lobby of our apartment building, she called down to me, "Peska, I want you to promise me two things. One is that when you get married one day, you will wear a *sheitel*. The other is that you will someday write a book about what happened to us during the war."

Of course, I immediately gave her my word. But I was too young then to understand the full implications of her requests. It did not make sense to me why, out of all the things on earth she could have asked for, she had singled out these two items.

Now that I am older, my mother's wisdom grows clearer and clearer to me with each passing day. She had no idea what would become of me when I left the ghetto illegally on that cold spring day in 1941. She was sending me out of a *rebbe's* household, away from an upbringing that glowed with the spark of the Forefathers and the love of G-d, into the unholy wasteland of the war. She knew that I would be exposed to dangers of all kinds, both physical and moral, and that she would no longer have any control over the person I turned out to be. So she did not focus on the backbone of my Jewishness, mainstays such as *kashrus* or Shabbos, which were ingrained in all her children from birth. She chose the *mitzvah* of covering the hair — the one practice that I might tend to regard someday as least important. Indeed, when I got married, it was very uncommon for women to cover their hair, especially in America. I think my mother also understood that if my standards were more stringent, I might marry more carefully and associate with a different element of people. Now I see what she saw. She was absolutely right.

She was very astute in her second request as well. Writing a book is a weighty task, something that cannot be requested casually. But my mother was searching for a way to keep my Jewish consciousness engaged, to keep the windows in my soul open to the utterly unrandom ways of G-d.

Events that occurred during the war strengthened many people's faith, including mine. Sometimes the split-second timing that kept one out of death's path or the fantastic circumstances through which people were sustained in the ghettos and concentration camps were so supernatural that they could not have emanated from any source other than G-d. But my mother knew that belief in G-d is not a foolproof guarantee of *frumkeit*. When she asked me to write a book, she was hoping that the awareness of the promise would live constantly in my mind, and that I would not only see the world around me differently but understand the past in a more profound way. She knew that I would have to justify every word I committed to paper and that I could not do so unless there was no disparity between my belief and my conduct.

I cannot begin to express the profound and loving influence that both my mother and my father have had on my life. One often needs the wisdom of age to make sense of the instruction he received in his youth, and it is a long but very rewarding wait. In completing this book, I can only hope that my mother will look down favorably upon me from Heaven, satisfied that I fulfilled my promises to her — and even more importantly, that I have tried to uphold my Jewishness in the way she would have wished.

Chapter One

My father's face shines over all the images of my youth and all the days of my life. To me it was the face of kindness, of love, of the goodness of the world. His hazel eyes smiled sweetly on us, his long white beard flowed regally below, his laughter sparkled. He ran our household in Siedlice with a stately and gentle hand; he was both prince and father.

He never raised his voice to us and never struck us, guiding us solely with the natural force of his personality. My earliest memory, in fact, is of his unique brand of reproof. When I was not yet three years old, I wandered off to the marketplace one Shabbos morning and found five *groshen*, the equivalent of about a nickel, on the ground. Enterprising even at that young age, I went straight to the nearest kiosk and bought myself an ice cream cone, which I enjoyed thoroughly. Then I marched home and boldly displayed the remnants of my prize to my parents.

That evening after *Havdalah*, my father asked all the other children to leave the room, as he did whenever rebuke was in order; he did not want to embarrass me in front of the others. Then he told me a story about a young girl my age named Ruchele, who had committed a deed very similar to mine. The story went something like this:

"There was a young *meidele* named Ruchele who went away from the house one day, and she went to places where she shouldn't have gone. She went to the marketplace, and there she found money. Instead of leaving it there, as she should have done, she picked it up — because the *yetzer hora* told her so." Those were the words he always used; he never condemned us, blaming instead the evil inclination that had persuaded us. At all times he protected us from shame.

The story would continue, repeating my own crime to the very last detail, when I had walked into the house with the evidence in hand. Somehow my father managed to turn even this act of brazenness into a benevolent lesson, telling me that my admission of guilt was in fact a *z'chus*, for otherwise there would have been no opportunity to correct the wrong.

"Do you think that 'Ruchele' did a bad thing?" he would prod gently; and when I nodded, the game was over, and there was no doubt that "Ruchele" and I were one and the same. "Why did my Pesok do it?" he would ask, using his affectionate nickname for me. I was hard-pressed to come up with an answer and had to admit that I really didn't know.

"One thing I want from you," he would close, looking at me with his sage and smiling eyes, "is that you should never do that again." And I am very happy to say that I always kept my promises. None of his children ever argued with him, for we had no greater pleasure than remaining in his good graces.

My father was Nosson Dovid Rabinowitz, a renowned *rebbe* in prewar Poland. He was the son of Rabbi Yitzchak Yaakov Rabinowitz, the Biale *Rebbe* and author of *Divrei Binah*, a man known for his warm heart and open house. It is said that my grandfather himself regularly sampled the dishes that were prepared in his home for the poor to make sure they were of the best quality. He transmitted his legacy of loving-kindness and Jewish unity to his three daughters and four sons, and I was privileged to watch my father carry on that tradition in our own household and to participate actively in it.

When the Biale *Rebbe* passed away, he left behind an ethical will in which he urged his children to set aside any jealousies and to remain strong in their love for one another. To this end he advised his sons, should they choose to enter the rabbinate, to settle in different cities. These four young men of prominence thus dispersed: Meir Shlomo Yehudah, the second son, to Miedzyrzec; Avraham Yehoshua Heschel to Lublin, where he spent his life attending to the publication of his father's writings; and Yerachmiel Zvi, the youngest, to Siedlice, where he was *Rebbe* for only six months before his passing in 1906. My father, the eldest son, went to Parczewo, where he married and raised a family of three children. There he gained fame as the Parczewer *Rebbe*.

My father's wife, Leah Reizel, unfortunately became ill in Parczewo and passed away. Some time later he wed my mother, Yitta Spira Horowitz, the daughter of Moshe Leib Spira, the Sassover-Strizhever *Rebbe*, and his wife Chana.* For my mother, the marriage was also a second one. She already had one child of her own, and she bore my father eight. The children were close in age, born across the continent during the travails of war and wandering. The first three, Tova Chava, Devorah Perel, and Yitzchak Yaakov, were born in Parczewo; the next three, Boruch Yehoshua Yerachmiel, Betzalel Eliezer, and Yehudah Leib, were born in Russia, where my parents had fled when World War I broke out. When they returned to Poland in 1919, they settled in Siedlice. Here they welcomed me and a little sister named Frima Rivka, who tragically did not reach her third birthday.

I was born a great-aunt, for by that time my half-sister Esther was already a grandmother. Although they left the periphery of

---

* My mother's siblings also merited to marry into very fine families. Her older sister Chasie was married to Rabbi Shlomo Teitelbaum; they lived in Gorlice (Reisha). A younger sister, Mindele, was married to Yisroel Chaim Shapiro, the Berczer Rebbe. My mother's brother was Rabbi Nechemiale Spira, who succeeded my grandfather as rabbi in Strizhev. His wife, Nechama Tila, was the daughter of the Dinover Rebbe, Reb Shaya. The youngest sister, Pesele, lived in Vielun with her husband, Reb Moshe Hirsh.)

our immediate family, my father's children visited our home frequently and always remained close to us.

All that I remember of my youth is from Siedlice, but I heard many stories about Parczewo, where my father had created a new rabbinic dynasty. Even after he moved away, he remained known as the Parczewer *Rebbe*. We children were the lucky beneficiaries not only of a fine lineage on both sides of the family, but of the combined influences of my parents' widely differing backgrounds.

My father was a unique blend of knowledge and compassion, a man of liberal mentality whose heart expanded to receive every Jew, no matter his background or station. His love for *Am Yisrael* radiated to every one of the many visitors he received in our home. In my mind's eye, he still represents the image of the benevolent patriarch.

My mother provided the sharp edge to my father's pacific manner. He was the voice of tolerance and humor; she, the wielder of practicality and discipline. She was of Hungarian descent, a darkly beautiful woman with a soul and will that had been toned by adversity. I remember her as the fortress of our household, a great manager who was able to handle any situation, any difficulty, with a steel surety. It was only much later, when I was grown and had a family of my own, that her son Chaim Shlomo, my half-brother, opened the door to her past for me.

From him I learned that my mother had been engaged at the tender age of four to the son of another prestigious rabbinic family. Her mother had come up to her while she was playing in the backyard of their home in Strizhev and made this momentous announcement. She had no idea, of course, what it meant; but as she grew older, she began to inquire about the *chassan*, to ask whether he was developing into a *talmid chacham* and a person of quality.

When she was sixteen and on the threshold of her wedding, she went to her grandfather, the Gorlitzer *Rebbe*, and told him that she had doubts. She declared her reluctance to wed; her

My father, Rabbi Nosson Dovid Rabinowitz, zt"l
Parczewer Rebbe

My mother, Yitta Spira Rabinowitz a"h
Parczewer Rebbetzin

grandfather declared his equally vigorous denial of her appeal. And so my mother went to the *chupah*.

A year later when she was expecting a child, she came home again to tell her *zeide*, in no uncertain terms, that the marriage was not viable; she and the young man were plainly incompatible. To take such a firm stand, at that age and in those times, required an iron backbone, but this time the *zeide* relented and immediately arranged her divorce.

At seventeen, my mother moved back into her parents' home. There she gave birth to a son named Chaim Shlomo, who later grew up to head a prestigious Chassidic dynasty and who left behind a very fine family of his own. My mother remained at home until her son was ten years old. During this time she educated herself in a manner most uncommon for a young woman of Galicia. Custom here did not sanction the intellectual development of girls, but my mother was intelligent and quick, and she did not have the patience for an idle mind. Her father gave her permission to work as a receptionist for a local doctor, where she gained a great deal of medical knowledge. She also worked for a

Chapter One / 17

time for a lawyer, and she taught herself *Tanach* at home. In addition to her intellectual pursuits, she was very skilled at cooking and handwork. She designed clothing, made her father's *bekashes,* and once even undertook the making of a *shtreimel,* which turned out typically flawless.

By the time she married my father, she was possessed of a rich background of knowledge and skills which stood her in good stead, for settling in a new home did not necessarily make her life easier. She came alone from Galicia to Parczewo, in the Russian area of Poland, to an entirely different culture, where custom and mentality were sometimes completely at odds with her own. She was forced to adjust not only to a new home, but to her sudden role as the *rebbetzin* of a fast-growing Chassidic following. In Parczewo, and later in Siedlice, she could not afford to show any vulnerability. She assumed her responsibilities with her characteristic granite grasp, and it is to her credit that she was admired and respected by virtually all of her husband's adherents.

My mother was an extremely resourceful and meticulous woman, with an artist's eye for detail. She taught us everything: to sew, to cook, to embroider, the thousand and one tasks that consumed the keepers of the typical rabbinic household of prewar Poland. She taught us well — but it was to my father that we ran for approval.

His praise was sweet and gratifying, and it is scattered plentifully over all the memories of my short childhood. He encouraged us constantly, lavishing his blessings upon even the most childish of our accomplishments.

When I was about six years old, I remember appointing myself the official caretaker of the *bechers,* the special wine goblets we kept for the many guests who came to our Shabbos table each week. I used to polish every one of those *bechers* until they gleamed; then I would wash them in the sink, standing on tiptoe on the small stool that was my constant companion. Afterward I would proudly present them to my father. Each week without fail he would inspect them and say with shining eyes, "These are beautiful! May your own children be blessed to do such a wonderful job."

I also remember the famous — or perhaps infamous — grits that I cooked every *Motzaei Shabbos* for my father's *chassidim.* They used to come up each week to have *melaveh malkah* with him, and they appointed me to cook the grits for this special meal. The making of the grits became a hallowed weekly ritual. There was a wonderful grocer in town who regularly donated all the food for the *melaveh malkah,* and a few of the *chassidim* would take me along to pick it up. The snow in Siedlice was neck-high during the winters, and there were no cars available in this small town. We would thread our way across the top of that white plateau in the pristine stillness of the Polish winter night, listening to the crackling sound of our heels in the snow. Those walks were among the greatest pleasures of my youth.

The grocer was a *chassid* of my father's, a slight man with a small beard and a very large heart. He always teased me fondly and exhorted the boys to take care of me: "Watch out for Pesele, *ze zul nisht shleppen* — don't let her carry the heavy bags!"

Nobody was allowed to help me make the grits; it was my job alone. I used to stand on my little stool and pour in the pepper and salt. The pot was so tall that it was impossible for me to reach in, even with a long-handled spoon, and taste my own concoction. I have no doubt that those grits were overspiced and barely edible, but there was never a word of complaint from the *chassidim.* They would take the pot and distribute the barley amongst themselves, and then they would sing and dance for a while in the day room. Soon my father would come in and spend some time with them, cherished time in that warm olive-colored room, where the men sat between the glowing coals of the ceramic oven and the huge picture window that looked out on a world of white.

When the meal was over, my father would ask the *chassidim,* "*Vi iz gevein de grits* — *bataampt?* Were the grits tasty?"

And they would answer: "*Az Pesele hut es gemacht, iz es gevein git*; if Pesele made it, it was good."

My father's *chassidim* spoiled me sinfully, not only with attention but with presents. Many of them traveled frequently on business, and they always returned with gifts. Among the most memorable ones were a big doll whose eyes opened and closed (a very exotic item at that time), a beautiful doll carriage with satin lining, and a smart blue outfit trimmed with gold piping. I soaked up all the benefits of being the baby of the family and spent my youth in the limelight of my father's household — and I am not ashamed to say that I enjoyed it thoroughly.

My father's children were his first priority, whether there were guests in the house or not. But the attention that we received was not mere indulgence. Through his love, we learned of the love of G-d. His behavior was full of compassionate instruction of the ways of a Jew, whether he was playing with us, speaking to guests, or sitting alone learning in his study. His unassuming gestures and gentle nods glowed with the sterling dignity of the Torah. All through the day, we learned from him.

Chapter Two

My father ran our household with a characteristic mixture of caution and liberality. Everything he did was carefully calculated, and he carried out his standards with a great independence of spirit, even though some of them sidestepped the mainstream current.

Siedlice was a typical European town, fairly well developed at its heart and trailing off to rural expanses at the edges. Although my father had many followers in Warsaw and probably would have done better financially in a large city, he had chosen not to move there because the Communist influence at that time was burgeoning. He felt he would be able to watch us more closely in a smaller town and keep us free of the blandishments of leftist thinking, which was then a serious threat to large portions of the European Jewish community.

Most of the people in Siedlice were *Shomer Shabbos* and quite poor. The influence of the *maskilim*, the more modern Jews who propagated a Western style of ideology, was beginning to be felt in town. My father tried to maintain a strong balance between sheltering us from the toxins of the Enlightenment and at the same time teaching us tolerance and love for all Jews. He wanted us to feel connected to the Jewish people as a whole.

He did not send any of my four brothers to *cheder,* insisting on supervising their education personally. To that end he searched high and low across the country to find suitable *talmidei chachamim* to learn with them privately. Every teacher was handpicked. I remember in particular one *rebbe* named Rabbi Mandel, a slender, pleasant man with a long beard, who had a great influence on the boys.

Although *chinuch* has never been an easy living, the *melamdim* of those days plied their trade with additional burdens. Sometimes it was impossible for them to move their families to the places where jobs were available. Rabbi Mandel left his hometown of Strizhev — which, incidentally, was my mother's hometown as well — and stayed with us for several years, returning home regularly to visit his family. The boys learned a full day in my father's *beis midrash,* which was upstairs from our apartment.

In contrast, my father was quite liberal when it came to his daughters' education. He insisted that the three of us have both Jewish and secular training, but, as with the boys, he did not send us to the local Polish public school. Most of my friends attended school, and some even went on Shabbos, sitting in class without writing just to show their faces, for the law about school attendance was strictly enforced. Because of his status, however, my father received dispensation from the city authorities and was permitted to educate his children at home.

Most girls then did not receive much formal Jewish education. Mainly they were taught Hebrew so that they could read and *daven,* but my father wanted more for us. My older sisters Chavcia and Devorah — ten and nine years older than me respectively — were eager to learn, but I cannot say the same for myself. The main thing I remember about the *melamdim* who came to our house is that I used to run and hide under the nearest bed to get away from them. My father tried out more than one teacher on me, but I was very particular about personalities. I am afraid I gave those poor men a difficult time; I was a feisty little girl, and none of them were quite sure how to handle me.

I must admit that I once did something quite awful. One day when the teacher arrived, I hid behind the thick, elegant drapes that hung across the bay window in our dining room. When they came to look for me, I threw a book at the teacher. It was quite some time until I heard the end of that episode. Now that I look back, it's miraculous how much remained in my head, in light of the fact that I was so resistant to learning. All through my life, although my memory was good, I was never able to adjust to formal instruction. But my father's great respect for education became ingrained in me, and to this day I am thankful for the breadth of awareness and understanding that I was fortunate to receive in his home.

In addition to the Hebrew language, *Chumash, Neviim,* and the standard *sifrei mussar,* my sisters and I also learned basic arithmetic, Polish, reading, history, and geography. And our schooling did not end there. My father wanted us not only to have book knowledge, but to be polished in other ways as well. I remember when he brought in a painting teacher to instruct my two older sisters. This was quite a sophisticated privilege for a rabbi's daughter, particularly since the painting teacher did not ordinarily make house calls.

The girls were taught in their bedroom, which was papered with lively hunting scenes and heated cozily by a large, ceramic-tiled oven. My sisters used to stand in front of their window as they worked, framed in a flood of honey-colored sunlight.

Our bedroom was adjacent to my father's study. During the lesson, the door between the two rooms remained open so that he could keep a gentle eye on the proceedings. Although I was too young to participate, I sat and watched in fascination as the painter taught Chavcia and Devorah how to mix colors and use perspective to create the illusion of depth. Under his tutelage, they collaborated on the design and painting of unusual murals. I remember one especially large, exotic oil painting in which peacocks and palm fronds were intertwined in a fantastic concoction of brilliant colors: orange, turquoise, yellows, greens. The painting was padded and framed, and it hung triumphantly in our dining room.

Among my father's *chassidim* were spice merchants who sometimes traveled to the Orient on business. Once they brought us a large supply of Japanese tea, beautifully encased in a tin canister which was decorated with scenic pictures. My mother copied the design and enlarged it on a velvet background so that my sisters could embroider it, another feather in their artistic caps. All of these creations are gone now; Hitler took care of them.

Next to make its appearance in our mildly unconventional household was a new Singer sewing machine, a modern sensation. Along with it, of course, came a teacher. My mother had always been our primary sewing and embroidery instructor, but the new teacher taught us many fancy, professional tricks on the machine.

When Chavcia, the eldest of my two sisters, got engaged, my father decided that we must have dancing lessons to prepare for the wedding, and he brought in a young woman to teach us to dance. There was no music, only the counting of steps: one, two, three, four. The dancing lessons also took place in the day room, but this time the door to my father's study remained modestly closed. This did not mean, however, that he had lost track of our progress. From time to time he would knock on the door and inquire in his smiling voice, "How are my children doing?" We never felt resentful of my father's supervision. Rather, we felt that his loving eye was upon us at all times, caring for every space of our lives. We were completely secure in his love.

My mother did not object in principle to a rounded education for girls, most probably because she was highly intelligent and educationally inclined herself. But she and my father came from entirely different backgrounds, and they disagreed frequently on aspects of their children's upbringing. He had come from *Russishe* Poland, she from Galicia, and they diverged in much the same way that the *Chassidim* diverged from the *Misnagdim*. Their differences were not ones of *frumkeit*, but of the culture and style of daily life.

My mother was loathe to depart from any small nuance of the external traditions of her youth; she had been brought up not to look too far past the boundaries of her own backyard. She considered it a heinous waste of time, for example, if my brothers wanted to play a little ball during the afternoon. While my father was rigid in matters of *halachah*, she was more deliberate about custom. Traditional dress was important to her; she was adamant that her sons' shirts be fastened with small string ties rather than with buttons, which were considered more modern at that time.

To my father, it did not matter so much what people looked like. He encouraged us to focus on a person's inner rather than outer appearance, to savor the jewelry of the soul. He was not particular about string ties or black stockings, and although he insisted on a rigorous standard of modesty, he was much more concerned that we be dressed comfortably and — yes — stylishly.

I remember the good-natured disagreement my parents had over boots. Fashionable beige boots for young girls had just come out in Warsaw. These boots had fur-lined cuffs, small heels, and side zippers, in contrast to the usual high-top laced shoes which were the normal style for girls of nine and ten. Against my mother's protests, he immediately sent out to Warsaw for two pairs of boots for his eldest daughters. Then he heard that they were coming out with matching shawls, gloves, and ski caps with pom-poms. He asked one of the *chassidim* who was about to depart to Warsaw on business to bring back two matched sets to go with the boots.

My mother, although she had excellent taste, would have preferred to wait until such accessories became more accepted fare in the Orthodox community; she was not opposed to her girls dressing well, but, as she told my father, she did not want them to be trendsetters.

Without a qualm, my father replied, "Nothing is too much when it comes to my children's comfort. So long as my girls are happy and warm, I don't care who talks about it." They had quite a debate, but my father prevailed. Soon we were parading our new winter ensembles in the streets of Siedlice.

My parents also had very different approaches to discipline. My mother's was of the more traditional variety. We knew with clarity when we had done something wrong; spankings ensued and privileges disappeared. It was only later, when I was more mature, that I grew to appreciate the depth of my mother's affection, expressed in the firm steering that kept us strong and uncompromising.

My father's disciplinary style, as I have mentioned, was enormously tolerant in comparison to that of the average European household of that time. He saw a gestalt, viewing the development of our personalities in a more holistic way, and was inclined to look away from what he considered minor infractions. Through all of his children's foibles, he forbore. He looked at us as being human, and he loved us for being human, and he tried to straighten us out in his own particular way.

I must say in all honesty that I kept my parents busy, for I wasn't an easy child to manage. I was always very high-spirited and enjoyed attention more than I feared punishment. I fought constantly with my brothers, stole pears from the priest's tree next door, and ruined plenty of good clothing — certainly not a model little girl by anyone's standards!

There were two particular episodes of trouble which I remember with a mixture of amusement and contrition. One had to do with a new coat that had just been made for me. It was a beautiful blue, yoked coat with pleats in the back that tucked neatly into a half-belt, a lovely collar, and two front pockets. I was quite impetuous when it came to clothing, and I insisted on wearing that new coat immediately. My brothers and sisters were playing hide-and-seek with some friends, and I went to hide under the shelf in the kitchen where my mother stored the flour and oil. The entire can of oil came down all over me, and the coat was soiled beyond repair. To this day I am sorry about it.

The second occasion was when I jumped off the bookcase in

the dining room. My oldest brother Yankel had once tried this feat from the top of the tile oven in the foyer; the entire oven came down on top of him, and I have no idea how he got out alive. But I was not concerned with the particulars of the risk. There was a spare bed in the dining room, my favorite sleeping spot, and I climbed to the top shelf of the bookcase and fearlessly dove into it. I went straight through the wire netting in the mattress and hit the floor. That was the last time I was allowed to sleep in that bed.

My mother withheld my allowance; my father said, "Don't do it again," and I never did.

Whenever I look back now on these youthful vignettes, I appreciate my parents more and more. I am grateful for their loving navigation — for my father's smile and my mother's stamina; for my father's elasticity and my mother's diamond chisel. Together, they cast us in a shining mold, and we grew and thrived.

Chapter Three

My father was at home all day long. He suffered from diabetes and a weak heart, and could not engage in strenuous activity. He spent much of his time in his study, a room that was very much like him — warm and comfortable, full of the rich evidence of a life well lived.

The first sound you heard upon entering that room was the soft, rhythmic murmur of a vast assembly of clocks and watches. My father collected timepieces. He loved listening to that insistent, pulsing sound; he liked to be reminded of the passing of time and of the need to spend it meaningfully. His minutes were counted as carefully as his actions, and he never sat idle.

By the side of the doorway between the study and the day room stood a tall wooden coat stand where my father's *bekashes* hung. There was a special one for each occasion: one for candle-lighting on Friday night, one for Rosh Chodesh, one for *Yom Tov*, each one elegant and neatly pressed. I remember that one Friday afternoon, a spark flew from the coal oven in the study and ignited one of the *bekashes*. My father did not panic. He quietly took down the *bekashe* and stamped on it until the embers were crushed. The odor of the smoke was awful, but even more impressive was my father's utter calmness. He had complete trust in the *Ribono Shel Olam* about all the matters of his life, great and small, and his inner security radiated to his children.

Against the soft beige walls on one end of the study were a rolltop desk and several beautiful wooden cabinets filled with *sefarim* and important papers. At the other end there was a couch, and next to it, in the corner, a *shtender* with a *ner tamid* hanging above it, where he used to *daven* when he wasn't feeling well enough to go out.

An enormous side table stretched across the opposite wall. At the head of the table was my father's tall-backed chair with armrests, where, ironically, he almost never sat. He preferred to sit at the side of the table, beneath the light of a beautiful, green-shaded lamp with his inkwell beside him, writing constantly in his precise, even script. The only time he moved to the special upright chair was when he received guests. In that case, the dignity of his position dictated that he assume the role of host.

When a woman came with a *kvittel,* a written request, I was always summoned into the room. My father did not want the *shamash* there in case the visitor wanted to discuss something confidential, but since I was so young, I would not be listening anyway. On those occasions the door was left open, and I would amuse myself by crawling under the table and playing on the carpet around my father's legs. As he spoke to the visitor, he would reach under the table from time to time and pat me on the head. Those moments were the treasures of my life. The table became a very pleasant haven for me; I used to sit comfortably beneath it while my father wrote or learned, sometimes until two or three in the morning, delighting in the warmth of his gentle caresses. He never sent me to bed; he enjoyed my company as much as I enjoyed his.

I remember one other fascinating thing about that massive table. It had deep drawers built into it on all sides, mysterious compartments about whose contents I was extremely curious. I was once allowed to take a peek inside, and I think I must have been the happiest child in the world at that moment, because now I knew the secret.

The drawers were full of money. Dozens and dozens of suede drawstring pouches lay inside them, each labeled with the name of a different *tzedakah*. Although the calculations for such an extensive network of charities really required the services of a part-time bookkeeper, my father did all the accounting himself. Once a month he would call in Ellenka, the *gabbai,* his loyal friend and *chassid.* "Ellenka," he would announce, "*men darf gein tzu di post* — it's time to go to the post office!" And the *gabbai* would race out with his customary alacrity to send off all the money. Another meticulously observed monthly ritual was the visit of the *sofer,* who came to inspect all the *mezuzos* and *sifrei Torah* in the house and in the *beis midrash.*

Each afternoon my father took a nap on the couch in his study. There was a pitcher and a basin for *negel vasser* on a stand near the couch, and when he rose at about three o'clock each day, I used to run in to help take the water out to the kitchen. The filled basin was much too heavy for me when I was small, so my father would help me carry it as far as the day room. He would call out, "Pesok is here with the *shissel*" and then quickly retreat into the study so that it would appear that I had carried the heavy bowl myself. The maid would come in and take it from me, and afterward I would retrieve the empty basin and return it to its stand in the study. The delivery of the water was a privilege that I relinquished to no one.

After this came the fascinating ritual of the tea-making, conducted by the *gabbai*. Ellenka was a fixture in our household. He was a *talmid chacham* of note, a small, fast-moving man in his middle years, with a peppery gray beard and a brisk wit. He always had a good word for the maid and the cook, a bit of affectionate teasing for the children, and an interesting *vort* for my mother. The house seemed to vibrate with a fresh surge of energy when he came walking in.

Ellenka was an efficient manager and an arch diplomat, two of the primary assets of a good *gabbai*. He was inexpressibly devoted to my father, who depended on him heavily. Ellenka would come to our house each morning and go into the study, where he and my father would engage in a lengthy Talmudic discussion. He would attend to any errands or duties my father had for him and go home to eat lunch with his wife and family; then he would come back at four o'clock to make the tea. Always underfoot, I loved to watch this remarkably detailed process.

First Ellenka would boil water in an earthen teapot, adding an egg white to the water to purify it. In a second pot, he boiled up the special, loose Japanese tea that the *chassidim* sometimes brought us from their business trips to the Orient. He let the tea brew over the steam of the first pot and then poured it out through a small strainer that was attached to its spout. He would serve my father the tea, scaldingly hot, in a crystal glass etched with flowers, on a crystal dish. My father would learn for a while until the tea had cooled off, and then he would slowly drink it.

My father had many beautiful *minhagim,* and we participated in them at a very early age. The preparations for Shabbos were especially precious to him, and so they became exquisite adventures to us. On Thursday afternoons we would buy the Shabbos fish and lay it out on a huge platter. We children would carry the tray to him, and he would lovingly salt it himself, *"l'kavod Shabbos Kodesh,"* in honor of the holy Sabbath.

When each girl in the family turned three years old, he bought her silver candlesticks, and all the girls would light candles together with my mother. An hour before Shabbos, the countdown would begin.

"Hurry," my father would say to me, "go tell *Mama'she* that it's an hour before lighting." In the meantime, he went over the weekly *sedrah* with all the boys.

A while later he would say, "Go tell *Mama'she* it's a half hour before lighting." And then he would send me again five minutes before Shabbos. The delicious anticipation of candle-lighting was exceeded only by the event itself. We would gather in the dining room, the formal reception hall for the Shabbos Queen, with its majestic bay windows, sculptured velvet couch, and carved book cabinets. All three girls — two large, one small — would stand with my mother around the mahogany table, I on my little stool as always, and my father would stand beside me as we lit candles.

My father hosted a separate *tisch*, or table, for his *chassidim* late on Friday night, and then again at *Shalosh Seudos* on Shabbos afternoon. Although we did not eat those meals with him, he insisted that our own family meal not be delayed on his account. He would assign someone to recite *Kiddush* for us, and he would look in on us from time to time to make sure we were enjoying a pleasant *seudah*. When we were finished, we would go to his *tisch* to listen to his beautiful *Shalom Aleichem* and *Kiddush*.

At the *tisch*, a whole, cooked fish would be brought in. My father would eat a bit and distribute the rest to the *chassidim*; then he would do the same with the *ferfel* and a broiled liver. I once asked my mother why she always prepared those two dishes. She told me that the *ferfel* symbolized *parnassah*, or livelihood, for everyone, and that the liver symbolized dignity and honor, since the Hebrew word for liver is *kaveid*, which is reminiscent of *kavod*, honor. My father would deliver a Torah discourse during the *tisch*, and Ellenka would designate *chassidim* to sing the *zemiros*. The other-worldly aura of those gatherings fills a luminous corner in my memory and is still warm in my heart.

On *Motzaei Shabbos*, my father would gather all the children together and say *V'yitein Lechah* with us. As the youngest, I occupied the seat of honor — my father's lap. I always loved to play with his long white beard; whenever he laughed, his shoulders rippled merrily, and I enjoyed the "ride." I felt wonderfully close to him at those times. Although I was so young, I remember them with a sweet clarity.

My father used to have fish for *melaveh malkah*, and he would cut up a number of small squares for the children. Apparently, this fish was a special *segulah* of some sort, because he would wake us up for it if we had already gone to bed. He would make us wash *negel vasser,* say a *brachah,* and give us the fish. I did not know the reasons for all his customs, but it didn't matter; I knew the outcome of his ways, and that was enough.

Occasionally my father would go on vacation with some of his *chassidim.* The *rabbanim* of those days would gather for Torah retreats in resort areas such as Marienbad or Carlsbad, where they would enjoy the healthful waters and exchange Torah thoughts. Before he left, my father always called in the children and took down a list of requests. He never returned from a trip without bringing us gifts.

I remember him as he looked when he went traveling: he was erect and princely, and his face glowed. He always traveled in a *statz-peltz,* the fur-lined coat that signified rabbinic status in the Torah circles of prewar Eastern Europe. The coat had a beaver collar and wide lapels, and it was complemented by a soft white shawl, leather gloves, and a Russian fur hat. His boots shone like lacquer. A carriage pulled by two horses used to wait for him outside our house to take him to the train station, and he would depart royally, an emissary of G-d.

While he was away, he would always shop for our gifts himself; such important errands were not to be left to the *gabbai,* even one as capable as Ellenka. Often he would return from his trips very late at night. If we knew that he was expected, we would put our hands under our pillows in the middle of the night, and there we would find our presents. I remember once receiving a lovely charm bracelet, just as I had requested, and another time a small basket-style pocketbook, beautifully decorated with painted flowers and closed with a stylish latch. My father took great pleasure in pleasing his children, and he was pained if the gifts were not exactly to our liking.

He loved us with all his might, as much as it is possible for a human being to love. He tucked us into bed at night and always made sure that the house *bachur,* the young man who attended to household chores, had brought in plenty of wood and coal for the ovens. He used to sit and learn until after midnight, and then he would come around to each room to feed the ovens himself and to check the thermometers.

We slept soundly, for there was nothing to fear. We knew that our father was watching over us, at night as in the daytime; he guarded us constantly, with words, with gestures, with smiles, and his presence warmed our lives.

Chapter Four

When I was young, I did not fully appreciate the enormous energy and vigilance that went into the maintenance of a rabbinic household. Only in retrospect do I see that what my parents —especially my mother — went through merely to keep the house running from day to day was extraordinary.

We lived on the second floor of a large, three-story house. The building was typical of the European residential set-up, with businesses occupying the ground floor. Downstairs from us there was a barbershop and a tavern, as well as the concierge's room and a small flat rented by a very poor Jewish family. Our own apartment, considered luxurious by town standards, occupied half the second floor. The other half was shared by two tenants, a grain dealer and a shoe manufacturer.

On the top floor was our *beis midrash,* a small kitchen, and a bedroom where my brothers slept. There was also a small apartment which was occupied sometimes by the *gabbai* and sometimes by a Polish woman who helped manage our household.

There were people in the *beis midrash* constantly. These were all married men from other towns who came to learn for a while and observe the *Rebbe's* ways, as was customary amongst *chassidim*. A few had undertaken vows to separate themselves completely from their homes for periods of three and four months at a time. Such people were commonly known as *yoshvim*, or dwellers. In addition, there were *chassidim*, both married and single, who came for the *Yamim Tovim* from the big cities — Lublin, Krakow, and Warsaw, as well as surrounding towns and villages. For Rosh Hashanah and Yom Kippur, we used to set up a tent on the wooden floorboards of our large courtyard as sleeping quarters for all the guests. Often there were so many men for davening that the *beis midrash* was not big enough to hold them all, and those who could not fit davened on the steps of the building.

My mother ran this twenty-four-hour household with an exact and magnificent competence. She was a very sharp-minded and capable woman, endlessly talented, endlessly busy. Her dark, strong-boned beauty was matched by an equally strong soul. I never knew her to complain or to show any visible sign of weakness. She imbued us with her most prominent qualities: a sense of excellence and the desire to work.

Although we were comfortable enough to afford help, my mother never allowed us to remain idle. She always wanted us to work alongside the hired girls. Needless to say, we were not fond of this approach, but she once took us all aside and explained her philosophy in a simple and matter-of-fact way: "You don't know what life will bring you. If you can't afford to have help in your own home, work should not be strange to you. And if, G-d willing, you are fortunate enough to have help, you should know what to expect from a good worker."

And work we did. We cleaned windows and floors, we cooked and baked, we hemmed and embroidered. Although sometimes we smarted under the demands of my mother's program, how thankful I was later on for her foresight! I still remember distinctly how we washed and waxed the parquet floors, which then had to be brushed until they gleamed. For this job we had large brushes with straps attached, so that we could wear them like sandals. We would insert our feet into the straps and glide back and forth over the wax. My sister Devorah tried to make this tedious task more bearable by reading while she did it.

On Thursday nights, my mother stayed up all night baking and cooking for Shabbos. The aroma of her gourmet cakes and cookies was ambrosial, so sweet that it used to wake me up in the middle of the night, as though from a pleasant dream. Her meals were custom made, and the many guests who sat at our table each week were treated royally. Her *minhagim* were also very sweet. She adorned my father's Friday-night *tisch* with twelve *challos* (*Yud-Beis challos*) every week, each one baked in a different shape, in remembrance of the *Lechem HaPanim,* or Show-Breads, in the *Beis HaMikdash*; and during the *Yamim Noraim* there were two special *challos,* one baked with a key inside and the other formed in the shape of a ladder. The key was meant to "open up" the gates of Heaven, as in the verse *Pischu li shaarei tzedek*, "Open for me the gates of righteousness." The ladder symbolized going up to *Shamayim* to receive a good *kvittel,* the figurative writ that promised a healthful and abundant year.

What strikes me most in retrospect about my mother's abilities is her unusual combination of creativity and practicality. The trite image we hold of the starving artist selling his paintings for pennies on the street corner is perhaps not so exaggerated, for art and management often do have trouble coexisting in the same personality. But my mother had strains of both. She had not only a very pure sense of the flavor and colors of Yiddishkeit, but the technical aptitude to make sure that *halachah* was observed to the finest detail in our house. The best example I can think of is the Shabbos oven she built for us.

In those days there were no ovens whose temperature could be finely regulated. In Siedlice, all the people sent their *cholent* to the baker on *Erev* Shabbos, and he kept it overnight in his large oven. There was an *eiruv* around our neighborhood, and after *shul* on Shabbos morning, you would see dozens of children carrying the *cholent* home in cast-iron pots. My father, however, did not send our *cholent* to the public oven, for he wanted to maintain a strict standard of *kashrus* and preferred not to mix our food with others'. My mother had to figure out another way to keep our food warm, so she did what she had to do — she designed and built an oven.

She took a wooden box and lined it with tin, dividing the interior into two halves with a wire mesh partition. The *cholent* and *kugel* were placed in one half, and bottles of hot water in the other. The oven was heated from below with two petroleum lanterns which kept the food perfectly warm until Shabbos day. My mother arranged pillows on top of the oven in a permissible manner in order to keep the heat in, and she covered the entire contraption with a beautiful afghan. We had only one small mishap with the oven; the pressure of the heat once caused the water bottles to explode, so after that my mother stopped up the openings of the bottles with paper rather than corks. Otherwise, the oven was a model of technology in the service of the Torah. We were the only family in town lucky enough to have a mother who was a self-made engineer!

Our daily schedule itself was an exercise in engineering. My mother was busy from morning till night. There were constant deliveries to our house. All the delivery men came to the back door; the front entrance was reserved for special guests. Ours was one of the few houses in town with an internal plumbing system, albeit a primitive one, and the water was delivered daily by the water carrier, or *vasser treiger*. Elucha, as we called him, was a tall and somewhat slow man who knew all of *Tehillim* by heart. He would begin hauling water to fill up our ten barrels at four in the morning, and all the time that he walked he said *Tehillim* under his breath. I am sure that the water was blessed because of it.

The laundry in our house was a two-week procedure. Linen had to be washed continuously, not only because our family was so large, but because we had so many guests. A Polish woman named Zosia lived with her family on the top floor of our house, and she managed the monthly wash. She would call in gentile girls from the neighborhood to help out, a service which very few people in town could afford. We used to hang the wet laundry in the attic, where it took eight days or so to dry during the damp winter months and as many days to iron. When it was especially cold outside, the linen used to get stiff as wood, and we had fun playing in the attic and banging into those frozen sheets.

Once a month a seamstress used to come to the house to mend the old clothing and sew the new, whether it was undergarments for the entire family or dresses for the girls. I remember that I was never happy with the outfits my mother and the seamstress designed for me. I was a very headstrong child at six or seven, and I wanted to create my own designs, but of course I never won those arguments.

There were many others who helped out part-time on our staff too, people who cooked, shopped, and plucked feathers from the newly slaughtered chickens and geese. Every year before Yom Kippur, the *shochet* came to the house after *chatzos*, and we children were awakened at around three a.m. to *shlug kaparos*. The chickens were *shechted* on the spot, and we watched the procedure as though it were the most natural thing in the world. My mother *kashered* the chickens right away, and the hired women helped pluck the feathers. Tables were put up in the backyard, and the chickens were prepared for a large number of poor people who came for the *seudah hamafsekes,* the final meal before the fast.

Perhaps the main event of the year was Pesach. As many survivors of prewar Europe can attest, Pesach was an ordeal that began at least four months earlier. Perhaps if we fully appreciated what our mothers and grandmothers went through in order to have a truly "kosher Passover," we would not be so quick today to complain about the work!

Absolutely everything for Pesach was made from scratch, beginning with the *shmaltz.* Around Chanukah-time, the fat of several large geese was melted over a small copper burner. The

Chapter Four / 39

shmaltz was then put away to use for cooking and frying for Pesach. The smell of the fats sizzling in the burner along with onions was heavenly; it gave the whole house a fragrance of warmth and provided a pleasant herald of the upcoming season.

Next came the potato starch. In the winter, farmers came to our house with several wagonloads of potatoes. Several gentile women sat for a week or longer in the small kitchen upstairs near the *beis midrash*, peeling and grinding and sifting those potatoes until the starch was as milky as snow. Afterward, it was put out in the sun to dry.

Eggs came from the farms too, fresh and dirty, and we children helped to wash them off. Coffee was roasted over an open fire; the sugar had to be sifted grain by grain, to make sure there was not a speck of impurity in it. We made our own butter (even my brothers took turns churning) and our own cheese, hanging it up in a cheesecloth wrapping until all the water dripped out, and then pressing it into shape under a stone. We made our own borscht, storing it in huge enamel barrels in the yard that were taller than I was. Before *Yom Tov,* a crowd of people used to line up in the yard, and my mother filled their cups from these huge vats. She also made her own drinks: apple cider, wine, and even a very sweet drink made from the grape stems. She bottled and sealed her wine with the date and stored it in the cellar. By the time Hitler came, the wine in our cellar was very old and very expensive.

Immediately after Purim, my father used to go out with a group of *chassidim* to gather the *mayim shelanu,* the special water taken from a well which was used to bake *matzos* for Pesach. The *matzah* bakery was in a nearby town, and the *matzos* were stored in the baker's attic in tall, covered baskets. Our family alone reserved about five or six baskets because of all the company we had. The special *matzos* used only for the two *sedarim* would not be baked until Erev Yom Tov.

A few days before Pesach, the pace became even more intense. Our kitchen was *kashered* completely every year, and we didn't eat regular meals for eight days or more until the oven was burned out to my mother's satisfaction. The *chametzdike* dishes were put away and the lovely Pesach dishes emerged: a set of white Rosenthal porcelain with a cobalt rim, imprinted with an elegant gold filigree finish. I still have a very warm and pleasant association whenever I see that pattern today.

We also had a special Pesach heirloom in the family, a red crystal goblet that was used as Eliyahu *HaNavi's kos*. The goblet, which my father had inherited from his first wife, had once belonged to the Kozhnitzer *Maggid, zt"l*. In order to protect it, my parents had made a special container of gold brocade for the glass, lined with red velvet. One year on *Erev Yom Tov,* my mother was taking down the goblet when the bottom of the box gave way, and the glass crashed to the floor.

I remember that my mother's face became pale and her hands shook. I heard her saying, "I'll fast tomorrow." And she did —not because of the cost of the glass, but because of the spiritual loss.

When my father found out about the accident, he insisted that he was not upset and told my mother that it wasn't worthwhile to suffer so much aggravation; we should be grateful instead, he said, that the memory of that holy *tzaddik* had lasted for such a long time in our family. Although my father's warm reassurance always set things right in our house, I was equally affected this time by my mother's "aggravation" — the deep sensitivity to *kedushah* and to the meaning of a *gadol's* life which gave objects a heightened importance in her eyes.

When I visualize my mother working, I see her firm hands and businesslike demeanor, but the older I get, the more able I am to penetrate the surface of that image. She was not a demonstrative person; even when my little sister Frimele, *a"h*, swallowed lye at the age of two and passed away eight days later, I don't remember that my mother broke down in any way. But although her emotions did not surface, her love and compassion were profound. The giving that she did was not mechanical; it was directly from the richness of her heart. We learned who she was not from word but from deed.

We speak freely nowadays of *chessed* and of "open houses," but my mother's was open in the truest sense of the word. One of her greatest gifts to me, in fact, was the presentation of hospitality as a given, as a prescribed staple of daily life. She made it so natural a part of our household routine that I was later able to carry on that practice in my own home; the role lay on me comfortably, like a perfectly fitting glove.

My mother's ordinary, daily generosity was expansive. She was extremely sensitive to those less fortunate than herself, but her definition of "unfortunate" extended past the normal parameters. Every Friday I was sent to various houses in town to deliver chicken and fish, but even more importantly, I remember the times I delivered delicacies such as ducks or geese to families who had fallen from their accustomed financial status. "They are used to having better food," my mother would tell me, "and now they can't afford it."

Her cooking made its way out of town, too. My father was a known *mohel* in our district and frequently traveled to other towns and villages to perform *brissos.* His custom was not to eat anywhere outside the home, so my mother always sent food along with him. It was never just a single portion, however. More often than not, there was enough to feed all the *ba'alei simchah,* especially if they were people of simple means.

My mother liked to involve herself in the less conventional areas of *chessed* as well, and she even dabbled in *shadchanus.* We knew a woman in town from a prominent family who was left with two daughters after her husband passed away. She did not want to be the recipient of charity, so my mother tried to ease her situation by discreetly mentioning that she could use some extra help at home. While the woman was working in our house, her daughters used to come in to visit her, and my mother once suggested a match for the older daughter. Needless to say, the widow was very grateful, and a meeting was arranged for the two young people at the widow's home.

Most houses at that time were lighted not by electricity but by kerosene lamps. On the evening of the meeting, the woman saw that her supply of kerosene was low, so she gave her younger daughter a glass and sent her to a neighbor to borrow enough to tide them over. The young man soon arrived, and the meeting seemed to progress pleasantly enough. After a while, the woman offered him a drink, and he accepted; but in her excitement and nervousness, she accidentally picked up the glass which had been filled with kerosene and unknowingly used it for her guest's tea.

The mistake quickly registered on the *bachur's* face. The woman remembered only one other remark that was made at that unlucky meeting; the young man said something to the effect that he might see another girl sometime, but he would *never* drink a cup of tea again in his life. The distraught woman came running into our house the next day, wailing bitterly, "*Rebbetzin*, I killed it! I killed it!" and my mother had no choice but to agree.

Fortunately, not all of my mother's matchmaking involvements had such disappointing results. In fact, the incident I am thinking of is also perhaps the most moving recollection I have of my mother's kindness. It concerned a man in town of about forty years of age who did not have all his wits about him. He was a very short, slight man who used to come to the house frequently and sit in the kitchen while my mother was working. He never asked for anything; all he wanted was to sit by our stove during the winter months and warm himself. Sometimes he would bring along an iron pot to cook himself some soup. My mother would clear off the entire stove to let him cook, and whenever he looked away for a moment, she would furtively add a little butter or a dash of spice to his hapless concoction. The man was not clean, and my mother did not want us to be exposed to him. She would send us out of the kitchen when he came around, but she herself stayed and kept him company for hours at a time. Now that I look back, I marvel at the things she did.

Day after day, the man would come and sit in our cheerfully decorated kitchen, comforted by the pleasant atmosphere and my mother's company. He would sit until the soup was finished, and the next day he would return to boil his laundry — in that

Chapter Four / 43

same pot. "I'll give you another pot," my mother always insisted, but he wouldn't hear of it. His pride was intact, and he did not want to be the recipient of any greater charity than his spot by the stove.

There lived in town a very tiny girl of about thirty, a midget. I don't know exactly who was responsible, but somehow a match was arranged between that girl and my mother's visitor. The *kehillah* of Siedlice paid for the couple's wedding, which took place in our house. I remember how one man called out the *drusha geshank,* the list of all the gifts the couple had received and who had given them, in traditional European fashion; they were not to be denied any of the customs of a full *simchah.*

The *kehillah* then set the couple up in an apartment in town and looked out for their welfare. The young woman was more intelligent than her husband, but this did not interfere with their happiness. Soon she became pregnant. She used to come visit us nearly every Shabbos; she was comfortable in our home because she was treated so beautifully, and none of the children laughed or made fun of her.

Unfortunately her child was stillborn, and the entire community felt the loss. I remember that couple well for several reasons: because the match was so unusual and so successful; because of the community's unstinting involvement in the couple's welfare; and because of my mother's steadfast attendance to their needs. There was a complete sense of commitment and responsibility for the happiness of others in those days, something we do not often see any more.

Chapter Five

Aside from my younger sister's tragic death, the first nine years of my life in Siedlice were the most sparkling days of my life. I roamed the fields and the streets of our town, carefree, mischievous, secure in the welcoming arms of my parents and in the illusory safety of the world. We did not have the electronic games or elaborate toys of modern times, but in my opinion we had much more fun. The town was filled with sights and sounds, infinite enchantments for a youthful curiosity.

We lived on the outskirts of Siedlice, closer to the fields and the train station. Although our neighborhood was not very crowded, there was no lack of activity. Across the street from us was the city hall, an impressive edifice with a sprawling front garden, where many functions took place. A little further down the road was the marketplace, a huge, open dirt square surrounded by small booths. The market was open on Tuesdays and Fridays each week, in all kinds of weather. It also carried the unique distinction of housing the nearest water pump.

The view from the large kitchen window in our house was

enormously entertaining. On one side were neighbors who owned a grocery store and, what was even more extravagant, a cow. I used to watch in fascination when the cow was brought in from the fields to be milked and fed. The grocer mixed her an atrocious combination of remnants from his store and his own dinner, and its smell was delightfully horrific.

On the other side of us lived the priest whose pears I used to steal. He would always yell at me: "If you take my pears, I'm going to tell your father, and he'll punish you!"

"He will *not* punish me," I would reply in total confidence.

"Yes, he will!"

"No, he won't!"

This childish exchange sometimes went on for minutes, and I must say in all honesty that although I was very confident of my father's love, my smug attitude did not reflect well on me.

Below us on the ground floor were two very intriguing sources of entertainment. One was a small alcove built into the wall of the courtyard. Two of my friends and I once cleaned out that nook thoroughly and set up a "store" in it. From bricks we made cinnamon, from sawdust, flour; many of our friends came to "shop" there. The alcove was so small that even as children we could not stand up straight in it, but this did not dampen our pleasure in the least.

The other fascination downstairs was the tavern. This interesting establishment might have become the gateway to a rather unsavory education if not for my mother's watchful eye. On Tuesdays and Fridays the *goyim* from the surrounding villages flooded the marketplace to sell their wares, after which they would come to the tavern to spend their money. We were not allowed to go out of the house on those days, not because there was any real danger but because my parents did not want us to witness any of the sordid goings-on below.

Once, however, I was standing on the dining room balcony when a man came staggering out of the tavern, bleeding from the forehead. A friend of his came after him and tried to plaster a piece of pumpernickel bread to the wound. I began screaming, partly from horror and partly from curiosity, and my mother came running out and snatched me inside. That was the last I remember of those inglorious patrons.

Of course, we had our own houseful of interesting people — friends, relatives, neighbors, *chassidim* — and we never lacked for stimulation. There was something going on in our house almost all day long. My father's married children used to come visit regularly and were very much a part of our household, even though the two sets of siblings were so far apart in age. The younger daughter, Faygele, was the one we saw most often. She was married to Reb Aharon Perlow, the Stoliner *Rebbe*, a great *talmid chacham*. They lived in Warsaw but used to come frequently to see us; Faygele was very close to my father. Unfortunately, she had no children. I remember her as a very gentle, reserved person who often seemed sad.

Her husband — Reb Arele, as he was called — was an unusual *ba'al chessed*. In Warsaw, he was known as the champion of the *kimpeturen*, mothers who had just given birth. Reb Arele had made the new mothers his mission in life. He used to visit the city hospitals daily to make sure their needs were met and to find out if a *bris* or *kiddush* had to be organized or paid for. He also made certain that the other children at home were taken care of and that the families were well supplied with wood, coal, and food. Reb Arele was very comfortable in our family. I remember that he used to love to tease me; he would chase me from room to room until he caught me and then pinched my cheeks. I didn't like the pinching, but I was always hard-pressed to refuse attention of any kind.

Faygele and her husband later met a tragic end, dying *al Kiddush Hashem* in the Warsaw ghetto. They were hiding in a basement when they heard the screams of a mother and her child, who were being held at gunpoint by a Nazi in the street. Heedless of his own safety, Reb Arele raced out to help, and Faygele followed, trying to restrain him. Both were killed on the spot by the Nazi.

My father's youngest child was a son named Meilech. He was

married to the daughter of the Grozhitzer *Rebbe* and lived in Levertov, but he often came around to visit us. Meilechel, too, was sacrificed on the altar of the Holocaust when he was found in hiding during the Nazis' search for local rabbis. His entire family was wiped out on the same day.

My father's eldest daughter, Estherel, was married to the Drochobitzer *Rebbe,* Yaakov Spiro. They had lived in *Yerushalayim* since the early twenties, but they were very much connected to us in spite of the distance. Esther's husband carried the unusual distinction of being not only a great *lamdan* but a landscape painter of considerable talent. I was to see more of Esther in later years.

Of all my siblings, however, my own two sisters played the largest and most penetrating role in my young life — and perhaps in each other's as well. It has often been said that opposites attract, but it is still fascinating to me that these two were so close even though their natures were at opposite poles. Chavcia, the

Devorah, Chavcia, and me in Siedlice

oldest child in our family, was a pale princess, a brown-eyed, gentle soul who was content with duty and tradition. Devorah, on the other hand, was a fiery rebel. Her striking green eyes glittered against the whiteness of her skin, and she was anything but complacent. She hungered for knowledge, for a broad scope, for perfection.

Devorah was an impassioned writer. I saved several of the pieces that she wrote in her youth, all of which were originally written in Hebrew and later translated. Her account of the Pesach *sedarim* in our home still moves me to tears today, because it is so true and so telling of the depth of her feeling. She wrote it when she was seventeen years old:

> *Siedlice, 3 May, 1928*
>
> *On the first eve of Pesach at the ninth hour, Father returned with the two boys from evening prayer. The large dining room was already prepared for the Seder: a set table, covered with a tablecloth white as snow, was placed in the center of the room. At the head of the table was Father's seat, a soft couch with a cushion covered in an embroidered silk cloth. Around the table were chairs for the boys and the guests. There were candles lit in sparkling silver candlesticks that burned and radiated in all corners of the room. Before each seat, silver cups were set on small silver trays, and wonderful bottles of wine shone in the light of the candles. The sight of the table, bathed in the abundance of light and decorated with various dishes of silver, gold, and glass, was exquisite in the full sense of the word.*
>
> *On the side was placed another table for the women. This table was also set like the first. In the bedroom, all the candles burned in the electric chandelier, and they added so much light that the light in the house was like the sun that shone during the day. Mother, dressed in a silk dress, sat at the head of the table and we sat around her: I, my sister, and also little Pesele. We were all dressed in the finest dresses that we had in our wardrobes.*
>
> *Around the men's table sat the older boys and the guests. Their faces and hands were freshly washed, and their clothes*

were clean and lovely. Everyone sat at his place, waiting for Father to appear. The older boys reviewed the Haggadah, and the younger ones memorized the Kushios (the Four Questions) so that they would remember them well. Father entered, wearing a black silk kapota and a white kittel embroidered in silver, with a sash made of silver; on his head was a silver yarmulka and a shtreimel. His scrubbed face, full of charm, glistened with a light sweat, and the gentle smile on his lips expressed satisfaction and the joy of the holiday. His entire appearance was like that of an angel of G-d.

When he entered, we all rose from our seats. Father sat at the table and began to arrange the k'arah, and in a pleasant voice he said, "Bless and wash." Afterward he made the blessing on the first cup, and we all stood and listened to his sweet words. When we reached the section of asking the Kushios, Leibel began, followed by Eliezer, and afterward the older boys. When they began to say, "Tatte'she, I will ask you four questions," their faces blushed above their ears and their voices trembled at first, but the Kushios went smoothly, without any faltering.

Then Father began to explain the questions by saying, "Slaves we were in Egypt," after which the entire family recited the Haggadah out loud. But Father's voice could be heard amongst the many voices, like the sound of a violin or an organ. Yaakov sang, "All achas kama v'kama . . ." His voice sounded like a small bell, but the younger children came to his assistance and the singing went well . . .

At twelve, people came from the town. Some of them came out of sheer curiosity to see how the Seder is held in the house of the Rabbi. But there were also those who came to hear Torah from Father. The group of curiosity-seekers was more interested in the table. They most probably wanted to see how the Rabbi's wife and daughters behave . . . but when they saw us reciting the Haggadah with great interest and not paying attention at all to their piercing stares, they slowly dropped their eyes from the table.

> When Father began to recite, "Pour out Your wrath upon the nations," I already felt a tiredness in my body. I closed my eyes and took pleasure in listening in my dream to the rustling of the wings of the angels of G-d who came to see the abundance of light, the splendor and the sanctity that spilled into each corner of the house. My heart was filled with secret yearnings, very pleasant yearnings . . . When I awoke, I heard the singing of "And It Came to Pass at Midnight," and suddenly I was overcome with drowsiness again. I placed my head on the table and slept, and in my dream I saw amazing pictures. I saw a large and mighty nation going forth from slavery into freedom. The nation wandered in the desert surrounded by darkness, but in front of them shone a bright light. At the head of the camp walked a tall man, his face glowing like an angel of G-d, and in his hand a wonderful staff. [The nation] was humming and singing words and praises to G-d, Who delivered them from their hard labor and was leading them to the land flowing with milk and honey.
>
> I started to shout with all my might: "Moshe, our master! Shepherd of Israel! When will you also come to us and deliver us to the Holy Land? . . ." And suddenly I heard a pleasing voice at the table: "Next year in Jerusalem!" I looked up with happy eyes because I remembered the dream, and my hope was strong that it would come true, since these words were like a resolution of my dream . . .
>
> On the first night of Pesach, the Seder ended at three in the morning, and on the second night it ended at five in the morning, before the break of day.

Perhaps because of her thirsty intellect, Devorah was extremely close to my father. She gave her life for him; she was his confidant, his nurse and friend. Energetic and cerebral, she spent hours engrossed in conversation with him, often in philosophical debate. I remember that she wanted to learn *Gemarah* but that he was very much opposed to it.

Devorah knew where all my father's things were kept, and

her constant attendance on him was a great help and relief to my mother. She helped him dress, brought him his *sefarim* and his meals, and monitored his medication. He did not want any of the children to know how sick he was, but Devorah knew. I remember how she used to crawl into his bedroom at night so that he wouldn't see her and lie at the foot of the bed, waiting for the moment when he might need something.

Each night I slept with one or the other of my sisters, for there were only two beds in our narrow room. Devorah was an incorrigible reader, and she used to sit up at night with a flashlight and devour book after book, long after the three of us were supposed to be asleep. Once while she was reading by the light of a candle, she dozed off and the curtains caught on fire. Luckily, she pulled them down and stamped out the flames before any serious damage was done. My guess is that she considered it a small price to pay for the expanded horizons of reading, but I have some doubt my mother would have agreed.

Our bedroom was a snug, pleasant European room, with a tile oven and the famous Singer sewing machine nestled neatly into its corners. Overhead were dozens of Devorah's books, in Hebrew, Yiddish, and Polish — all approved by my father. When I lay down to sleep at night beneath our down comforter, the ornate hunting scene that adorned our wallpaper seemed to become animated; the dogs and horses, by a very effortless turn of the imagination, trotted briskly across the walls in the dusk, the hunters in their red caps bobbed up and down among the greenery . . .

The winters in Siedlice were miserable. The water froze and the sink pipe burst on more than one occasion, but I never noticed. I thought only of the joy of the snow. I was perhaps the only child in history who actually enjoyed going to the dentist, because the trip was so much fun. I loved the crackling sound of the frozen crystals, the wonderful grip of the snow on my heels when it was packed just right. Sometimes the ice was so thick that it was impossible to walk down the steps. There was no salt then, and you needed professional acrobatic maneuvering to get across the yard. I reveled in the weather, though, as in everything else; small discomforts were an easy exchange for the splendid freedoms of a village childhood.

In the summertime, when my parents wanted a little rest from the hectic pace of the year, we children enjoyed the special treat of several weeks' vacation in the nearby village of Roskoshe (which, ironically, is the Polish word for "luxury"). A nanny came along with us, and we stayed in the home of one of my father's *chassidim*. My mother sent out care packages full of treats every two days or so, and she would come out periodically with a horse and buggy to visit us.

In Roskoshe we had the run of the fields and woods. We chased after butterflies and chipmunks, got lost in the forest, sat in the grass and daydreamed. The boys climbed the columns from the porch to the second floor and especially enjoyed turning us over in the hammock. I remember one particularly daring night when I slept outside on a cot, close to the woods — something my mother certainly would not have allowed. Truth to tell, I was petrified, but I would not deny myself the pleasure of the challenge. Those were glorious days, full of the insouciant laughter of a secure childhood, the love of brothers and sisters, and the spangle of innocent mischief.

The summer when I was eight years old was the beginning of change in our lives, the first awkward tug toward adulthood. That year, instead of going to Roskoshe, my sisters and I went to stay with my grandmother in Strizhev, the town where my mother had grown up. It was a memorable summer, with an unexpected ending.

I remember that little town so well: the narrow, monotonous dirt streets, the piazza, and, of course, the train station, which was the major gathering place in all the small villages of Europe. I remember how everyone used to run to the station the minute a train pulled in, to meet new people and to hear the news.

Bubba Chana, a"h, Strizhever Rebbetzin, in Strizhev

My *Bubba* Chana — "Bubbe'she," as we called her — was a quiet, patient woman, with the same combination of intelligence and industriousness that she had bequeathed to my mother. She was a patriot of the town, the daughter of the Gorlitzer *Rebbe* and the wife of the Strizhever *Rebbe*, who was no longer alive. *Bubba* Chana's two sisters had also married Torah giants; one was the wife of the *tzaddik* Reb Shayale Czechower in Krakow, and the other had been married to the *Sfas Emes*. *Bubba* Chana lived in a two-story house which contained a *klauz*, the Galicianer term for a *beis midrash*, and a built-in *succah*. The house was quite impressive in comparison to the tiny wooden dwellings across the road; my grandmother, however, lived very simply, without luxuries and without pretenses.

The one piece of furniture in that house which I remember most clearly was the carved, antique day bed that I slept on in the dining room. Its hard wooden cover lifted to reveal a straw mattress. The bed had a special significance, not because of its beauty but because of its history; for it was known that my grandfather, *zt"l*, had slept on it all through the years — not on the mattress, but on the hard wooden lid, with a stone beneath his head, in memory of the *Churban*.

My sisters and I enjoyed leisurely days in Strizhev, where time seemed immobilized. We used to take long walks to the fields outside the town and spend the day in the open air and sun, each absorbed in her own projects and her own dreams. Chavcia would sit with dovelike simplicity, doing embroidery or other handwork. Devorah, the perpetual student, took her education into the fields; she was very intent on learning Hebrew and would consume one Hebrew journal after another. My grandmother always sent along wonderful lunches on our outings: home-baked whole wheat rolls, fresh cheese, and jugs of cold milk. We sat for hours in the outdoors, with the sun gliding above us in a timeless golden bath. It was hard to imagine that life could ever be any different, any less sweet.

When we were not outdoors, I spent a great deal of time indulging in my favorite pastime: the culling of attention. I was extremely jealous of my sisters because they knew my grandmother better than I did, and in spite of *Bubba* Chana's protestations that all her grandchildren were equally loved, it seemed to me that my sisters were closer to her.

I annoyed them constantly. There was a tiny room in the women's section of the *shul* upstairs where my grandmother *davened* separately, and I more or less appropriated that room. I would lock myself in there and play for hours, without letting anyone else in. When my sisters complained to *Bubba* Chana, she laughed tolerantly and asked me a question that pinpointed one of my prominent shortcomings: "You want to take *everything* for yourself?"

As though my father sensed that I needed a gentle chiding, he wrote a letter to all of us that summer. It came from Marienbad, where he was vacationing. He wrote partly in Hebrew, mostly in Yiddish, addressing both my grandmother and the children:

Nosson Dovid Rabinowitz, Siedlice
Marienbad, 5688
HaRabanis Hayikarah MiStrizhev:

I received your letter and was very happy to read it. Thank G-d you are well; I hope to hear good news from you very soon. Hashem Yisbarach should grant you satisfaction for the good in all your endeavors.

And now I would like to ask you: Is Pesele straightening out a little bit? Perhaps you would be kind enough to teach her to write a little Yiddish, because I would like very much for her to write me regards.

I hope that you girls are enjoying your stay. I heard from Mamma that you want to fast on Shivah Asar B'Tammuz. I do not want any of you to undertake to fast . . . Conduct yourselves

> *properly and enjoy yourselves thoroughly; do as you please, only do not give a lot of trouble to the Bubbe'she. I wish you all the best. I am staying here in Marienbad another two weeks.*

One day in the middle of this idyllic interlude, a man arrived at the railroad station. His name was Avrumale Weinberger, a spirited, middle-aged man with a long red beard who was one of my father's trusted *chassidim*. He came to my grandmother's house with a message for Chavcia from my parents: it seemed that a match had been arranged between my sister and Yisroel Danziger, the son of the Alexander *Rebbe,* and Chavcia was to come home right away. Alexander was a small town on the outskirts of Lodz, and the prospective groom was from a distinguished line of *rabbanim*.

Chavcia was seventeen years old, and she did not want to go home. She had known all along that her carefree days were drawing to an end, but she had thought she would at least have the summer to herself, and she was taken aback to be pulled up short in the middle of it. Chavcia was still enjoying the bloom of her youth, and the last thing she wanted right now was to become a *rebbetzin*. "I have time! . . ." she kept repeating over and over again.

Avrumale Weinberger had been given specific instructions

The Alexander Rebbe, Rabbi Menachem Danziger, zt"l, with his son Yisroel to his left, in 1937.

not to return home without my sister. He sat in my grandmother's house for a very long time, and it was clear that he had no intention of reneging on his mission. Chavcia's sense of duty finally ended her dilemma, and she packed her bags and went home. Devorah and I followed soon afterward.

So that summer of endings and beginnings came to a bittersweet close. I was not nine years old yet, but somehow I sensed that other changes would follow in the wake of this one, that I would not be able to float in my golden family bubble for much longer. Sadly, my intuition soon proved true.

Chapter Six

Chavcia's future mother-in-law arrived at our house from Alexander a few days after we returned home. The occasion was the European tradition of *beshoh*, the initial meeting of the families of a prospective match. She brought along two of her eleven children, both daughters, and her husband's *gabbai*.

I had an ingenious knack for sniffing out the advent of an important episode, and I sought out a strategic position from which to watch the proceedings. I remember distinctly how those three women walked in through our front door. They were tall and beautifully outfitted, and they carried themselves imperially. The *rebbetzin* wore an elegant blond wig, which seemed very sensational in comparison to my mother's simple hat and homemade frisette. I was quite impressed with these regal-looking women and much too young to understand what my father had always known: that aristocracy is an inner quality which cannot always be judged by outward appearances.

The *rebbetzin* asked Chavcia to walk around the room so that she could observe her carriage. This was not at all an uncommon feature of the protocol of a *beshoh,* but Devorah told me many years later that she nearly exploded when it happened. Devorah had always been the proud rebel in our family, and she was outraged at the very idea of her sister being put on display. It is probably fortunate that she herself had not been chosen as the bride; one can only imagine what might have resulted.

My mother designed Chavcia's trousseau and brought in dressmakers from Warsaw to sew all the outfits from scratch. This was not our first wedding — my mother had already married off her son from her first marriage — but it was an important one, the marriage of her first and oldest daughter. She went to great lengths to match up every detail and accessory of that trousseau. Among the outfits she created was a magnificent green suit with a three-quarter-length jacket and a matching blouse with a jabot. She sent me from store to store to bring back button samples for that suit, and the ones she finally chose were black, cube-shaped buttons made of lucite. They were quite artistic and somewhat bold, but in that sense my mother and father were very much of the same turn: modest and tasteful, yet quite esthetic, with a sense of elegance that radiated from within.

During this time, our supply of guests did not slacken. My father's daughter Esther traveled all the way from *Yerushalayim* to see us, bringing along her own two daughters. They stayed with us for quite a while, for to make such a trip in those days was no small feat. Esther's presence left a bittersweet aftertaste in our house, for her children were no longer quite to my father's liking. They had lost the special gleam of the *Rebbe's* household, the crest of spiritual refinement that was so sacred to my father.

Chavcia's wedding plans proceeded apace. My father went with Devorah and the *gabbaim* to the hall which we had rented in order to arrange the seating. He pointed out to her where each of the attending *rabbanim* would sit on the dais.

"And where will you sit?" she asked.

My father replied in a strangely quiet voice, *"Mir vellen shoin zei'en vi ich vell zitsin shpeter. Zorg zich nisht.* We'll see about the

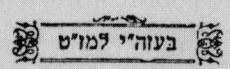

The invitation to my sister, Chavcia's wedding

seat later. We have time for that; don't worry. Just make sure everyone else has a place."

Three weeks before the wedding, on a cold winter Tuesday, my father didn't feel well. It was late in the afternoon, the seventh of Shevat, 1930. I was not at home for most of that day; my half-sister Esther had decided to take her two daughters for a sleigh ride in the morning and had asked me to come along. My father had allowed me to go, but had kept Chavcia and Devorah in the house. I assumed that he wanted to learn with them.

My father lay down on the couch in his study and called in Devorah. "There is a set of papers in the back of the cabinet," he said to her. "Bring them out, so that we will have them when we need them." Perhaps Devorah understood that this was his will.

They sent for a doctor, and my father removed his shirt and *tallis katan* for the examination. When the doctor left, my father asked for the *tallis katan*, but Chavcia suggested gently that since he was about to retire for the evening, he might want the one that he normally wore when he slept. He refused.

"Let me have it, mein kind," he replied. "They will take it off later."

After the doctor left, one of the *chassidim*, a *Kohen*, came to visit. They sat talking together in learning for a while, and then suddenly my father closed his *sefer* and asked the visitor to go home. He knew that this would not be the place for a *Kohen*.

He remained lying quietly in the study, dignified in repose, with the clocks murmuring their endless lamentation around him. He did not tell anyone how ill he was feeling; he did not want to raise an alarm.

When Esther and her daughters and I came back up the road after our outing, we saw my two sisters racing out of the courtyard in a frenzy. They were going for the doctor, but it was too late.

My father was sixty-two years old when he passed away. He died at exactly nine-thirty in the evening; I know, because all the clocks in his study stopped at the same moment.

Before the *levayah*, my father was laid on the floor of the dining room. He was draped in black shrouds, with a candle lit at each side of his head and another at his feet. Someone announced that my father's son Meilech would be the new *rebbe*. I remember these things happening, and I remember feeling an odd vacuum in my chest, but I was not afraid. My father was still there. Even from the next world, he sent his security to us. I felt sad, but I did not panic.

On the day of the *levayah*, something so extraordinary happened that the local paper carried a news item about it. They took my father's *aron* out into the courtyard, prepared to be carried to the funeral. Women customarily did not go to the cemetery at that time, so Devorah came out onto the balcony to say goodbye to her father. The courtyard below and the surrounding streets were so packed with people that it seemed as though a sea of rolling black waves was pressing against our house, threatening to flood it.

Suddenly, Devorah came forward, grabbed the railing of the balcony with both her hands, and began to speak about my father. Her *hesped* was spontaneous, uncontrollable, a fountain that surged up from the deep with such power that it could not be held back. She was only seventeen years old, and I do not remember exactly what she said; but I remember that she spoke with such passion and such a strong understanding of my father's character and ideas that no one stopped her. Not one of the *chassidim* interrupted her. When she had finished, the procession continued into the street.

My father's mother, Rochel L'via Rabinowitz, a"h, the Biale Rebbetzin, in Warsaw.

Much later, Devorah revealed to me another of the many secrets that had passed me by in my youth. My father had always written weekly to his mother, who lived in Warsaw, and when he felt that he was going, he had prepared enough postcards to last for about three months. He was the much-beloved son in his family, and he did not want her to know of his death. Devorah told me that the last postcard arrived in Warsaw a week before his mother passed away. Even after his death, my father had done *chessed*.

In 1977, my father's remains were brought to *Eretz Yisrael* for burial by Rabbi Pinchas Mandel. He was laid to rest in Petach Tikvah, where my brother Boruch was the rabbi, in a cemetery where many *gedolim* were buried, including the Spinka *Rebbe* zt"l, the author of *Imrei Yosef*. My father's plot is near the wall at the entrance to the cemetery, so that whoever comes in has to pass by his *kever*; and even today when I am there, I am reminded of the *kever* of Rochel *Imeinu*, who watches all her children as they pass by on the road and prays constantly for their welfare.

There is one very unusual thing about my father's *kever*: it has more space around it than the others, which are crowded very closely together. My brother was able to make this special arrangement only because of his rabbinical position, for it is very difficult to secure extra space in *Eretz Yisrael* at any price. My father had specifically requested this in his will. His reason was that people might not know who he was, and he — a person of doubtful merit — did not want to shame those buried near him by encroaching on their territory.

Pinchas Mandel might have taken issue with him on this matter, for he wrote in a newspaper article that out of the nearly five hundred bodies he had exhumed and brought to Israel, my fa-

My father's kever in Petach Tikva

ther's remains were the only ones he had found that were nearly intact.

Ellenka, our devoted *gabbai*, took over all the preparations for my sister's wedding. He was capable, a good manager, a personality inseparable from our household. My mother coped somehow, never relaxing her grip on life, but I don't know how well she would have managed without him.

Three weeks after my father's death, Chavcia was married. We went to our *simchah* from sorrow, to a wedding joyful yet strained. There were lavish *sheva berachos* every night that week; Chavcia's new life was not to be diminished in any way.

My sister Chavcia after her marriage to the Alexander Rebbe's son.

The last festivities took place in a spacious hall that we rented from the local orphanage. Toward the end of the meal, the gabbai began to rush us.

"Let's hurry and finish quickly," he said. As he handed out the last *kibbud* of the *sheva berachos*, he remarked almost casually to some men who were standing nearby: "*Mein rebbe rift mir; mein rebbe darf mir.* My *rebbe* is calling me, my *rebbe* needs me." Ellenka then said that he didn't feel well and went into the cloak room to lie down. When the doctor came, he was already dead. Everyone at the *shevah brachos* that evening saw what happened. Apparently, the gabbai too had known.

A year later, a man named Leibele Malritter came to our door. We knew him well. He was a lumber merchant who traveled to ussia frequently on business, and he was also a loyal *chassid* who ad often spent hours in conversation with my father. He had built one of the most unusual clocks in my father's collection; its numbers were Hebrew letters, an extravagant curiosity at that time.

Leibele stood on the doorstep, his face sallow and thin. "I am very sick," he announced to us in a muted voice. "If I have to die, I want to die in my *rebbe's* house and be buried near him." He went into the dining room and lay down on the spare bed, the one I had slept on as a small girl. My parents called the doctor in to see him a few times, but Leibele Malritter did not get better.

One afternoon when I came into the house, I saw someone putting a feather under the *chassid's* nose. I had never seen that done before and did not understand what it meant. Then I saw them pulling a cover over him, even over his face. The *chassid* had received the first half of his wish.

The *gabbai* and the *chassid* were members of a generation of people we do not understand today. Their roots went deep into the earth and reached deep into the heavens, binding them firmly to teachers, to parents, to G-d. All through their lives, they played out the modest, sacred pageantry of the spirit, showing us how to be loyal in this world and in the next. I am very grateful that I was privileged to witness their conduct, in life and in death.

Chapter Seven

My father's passing was the beginning of many ends. The luster in our household faded after he died. Shabbos and *Yom Tov* were no longer the same; the longed-for approval was no longer ours, for there was no one to run to. Worries seeped in and began subtly to streak the smooth tapestry of our lives.

My mother lived through a period of quiet devastation. Fortunately, she received emotional support from the extensive circle of *rabbanim* and *talmidim* who frequented our home. Some of these people, who knew my mother well and understood the depth of her predicament, suggested that she send the children away for a while. In Myleeczyc there was a *dacha*, a vacation rooming house, which catered to members of the yeshivah world, and at least for a while she would not have to cook for us or keep house.

The boarding house in Myleeczyc was host to some of the most outstanding *rabbanim* of prewar Europe. Among the people I saw there were Rabbi Michel Feinstein, Rabbi Shmuel Harkaver, Rabbi Beinish Finkel, and Rabbi Elya Chazan, all of whom were

My brother Boruch as a young chassan, age eleven.

to become famous *roshei yeshivah*. I was only nine at the time and did not appreciate the full significance of this assembly, but I do remember the beautiful atmosphere that saturated that place. It was a melding of the majesty of a Torah presence with the wonderful, rich humanity of everyday life. Great thoughts were exchanged daily on the lawns beneath the trees, discussions that were graced with dignity, broad humor, and broader smiles. The teenage boys in the group played chess and chased each other across the porches and yards; there was a camaraderie and closeness among the people, old and young. We were privileged to enjoy a telescopic view of the daily lives of these great Torah personalities, lives that were a beautiful blend of spirituality and down-to-earth warmth.

The visit was something of a reprieve for us children, but it ended as soon as we returned home. Quiet cracks had opened up in the earth of our home. My father's son Meilech, the Levertover *Rebbe*, had been named to take over the dynasty, but he did not want to leave the town where he had settled. Many of my father's *chassidim* began to disappear, little by little, to Levertov, siphoning off the reserves of our family's network

At Boruch's wedding in Munkatch.

Chapter Seven / 67

of support. My mother worried more and more about how she would manage financially without the fulcrum of her husband's vast following.

While we hung suspended in this murky limbo, my brother Boruch was married to the daughter of the Munkatcher *Rebbe*, who was a cousin to my mother. Boruch had been engaged since the time he was eleven. After his *bar mitzvah*, the *Rebbe* had taken his future son-in-law to *Eretz Yisrael*; the trip in those times was a rigorous one, to say the least, but the Munkatcher felt that it was important for a Jew to see the Holy Land, and he wanted Boruch to have that experience. As Boruch grew up, the *Rebbe* had maintained contact with us, and he had even come from Hungary to visit my mother during the *shivah*.

My family went to Munkatch for Boruch's wedding — all except for Lazer and me, the two youngest children. I learned later that it was one of the weddings of the century. Triumph arches were put up throughout the city of Munkatch, and six white horses pulled the carriage that took Boruch to his *chupah*. The wedding was even filmed.

Although my mother had the satisfaction of knowing that two of her seven children were safely married off, her financial and emotional burden grew heavier by the day. Our resources were now very strained. Most of the tenants in our building were so poor that they only paid rent infrequently. This had not mattered much when my father was alive, but now there was no source of income to compensate for the loss. My mother did not want to be dependent on anyone. She had several favorite phrases from *Tehillim* which served as her banners in life, and one of them was: *"Al tivt'chu vin'divim* — Do not place your trust in donors." My mother took these words of *Tanach* most literally.

Some of my father's closest *chassidim* began to advise her to move to Warsaw. The idea of uprooting after so many years, of leaving the home where she had raised eight children, was mind-boggling for my mother, but the *chassidim* reminded her that in a large city there were more people from her husband's following who could help her out, as well as more opportunities for

My brother Lazer.

income. Prominent among the advisors was Munish Ridel, the banker of Siedlice. Ridel was so devoted to my father that when he was later released from a prisoner-of-war camp in Russia in 1945, he came back to Siedlice before going on to Israel to see if my father's *kever* was still intact. He found that the *matzeivah* was broken, and he paid to have a new one made. When we brought my father to *kevurah* in *Eretz Yisrael* many years later, that *matzeivah* came along and was set up next to the new one, a tribute to Munish Ridel's compassion and sense of responsibility. Apparently my mother must have trusted Ridel's opinion, for not long afterward she began to travel to Warsaw to look for an apartment. It took two months until she found a suitable place. My father had stipulated in his will that we continue to maintain a *minyan* in our home, so we needed a place large enough to house a *beis midrash*.

The moving van that came to our house was the first truck I had ever seen, for Siedlice was strictly a horse-and-buggy town. The van was a monster, a huge, living thing that had to be cranked up in the front. My mother took along everything from the house that she could possibly take — my sisters' paintings, lamps, trinkets. She traveled with the van and sent the rest of us to Warsaw by train.

After the transition, our family further dispersed. Lazer and Leiby, the younger two of my four brothers, went off to the Mir to learn, and Yankel, the oldest, went to the Lubliner yeshivah. Only Devorah and I remained at home for the time being. It was as though my father, in his passing, had removed the iron anchor from our household, and now the pieces, too weightless to hang together, were loosening from the framework and chipping off toward scattered destinies.

The new city was an explosive change from Siedlice. It was

Chapter Seven / 69

like entering the din of cymbals after being accustomed to the delicate tappings of a triangle. The streets were paved and milling with movement. No doubt the change was harder on my mother than on me; to this day I enjoy big cities. The bustling flow of action exhilarated me. There was constant stimulation and interest, new happenings on every corner.

Warsaw was a very sophisticated city culturally. The life of the mind flourished here, and with considerable prestige. Clubs of all types — political, literary, artistic — thrived, and young people considered it stylish to have a book in hand. At this point, my mother was no longer very worried about the danger of modern influences on us. We had been involved in Bnos Agudath Israel (a youth organization for girls) since the time we were small, and we were already formed in my father's image, morally and mentally bound to his ideals. The intellectual ferment in the air, however, was invigorating and added a certain zest and sense of purpose to the cycle of daily life. The *frum* people, too, walked the streets with a *sefer* in hand.

Our new apartment, a large and comfortable one with twelve-foot-high ceilings, was at Gensia Street 7A, in the heart of the textile district. There were no private houses in the metropolises of Poland; the wealthy and the not-so-wealthy alike lived in huge apartment houses, each of which ran the length of a block and had its own cobblestoned courtyard, enclosed by an iron gate. The ground floors of these buildings typically were commercial. Below us on Gensia Street were several shops, including a well-known kosher restaurant called *Maadan*, the Hebrew word for "delicious." It was owned by a man named Mr. Gefen. The intertwining of residential and commercial life made for a constant revolving door of activity, which I thoroughly enjoyed.

Our section of town was almost totally Jewish. It was more or less an open ghetto, subdivided by the trades that concentrated on each street. The textile district, where we lived, was inhabited by a fairly wealthy population; parallel to us was Nalevki Street, the garment district; then came leather goods territory; then the

Reuven Kleinsinger, our family friend, in Warsaw.

schools. The adjacent neighborhood was a poorer one, where peddlers and old clothing merchants hawked their wares in a more hybrid, market-like atmosphere.

The streets of the textile district were peppered with a special breed of Jews called *treigers,* or workers who carried loads. A *treiger* wore a beard and a *Yiddishe hittel,* the brimmed cap associated nowadays with the Jewish face of Eastern Europe. Hundreds of these porters trudged the streets of our neighborhood, their huge rolls of twine on their backs, muttering chapters of *Tehillim* by heart. They were poorly educated and toiled in sweat for their bread, for competition among them was very stiff.

In nearly every building there was a *beis midrash.* At *Minchah* time, all the merchants would leave their stores and fly to the nearest *minyan* to *daven* — to *"chap arein a Minchah,"* as the men used to say — and to say *Kedushah. Shtiblach* dotted the buildings, those of Ger, Alexander, and Radzimin among the most populated. On Shabbos, virtually all of the businesses closed up, and you could feel a palpable sense of rest in the streets. Jewishness surrounded us, like the *Ananei HaKavod* in the desert.

All of the Jewish groups were organized under the strong central authority of the Warsaw *kehillah,* also known as the *Gemeinde,* or community. Even the more modern element subscribed to its authority. The streets of Warsaw were eminently Jewish; the community was rich and flourishing.

The *chassidim* in Siedlice had been right about one thing: we did indeed find many welcoming arms in our new city. My father had many followers in Warsaw who received us beautifully. One of them was Reuven Kleinsinger, a tall, imposing man with striking black eyes. Kleinsinger owned a profitable antique *seforim* store in town, where he collected and sold old and out-of-print volumes.

I remember how fascinated I had always been when I had visited his married daughter on our trips to Warsaw. Because of her father's profession, she had several pop-up children's books on her shelves, an unusual novelty at that time. This daughter also has a special place in my memory because she and her husband did not have children for seventeen years. My father used to tell Kleinsinger constantly that he should never give up hope of having grandchildren, and his daughter was a model of faith; she kept children's books and toys in her home all through the years, preparing for the *brachah* that she knew would one day be hers. And she did indeed have two children. We were already living in Warsaw when she gave birth to the first one, and I remember how excited we were.

Kleinsinger was very concerned for our family when we came to town, especially because he knew that we no longer had money. He used to come to the house every Sunday on his way home from the store and bring us huge baskets of strawberries, which were a lavish delicacy. We children used to sit on the porch, dunking the strawberries in sugar and eating them while Kleinsinger and my mother talked. His visits were always a treat.

My mother began to scour the city for ways to earn a living. Her resourcefulness stood her in good stead. First she went to local government officials who ran the city lottery and explained to them that she was a widow with several children to support. She asked permission to sell lottery tickets for a small profit, and they agreed. She also received a percentage of the winnings.

The next project she undertook was to open a boarding house, using the extra rooms in our spacious apartment. This had actually begun on an informal basis when friends of my brothers from the Mir came to Warsaw, looking for a place to stay. There were dozens of foreign students in the Mir, many of whom had occasion to come to the capital for various reasons; one needed to see a doctor, a second to buy clothes for *beshoh,* a third to arrange papers at one of the embassies. Lazer and Leiby began to make a habit of sending their friends to us, and before we knew it, our apartment had become a *"stanzia"* — a station for wayfarers. We provided breakfast as well as beds and sent the visitors downstairs to the restaurant for their main meals, but there were always those who elected to eat dinner with us too.

Among the *bachurim* who frequented our household was a young man of nineteen or twenty named Volvy Friedman. Volvy was a student in the Mir then. He was a very outgoing, self-sufficient young man who had already traveled through many yeshivos in order to gain an eclectic learning background. Originally from Munkatch, Volvy's lineage was a distinguished one. He was the son of Rabbi Naftali Friedman, who in turn was the son of Reb Chaim, the Rav of Dombrad. Reb Naftali's wife Zissel, the daughter of Reb Leibish Ackerman of Strobiczow, had passed away while the children were still quite young, and he married her sister Leah, who became a second mother to the children. Thanks in great measure to her, Volvy and his three brothers had grown up very independent and secure. All of them were involved in various business ventures.

Volvy Friedman became a prized visitor in our home because he provided my mother with the link to her past that she longed for so desperately, a window to the life of her youth. They both had ties to the background and values of the Munkatcher world, and they shared a common taste and understanding. They enjoyed discussion about the small things that glowed with the familiarity of home; even the mention of the Munkatcher *nussach* of davening brought a smile to my mother's face. She needed this all the more now that she was drifting further and further from her roots. Volvy and my mother got along famously.

Our apartment became known not only to the yeshivah students who trekked in from all corners of the map, but to the local thieves who often robbed them on their way in from the station. There was an organized theft ring in the poor neighborhood adjoining ours. Its members bore no resemblance to the psychotic criminal of modern times; rather, these hooligans were more akin to the Artful Dodger, crafty masters of the art of snatching suitcases from naive young men whose faces betrayed their awe of the big city. Although these robbers were non-violent, the aggravation they caused was beyond measure. The gang even had a mediator who used to come up to our apartment to claim ransom for the stolen luggage. When the bags were returned — as they invariably were, upon the word of the thieves — the valuables inside them were inevitably gone, but they always left passports and important legal documents; they were thieves with a heart.

Guests sometimes showed up at our apartment in the middle of the night, and I frequently had to get up and move to another bed. We had a few extra crude cots made from lumber, and when those ran out, I slept on the dining room table under my coat, or occasionally in the bathtub. There never seemed anything unnatural to me about this. My mother's door was wide open, just as it had always been, just as it should be. I never thought of the bathtub as an inconvenience, but simply as part of the package.

My mother earned a living from the combined income of the lottery ticket sales and her impromptu rooming house, but it was not as much as we were used to having, and the work was hard. She once mentioned that she could not go on doing this forever.

After a while, students were not the only ones who came to our door. Word of mouth and my parents' reputations soon transformed our apartment into a magnet for some of the greatest Torah personalities in Europe. Gensia 7A, little by little, became a landmark. One had only to mention the address to evoke a spark of recognition on the listener's face. I remember *bachurim* in the apartment whose mouths hung open when they saw the people who sat down at our table.

The list of Torah luminaries who passed through our doors was an impressive one. Among others, we were privileged to host Rabbi Elchonon Wasserman and his son; Rabbi Yerucham Levovitz, the Mirrer *mashgiach*; Rabbi Aharon Kotler of Kletzk (and later of Lakewood) and his wife; Rabbi Boruch Ber Lebowitz;

Rabbi Avraham Kalmanowitz of Tiktin and the Mirrer Yeshivah; Rabbi Fishel Goldfedder; Rabbi Gedaliah Schorr and Rabbi Elya Chazan, who were later *roshei yeshivah* of Yeshiva Torah Vodaath; Rabbi Dovid Snow and Rabbi Moshe Yehudah Blau, both *bochurim* at the time; Rabbi Joseph Baumol, a *musmach* of Lublin, who later took over the Crown Heights Yeshivah; Rabbi Avrohom Bender of Yeshiva Rabbeinu Yitzchok Elchonon and his wife; Rabbi Chaim Pincus of Yeshiva Torah Vodaath; Rabbi Shmuel Pliskin, who later became a rav in Baltimore; and Rabbi Yechezkel Abramsky, who became a rav in London. Gensia 7A developed into a focal point in town, a place where people came for a meal, for a word of Torah, for a word of comfort, for news of friends and relatives. At a time when traveling was strenuous and conveniences limited, our apartment was a beckoning lighthouse in the travels of the European Jewish world.

In addition to the boarding house, my mother later decided to earn extra income by renting out two rooms of our large apartment as a wedding hall. This began much later, after I had already gone away to seminary. I remember the first time I went home for *Yom Tov* and opened the front door of our apartment, only to wonder if I had come to the right place. My mother had renovated our house completely during the short time I had been away, and it did not look anything like the home I had left.

Two rooms had been set aside, one for the *chupah* and one for the *l'chaim* after the ceremony. No meal was served afterward in those days; weddings usually took place in the afternoon, and the meal was served elsewhere in the evening. The *chupah* room was decorated with my mother's characteristic good taste. A large white chair had been set up for the bride, with a white crown and two snowy doves affixed to its back. The *chupah* itself was a creation of beauty and innovation. Beneath a canopy of navy blue velvet trimmed with gold, my mother had attached silver stars, in the centers of which were tiny electric bulbs that twinkled delicately. The two rooms remained in order at all times.

The venture, thank G-d, was a successful one. Sometimes there were two or three weddings in our apartment in one day.

In my Bais Yaakov uniform in Warsaw.

My mother's financial burden was greatly eased, and as a bonus, the colorful cast of characters passing through our home continued to grow.

In Warsaw I began to attend Bais Yaakov. The elementary school was quite well established; both Hebrew and secular subjects, including the Polish language, were taught, and the school day lasted until three o'clock in the afternoon. Education for younger children was much more of a priority in the large cities than it had been in the rural culture of my childhood. We even received an official children's magazine called *Kindergarten*, a very prestigious item at that time, published by Rabbi Eliezer Gershon Friedenson. He also published *Bais Yaakov*, the official organ of the Bais Yaakov movement. Rabbi Friedenson ran a trade school for girls in Lodz under the auspices of Agudath Israel, and his magazines circulated all over Poland.

Spending the day in a formal classroom was a very difficult adjustment for me. Structured learning had never been my cup of tea, and I found the environment very confining in contrast to the freedom I had always enjoyed. Even worse than that was the discomfort of having to share the attention with nearly twenty other girls. For nine years of my life I had been the diamond in my father's household, and now I was only one of many. I did not have the same confidence now that my father was no longer behind me, and I had to work very hard to settle in. Two blessings pulled me through the double nets of social and academic adjustment: a naturally outgoing personality and a good memory.

After I completed the eighth grade, I attended a city trade school for a year. As always, I did best at those subjects which did not require an exact attention to dry facts. I enjoyed anything that engaged my imagination and my hands, and I remember winning awards for window-decorating projects.

My sister Devorah.

Jacob Landau,
Devorah's future husband.

In 1934, less than a year after we had come to Warsaw, my sister Devorah left for Israel. She was twenty-three years old. Her move was not only pioneering but daring; as a rule, single girls at that time did not take off by themselves to resettle in other countries without a very pressing reason, and Devorah had none other than the longings of her soul. She could justifiably have blamed her ambition on heredity. From her mother she had received her backbone; from her father, her idealism. The ceiling in Poland was too low for her — there was nothing to reach up to. In her thirst for a broader horizon, she had spoken to many people and read a great deal about *Eretz Yisrael*. She knew that this was the goal she was seeking, the project that would give meaning to her life.

Devorah's *aliyah* was arranged by a man named Jacob Landau, the son of the Czechonower *Rav*. He had emigrated from Poland to Israel and was now active in the affairs of Poalei Agudath Israel. He was a very educated man who had already written several books and had acted for a time as secretary to Jacob Rosenheim, the president of the Agudath Israel world organization, who resided in Frankfurt-Am-Main. Landau and Binyomin Mintz, also a Poalei Agudah activist, once came to stay with us during a tour of countries where they were trying to rally

Chapter Seven / 77

support and raise money for the Agudah. It was at our table that they turned Devorah's dream of the Holy Land into a reality. When Jacob Landau returned to Israel, he arranged for Devorah to make *aliyah* through the Agudah.

My mother did not understand why Devorah wanted to leave so badly. She only understood that her family seemed to be disintegrating in front of her eyes. She could not see deeply into that part of Devorah's being that was a spiritual inheritance from her father, the part that longed with divine passion for a greater Jewish dream. But she saw that she could not keep her strong-willed daughter at home.

Devorah left Warsaw along with several other *olim*. The train station was packed with thousands of well-wishers who had come to see the young people off. A radiant sun filtered through dispersing gray rain clouds, and music issued merrily from the midst of the throng. The *olim* were happy and confident; they had not the slightest doubt that they were going to a better place. A great wave of enthusiasm burst from the crowd as the train pulled out, and handkerchiefs waved overhead. I think that even my mother was uplifted by the infectious wave of good cheer that pulsated through the crowd on that platform.

Devorah was completely fluent in Hebrew by this time, and she had armed herself to earn a living by taking a sewing course in Warsaw before her departure. She was not afraid of hard work, and in fact that is exactly how she began her life in the Holy Land, splitting stones to build roads. In 1936 she married Jacob Landau, who, after the establishment of the State of Israel, became the director of the Social Ministry of the Israeli government. A year later she sent my brother Lazer a certificate; he came home briefly from the Mir and then followed her to Israel. Neither he nor Devorah ever saw my mother again. My eldest brother Yankel returned after a time from the Lubliner yeshivah, and he and I remained at home, alone of seven children.

When I was in my fifteenth year, I began to think seriously about attending the famous Sara Schenirer Beth Jacob Seminary in Krakow. The school had been open for more than fifteen years, and although it had an established reputation, the notion of sending young girls away from home was still a foreign one in most *frum* circles. It was no easy task to win my mother's consent. In addition to the expense, my mother was reluctant to part with another child, especially a daughter. To her, sending a girl away from home was tantamount to abandoning her responsibilities as a parent. But there was really nothing for me to do in Warsaw at this point; I was not of age to marry, and I was eager for new stimulation and adventure. I remember how thrilled I was to be accepted to the school, a prestigious accomplishment not easily won.

Sara Schenirer had already passed away, but I still remembered the time she had come to visit us not long after our move to Warsaw, when I still quite young. She had asked me some questions from *Chumash,* and I answered them. Then she had put her hand on my head and said, "You are going to be my good student one day." Perhaps she had planted a seed all those years ago, and the seed had now flowered.

Chapter Eight

In September of 1937 I went to Krakow, six hours away by train. I had no friends with me, and only a few distant relatives in the new city; but I was ambitious and eager for change.

Krakow was a much older and more romantic city than Warsaw. It had once been home to the Polish kings and still retained a dignified historical flavor. Elegant stone buildings, old and beautifully kept, lined its hilly streets. I remember in particular a stately palace called the Wawel, which was open to the public. Students often sat on the curving steps of its sprawling piazza, doing their homework while the pigeons circled overhead. The river Wisla meandered along the outskirts of the city, which was set against the picturesque backdrop of a lofty mountain range.

In spite of its traditional appearance, however, Krakow was culturally more advanced than Warsaw. The Orthodox community had a much more modern veneer; many of the *frum* women did not cover their hair, and Polish rather than Yiddish was the spoken language, which lent quite a different cast to the atmosphere.

Sara Schenirer had acquired a building of her own on the outskirts of town, where her students would not be caught up in the social whirlpool of the city. She had traveled for several years to raise money for this important project, a place where she could shelter and supervise her charges in complete privacy. Architecturally the place was unattractive; it was a three-story gray stone building with high ceilings and resembled a warehouse more than a school. Neither did it have much to recommend it in terms of its surroundings, situated as it was on a dirt road near the Wisla in a flat, non-residential area, and saturated with the fumes of raw hides from the leather factory next door. But Sara Schenirer was not concerned with surfaces.

The entire institution was housed in that drab stone building: classrooms, offices, dining hall, and dormitory. Two hundred students lived there, in large rooms shared by twenty girls or more. The school was well run and rules were strictly enforced. Lights went out at ten o'clock in the evening and on again at six in the morning, when we arose for *davening*. Three meals were served daily, and all the students were given assignments on a rotating schedule to assist with the serving. Our Shabbosos were spent together in the dormitory; only once a month, on Rosh Chodesh, we had the day to ourselves.

Classes were excellent, standards demanding. Two to three hundred students were present at the average lecture, many of whom came to classes from their homes in town. Tests based on the lectures were given regularly. Among the constellation of outstanding teachers who took the podium each day, Rabbi Yehudah Leib Orlean is the one who shines most brightly in my memory. He was a very famous thinker, educator, and author at that time, a distinguished-looking man in his forties with an aristocratic black beard. He taught us a course which he called *"historiosophia,"* history which focused on *hashkafah*, and his lectures were fascinating. As always, I was most absorbed by topics that were less factual and more ideological. I listened raptly, but I simply could not take notes;

I was no more disciplined a student now than when I had attended the Warsaw Bais Yaakov, and I still depended heavily on my memory.

Another famous *mechanech* was Rabbi Deutscher, who was also the school administrator. He was German, a man of very precise and uncompromising principles. He wanted us to reach for a higher Jewish standard than the one visible in the Krakow Jewish community, where custom was more relaxed. Rabbi Deutscher drew crisp lines for us among the gray shades of these varying values, and he let us know clearly where we stood.

Among other notable teachers on the faculty, we had *Rebbetzin* Gittel Pas for *Beiur Tefillah; Rebbetzin* Weitzasch for *Shulchan Aruch;* Mrs. Ida Bauminger for *Ivrit; Rebbetzin* Esther Beigun for *Chumash;* and Rebbetzin Rottenberg. We learned *Chumash* with *Rashi* and *mefarshim, Neviim, Dinim,* and the classic *sifrei mussar.* The curriculum was excellent, and in spite of the discomfort of the regimentation, I benefited greatly from it.

To me, the most beautiful experience of seminary was Shabbos. It was a time of closeness, of community, of true rest and spirituality. Every week a different faculty couple used to stay with us in the dormitory to make us feel more at home. The rabbi would make *Kiddush* for us, and later on *Havdalah.* I remember how we all used to congregate in the dining room in the afternoon; girls would drift in from various pursuits, some from a nap, some from visiting family or friends, some from reviewing the *sedrah.* We would sit and talk for a while until *Shalosh Seudos,* when Rabbi Orlean came in to give us a *mussar shmuess* based on *Chovos HaLevavos* or *Mesilas Yesharim.*

When the men left the hall, we girls would begin to sing. We sang all the *zemiros* and songs that we knew, one by one. As daylight waned, our mood would soften and turn more solemn; and finally, when the first stars flickered in the night sky, our voices would swell with the special *Motzaei Shabbos* Yiddish *zemer* full of prayerful hope for the coming week:

עס גייט שוין אוועק דער הייליגער שבת
אין שטיבל איז פינצטער אין שטיבל איז שטיל
עם שעפשעט די מאמא דעם ג־ט פון אברהם,
זי שעפשעט א תפילה פון הארץ אין גיפיל
גאט פון אברהם פון יצחק און יעקב
פארנעם שוין מיין תפילה אין דיין הימילישע געצעלט
און שענק מיר דיין ברכה, און רופט אויף מיין מזל
אז ליכטיג זאל ווערן אויף דעם גאנזער וועלט.

The holy Shabbos turns away;
In the little room, it is dark and quiet.
The Mama whispers the "Gott Fun Avrohom"
She whispers a prayer from her heart and feelings
And she says, "G-d of Avrohom, of Yitzchok, and Yaakov
Take my prayers to Your Heavenly Tent
And give me Your blessing and perfect my mazel
So that the entire world should be full of light."

As soon as we were finished singing, as though on cue, the dining room lights would go on and *Havdalah* was recited. The girls then went off to various corners to write letters, to do homework, or simply to sit at the window talking lazily and dreaming about the future. The sweet and refined taste of the Shabbos *Kallah*'s presence lingered pleasantly over our evening activities and filled the ensuing week with an echo of otherworldliness.

The student body in Sara Schenirer was truly distinguished. It included the daughters of some of the outstanding Torah personalities of Poland, many of whom became leaders of the next generation. Among these fathers were the future Gerrer *Rebbe*, the *Beis Yisrael*; Rabbi Aharon Kotler; and Rabbi Zalman Sorotzkin.

Sadly, of all the girls that I met in the seminary, I remember very few names. The war scattered us; distance and death prevented us from forming lasting relationships. The girls were from mixed *Litvishe* and *Chassidishe* backgrounds, and although

Chapter Eight / 83

we came from so many different countries, we had the Yiddish language in common.

One girl with whom I was quite close for a time was Miriam Alter, a niece of the Gerrer *Rebbe,* the *Imrei Emes,* who had come to seminary from *Eretz Yisrael.* She was a lively, intelligent girl with a lyrical nature who played the harmonica. Miriam and I used to sit by the window in the dormitory at night (sometimes after curfew) and talk about Israel. Somehow, we felt that we were related.

Another friend with whom I spent a lot of time was a native of Krakow, a blond, blue-eyed girl with very gracious manners who came to classes from her home in the city. Her name, unfortunately, is lost to me, but her home is not; it was a place of good taste and traditional values, a blend very familiar and important to me. The house was full of exquisite antique furniture, but more importantly, it was rich with the values of Jewish antiquity. I was comfortable there and visited often.

My friend was an only child, and she was glad to share her parents' attention with me. This was something for which I hungered, the attention I so desperately missed from my own parents, and it was the best gift she could have given me. On Shabbos afternoons the two of us used to walk to the park, talking and dreaming about the things close to the heart of a sixteen-year-old girl: marriage, a home, hopes for the future.

My mother sent me packages frequently while I was away. Sometimes they came by mail and sometimes with people who traveled to Krakow. Volvy Friedman, one of our frequent guests in Warsaw, once arrived at the seminary with a special delivery from my mother. When I learned that there was someone from home downstairs, I was very excited — but I was not altogether surprised when Rabbi Deutscher told me unequivocally that I could not come down to receive the package. The young man would have to leave it for me in the office.

It is very interesting to me now to think back on that incident. Socializing without *tachlis* was no more acceptable in *frum* circles then than it is now, but it is the difference in mentality that is so remarkable. As a girl, I was in a unique position; *bachurim* were not a strange sight to me. They had been in our house ever since I could remember, almost like part of the furniture, and there did not seem anything so terrible to me about receiving a package from a trusted family friend.

But the main issue is that there was never any thought of impropriety. People then maintained stricter inner boundaries in their interactions with both men and women; they treated each other with greater respect and kept their distance even when they were together. It is this respect of boundaries — and the utter inconceivability of trespassing them — that impress me so much looking back.

Needless to say, though, I did not go down to see Volvy Friedman — but it was quite some time before I was free of my friends' ribbing about the "young man who had delivered the package"!

In fact, viewing the overall picture, it seems to me that dangers in general were of an entirely different sort in those days. I am thinking in particular of one incident, perhaps the most memorable episode of my two years in school. It was the time we received an unexpected visitor in the dormitory.

One Friday night, just after candle-lighting, there was a knock on the front door of the dormitory. We went downstairs to find a boy of about eighteen clutching the doorpost, swooning. One of the girls, a tall red-head who came from a prominent family in Lithuania, insisted that we allow him in, for he looked about to faint. A few of the good-hearted among us encouraged the boy to come sit down in the hallway. There was no fear of abuse of any kind; our heads were not filled with the licentious criminality of modern times. The threat here was a much more subtle one — and, in a way, much more dangerous.

As soon as the door was closed behind him, this poor young boy had a miraculous recovery. He got to his feet and immediately began to distribute Communist literature.

Communist influence was spreading rabidly in many circles at that time. Europe, in fact, was a hothouse of leftist and radical ideologies whose organizational centers flourished in the big cities. Many Jews were attracted to Communism because of the social and economic oppression they felt under the anti-Semitic regimes of Eastern Europe, and they were eager to place their trust in any system that offered them — at least theoretically — equal treatment. My friends and I had heard quite a bit about these poisonous ideas, but we had never expected them to penetrate the walls of the seminary! Our girls were soft-hearted but not blind, and they quickly turned the young man in.

The red-haired girl was sent to the office and kept under observation. Marxist literature was found underneath her mattress. Most likely she had come from Lithuania already infected with these new ideas and had been recruited by her cohorts even before she set foot in the dormitory. The girl was sent back to Lithuania, and from then on there were regular mattress checks in the dorm; but fortunately the seminary did not have much to fear from the rest of us, and no such flagrant incident occurred again during my time.

There was actually only one very black hole in the richness of those years in seminary — but it was black indeed. It began when I contracted rheumatic fever in the dormitory, during the winter of my second year. Our building was poorly heated, and we were able to bathe only once or twice a week in cold water, so it is not surprising that I got sick. I had never been seriously ill before, though, and I had no idea what was happening to me. My hands swelled up strangely, and a fever threatened to consume me. I was in such great pain that it hurt if anyone so much as laid a hand on the bed.

My mother arranged for me to travel by train to the village of Wapyene, where there were mineral waters that were reportedly therapeutic. It seemed a little strange to me that she did not bring me straight home, but I did not question her judgment; I was too sick to think. My mother's sister had a close friend in Wapyene who took me in. When I was feeling a little stronger, I traveled home.

It was only after I had returned from seminary months later that I discovered the reason for the detour. My sister Chavcia had died in Alexander right before I got sick. My mother did not want me to find out so that I would not have to sit *shivah*. By the time I came home from Wapyene, the *sh'loshim* had already passed. Chavcia's husband and children had contracted typhoid fever, a dreaded infectious disease. She had nursed them all back to health and then succumbed to it herself. She was twenty-nine years old. Hadassah, one of her sisters-in-law, took over the care of her three children, all of whom were lost later during the war. That entire episode was a blank to me. I only remember that Chavcia disappeared from my life as quickly as a dream.

My illness, thank G-d, was the only serious one I suffered for many years afterward. Aside from the tragedy of my sister's death, my stay in the Krakow seminary was a relatively peaceful one. We lived in our own private enclave near the river Wisla, absorbed in the life of the spirit, thinking little about the events of the outside world.

During my second year, we began to hear rumors about a war, but these were remote fantasies and did not touch us in any real way. The teachers and administrators knew more than we did, but they did not discuss it with us. Partly they did not want to arouse panic, and partly they honestly did not believe — no one, in fact, believed — that any very severe crisis would develop. The concept of a Jewish holocaust, or even of another world war, was beyond the scope of even the wildest imagination. I had gone home twice each year to Warsaw, and I did not hear or see anything there either, other than a lot of wispy rumors. It was because of our false ensconcement in this comfortable complacency that the term *blitzkrieg* later became so apt: we were indeed struck by lightning.

During the winter of 1938-39, we had our first suggestion that there might be some basis to the rumors. Several girls from Germany who were of Polish birth came to Krakow, and six of them stayed in the dormitory with us. It seemed that all residents

With a friend of mine (right) in the Sara Schneirer summer camp.

of Polish birth had suddenly been expelled from Germany, told to pack their bags on short notice and to get out of the country. The girls who came to us were totally alone. The majority of them were suffering from malnutrition and had to be taken to the local hospital.

Among these unfortunate girls were two sisters who had lost their vision from hunger. I remember going with some of my friends to visit them in the hospital. They were about our age, very pale and very fragile; they did not even have the strength to speak much. They gazed aimlessly at the walls and ceiling, blinking frequently, and there was a terrible emptiness in their eyes.

The sister near whom I was standing suddenly said to me, "I want to touch your face."

I leaned down, and she touched my face. I cried like a baby — but she was the greater optimist, for she said, "One day I'll be able to see you." And both sisters did indeed recover their vision, after a very long stay in the hospital. I did not see them again after that and had no idea what became of them, but I remembered their haunting, empty eyes.

The German girls were unofficial heralds of the coming

storm, but we let the ill winds blow over us and finished the school term smoothly. In the summer of 1939, the entire seminary adjourned to the countryside, in the area of Chrobacze, for the summer program. Seminars were given on the grass in a rustic farm setting, and we enjoyed the fresh air and the relative relaxation.

Toward the end of August, in the middle of a tranquil afternoon, one of the administrators announced to us suddenly that we were to disband the camp immediately. The message fell from the sky, without warning of any kind. We had no idea what to think. Alarmed, we threw our belongings together as quickly as we could and scrambled out to the collection of horse-drawn buggies that had been rounded up to take us back into town. We did not know it at that moment, but Poland was mobilizing in anticipation of war; and the German invasion, in fact, would begin in a matter of days.

When we arrived at the dormitory, we were greeted by panic. There was a mad scattering of people and baggage in every direction. Supervision had evaporated, and every girl had to fend for herself. I had never seen such mass hysteria before. The principals were already gone; even the cook had left. No one stayed to see us off. We set our bags down in the dining room, wondering what to do.

In the space of a few short hours, the building became a shell; the world of the seminary was turned out into the street. Doors had been left carelessly unlocked, and there was not even any food in the kitchen. The hallways were emptied of glory, and in its place reigned a stiff, quiet fright — the quiet of the unknown.

I found a message waiting for me in the office, informing me that a telegram had arrived from my mother along with twenty-five dollars to come home to Warsaw. There was no telling how old the message was. The money, it seemed, had been forwarded to my cousins, the Levys, a more modern family with whom I had not kept up much during my stay in Krakow. I raced to their house now —only to find it empty. A neighbor told me that the Levys had left for South America. They were gone, and so were my twenty-five dollars. I had seen newly mobilized Polish soldiers in the streets on my way here, and I felt a brief streak of horror.

That night several of us slept in the dormitory. We did not unpack any of our things because we were hoping to get out of Krakow as soon as we could. When we came down to the dining room the next morning, our bags were gone. Every last thing had been stolen. I did not even have a spare pair of stockings.

Two paradoxical feelings flashed through me. The first was a feeling of doom, of being a helpless victim in an atmosphere of chaos. There was no one to appeal to for help. We were now in a lawless vacuum, with no one to defend us. The second feeling I experienced was a sense of relief. I had to get home quickly, and now I would not have to worry about transporting my baggage.

After a few days of luckless attempts to make arrangements to get home, only two girls remained with me of my entire group of friends. The first was a tall, blond American named Bertha Goldfedder. Bertha's brother had also spent some time in Europe learning in the Mir, and he had visited our apartment in Warsaw on several occasions. By this time he had already returned to America, and his sister was not as frightened as she should have been.

"Listen, Peska," she said to me in her typically upbeat manner, "how long could the war last? A year or so? What if I came to stay with you in the meantime? Then, when it's all over, we can go back to seminary."

Bertha's rosy projections were tempting, but my intuition told me that they were probably naive. The Germans were in town, and the air was brittle with tension.

"I don't know," I replied hesitantly. "This doesn't look like a joke — it's for keeps. You have a passport, Bertha. I think you should take it and go home."

Bertha's brother wired her to make the travel arrangements. He apparently had the same ominous hunch as I did, for he urged me to come to America as well, using his papers. But I had no intention of abandoning my mother. Bertha Goldfedder, with the greatest good luck, took my advice and went home just in time.

My second companion was a girl from Berlin named Ruth Nussbaum. Ruth was one of the sincerest people I had ever met, a girl of straightforward, Germanic manner and deep religious conviction. She was a very devoted student and was thrown completely off course by the emergency; she had wanted so much to finish school. She was totally lost. I remember how she looked at me pleadingly and said with simple terror, "Peska, what should I do?"

At that moment, Ruth Nussbaum became my ward. I had connections in Poland, and she had none. Within a few hours' time, it had become extremely dangerous to have German friends, but I could not abandon this girl to her fate. The only problem that remained was how to get home.

A messenger came to the dorm a day or two after our return, bringing a note for me from an elderly aunt of mine, the wife of the famed *tzaddik* Reb Shayale Czechower, *zt"l*. This aunt was a great woman, the daughter of the Gorlitzer *Rebbe* and a sister to my Bubba Chana — the grandmother who had once made us sandwiches in Strizhev, a hundred years ago, on a different planet. My aunt had heard that all the seminary girls were back in town and that there was no food in the dormitory, and she invited me to come up to her house for a meal. I had visited her a number of times during my stay in seminary, and I was enormously relieved to hear from her. I took Ruth Nussbaum along with me.

My aunt was the perfect embodiment of a *rebbetzin*, an intelligent, compassionate older woman who was extremely devoted to her husband. When we came to visit, Reb Shayale had just given her twenty *zlotys* to buy food for Shabbos, and she insisted that I take it and use it to get home.

Before I left the house that day, I took five *zlotys* of the money and asked the *gabbai* to write a *kvittel* to the *Rebbe*. The *gabbai* obliged and soon ushered me in to see my uncle.

"I'm going away now," I told him simply, "and I have no idea where I'll wind up. I would like to have a *berachah* — that everything should be all right."

The *berachah* I received from Reb Shayale Czechower was very different from what I expected, and it turned out to be one of the greatest and most powerful gifts I ever received. He said: *"Zolst nosei chein zein in die oigen fun Hashem Yisbarach und die oigen fun mentschen* — you should find favor in both Hashem's eyes and the eyes of people."

I could not have imagined how often this blessing would save me from grief in the years to come. I laid down the five *zlotys* on the table; even though Reb Shayale was my relative, it would not have occurred to me to request a *berachah* without giving a *pidyon*. How surprised the *Rebbe* might have been to learn that he had been given his own money!

I had decided by now to take Ruth Nussbaum home with me. It was playing with fire to risk traveling in the company of a German citizen, but I put my trust in G-d and insisted that she come along. It seems now, looking back, that we were the last two people to leave the Sara Schenirer dormitory.

There was a frantic atmosphere in the streets now; the patterned bustle of daily routine had been replaced by an aimless frenzy. People rushed back and forth in a disoriented flutter, like wingless birds looking for shelter.

The train station was full of Polish soldiers going to the front. When we went to the window to purchase tickets, we were told that there was not a single seat left on the train. The soldiers had filled them all.

We wandered out to the platform in a daze. Tall khaki uniforms thronged coldly about us, faceless and threatening. We saw the red cap of the conductor above the crowd, near the open doorway of one of the cars, and we pushed our way through to him. Was there anything that could be done? we begged him. Wasn't there even one seat left anywhere on the train? We would take anything — anything.

The conductor glanced down at our frightened faces. What

an odd couple we must have seemed to him! — two lost girls in a mob of men, one petite and energetic, the other tall and gangly, with the eyes of a lost kitten. Instantly he took pity on us. I thought to myself that Reb Shayale's *berachah* must already be taking effect.

"Listen," he said, "there is a very rich man on the train who hired an entire car for himself. He fell down skiing in Zakopane and broke his back. He can't move — and I bet he could use some company." The conductor took us around to the window of the rich man's car. He boosted us up and actually pushed us through the window, and he did not take any money from us.

The injured man, a husky Polish aristocrat with blond hair and a ruddy complexion, was lying on his back on a berth, covered in a body cast from head to foot. He was in agonizing pain. Rather than show surprise at the sight of two young ladies climbing in through his window, he seemed glad to see us. As the conductor had guessed, he was relieved to have company, especially since he had no attendant.

I thought of where I had been only a few short weeks ago — sitting in a field with my friends, absorbing an inspiring lecture in an atmosphere of detached tranquility. Now here I was, on a train packed with Polish soldiers, sitting illegally in a car next to a strange man with a broken back — riding, it seemed, toward the precipice of disaster. All normalcy had suddenly evaporated; the world had been turned on its head and was now a completely unpredictable place.

We tried to behave as though nothing extraordinary was going on. The Pole asked for some water, which we brought him, and he and I exchanged a little small talk. Ruth Nussbaum wisely kept silent. She didn't speak Polish, and the last thing she could afford to do now was speak German.

After a while, Ruth indicated to me that she wanted to go to the ladies' room. She opened the door of the car and began to thread her way gingerly through the masses of canvas-clad soldiers, a reed among cedars. She did not come back for a long time, and I began to panic. Ruth had a German passport. Not only that, but I had told the conductor that she was my friend. What if she had been discovered?

Finally I couldn't stand it any longer. I left the car and followed her to the ladies' room. The soldiers petrified me. Making my way through those pointed caps and even more pointed stares was like running the gauntlet. I did not see a single woman anywhere, which made me even more nervous. I knocked on the bathroom door. Ruth, thankfully, was still there, and she let me in. She had been too afraid to face all those soldiers again and had decided to remain where she was. I was not too eager myself to make a return trip through that sea of military faces. Ruth and I stayed in the bathroom for the rest of the trip, a journey of several hours, without letting anyone in. People knocked and knocked on the door, but we huddled quietly inside and did not respond. It was a miracle that nothing happened to us.

When we reached the station in Warsaw, the bedlam that greeted us on the platform was even greater than in Krakow. We could not get a *droshky* to take us home — they were all snatched up immediately, before we could blink. Then a second miracle occurred. A couple from our neighborhood who happened to be at the station recognized me and came over to us. Somehow, the husband managed to flag down a carriage, and he paid the driver to take us home. I still don't know how he did it, and I don't know what I would have done if he and his wife hadn't shown up.

We pulled up at Gensia 7 at about three o'clock in the morning. My mother was sitting on our balcony, looking down. She had been sitting there for eight days.

Chapter Nine

At seven o'clock on Friday morning, a few hours after I got home, my brother Yankel and I went out on the balcony of the apartment. It was September 1, 1939. We saw planes swooping through the air at dangerously low altitudes, spilling bullets on the city.

Yankel said uncertainly, "I think these are maneuvers."

I had a more ominous instinct. In fact, it felt very much like the intuitive chill that had struck me when Bertha Goldfedder had remarked blithely that she didn't think the war could last more than a year. "It doesn't look like maneuvers," I replied, half to myself. "I think this is the real thing — I think it's war."

We went back inside. The radio, which had been on constantly, was issuing warnings to the residents of Warsaw to board up their windows, store food, and prepare themselves for an invasion. The war had begun; Germany had attacked Poland.

Yankel and I were the only ones at home now with my mother. Devorah and Lazer were safely in Israel; Boruch was married and living in Munkatch as the new *Rebbe*; Leiby was still

My brother Yankel.

in the Mir; Chavcia was dead. Yankel was the head of our household now. He was a very clever and capable young man of twenty-four with considerable learning talents, and his outgoing personality had won him a large circle of friends. He did his best now to ease our distress. "Maybe it won't last too long," he told us. "Maybe it will pass." But it was obvious that he was not convinced of his own words.

On Shabbos afternoon, the bombing of Warsaw began in earnest. The bombs fell literally in our backyard. The sounds were morbidly fascinating, rolling toward us like a juggernaut in a strange science-fiction story. The whooshing and whistling wound about us in tangled loops, lacing us into the center of a fatal knot. Whenever you heard that whistling crescendo rising toward a shrill peak, you knew that an explosion would follow. The vibrations were earth-shaking, so close that sometimes you felt that you had been sucked into the very center of the explosion. Sirens would scream across the city when the raid was over.

Many people in our building began to rush downstairs to the basement, but my mother refused to go. Once again, the words of *Tehillim* were her practical guidelines, and she quoted them now with a simple sincerity that I will never forget: "*Anah mipanechah evrach?* Hashem, where can a person run to escape You? You are everywhere. If You come for me, come for me where I am." And she stayed upstairs.

The three of us did, however, prepare some basic necessities in case we would have to get out quickly. We each had a small tote bag filled with basic items — pajamas, a change of underwear, a sweater, a toothbrush, a *siddur*, a *Tehillim*, and some cookies. To her own bag my mother added the *sefer Shaar Yissaschar*, written by her *zeide*, the Gorlitzer *Rebbe*.

The bombing went on with a sporadic regularity for several more weeks. The Germans reached the outskirts of Warsaw, captured the airport, and began to close in on us with artillery. Whenever the explosions were close at hand, we moved out onto the back stairwell, where the walls were thicker and there was no danger of flying window glass. A few other tenants huddled together with us on the steps, but most stayed in the basement. We sat in that dark, curved hallway for hours at a time, just sitting, watching the paint peel and counting the minutes of our lives. Sometimes the bombing went on all through the night, and we would fall asleep out there on the steps, in our clothing. No one bothered to change into nightclothes in case a quick escape became necessary.

The raucous blaring of the bombardment was so continuous that eventually it deadened us altogether. Bizarre as it may seem, we became so desensitized that the noise itself sometimes put us to sleep. On most days we could not stay in our apartments long enough to cook a decent meal, so we kept hard candies and other non-perishables with us. I once fell asleep with a half-melted sour candy on my tongue. When I awoke, the acid of the candy had burned a dent into my tongue; it bled a little and ached with a raw soreness.

I remember being very disoriented when I opened my eyes. I couldn't remember exactly where I was. I saw dim figures scattered randomly on the dark stone steps, and I heard the thunderous rasping going on all around me, rattling the walls. I had to pinch myself to make sure I was still alive. That's what you did then; when you came to your senses, you touched yourself and you touched the people around you to see if they were still breathing and if the world still existed.

A few days after the war began, we were awakened at four o'clock in the morning by a new sound. The bombs were still falling, but a strange new noise was mixed with the clapping of the explosions, a sound like a jackhammer. We looked out the window to see hail falling, chunks of hail as big as softballs, smashing zealously against the roof. Nature was against us too;

it was as though the Accuser had battered through the gateway of Heaven, scattering our protection, flooding his wrath and vengeance upon our heads.

We asked G-d: Isn't the bombing enough? Do You have to send the noise of the hail upon us too? What have we done wrong?

During those few weeks, many Jews of Warsaw, from all ends of the spectrum, lost their faith. They were not strong enough to withstand the double fury; their anger was greater than their wisdom. Many others skated on thin ice, desperately clutching the threads of their heritage. My own questioning, thank G-d, was never of a serious nature. My parents' blood flowed strongly in my veins, and my father's image hung before me, a hallowed portrait. I only prayed that we would live.

During lulls in the bombing, we used to go out into the neighborhood and surrounding fields to scavenge for food. These trips were feats of daring — or perhaps they were simply exercises in the bravery of necessity. The bombing was more or less constant, with intervals of respite that teased us cruelly into false hopes. When you walked out the door you never knew if you would come back alive. You prepared yourself constantly to die. The line between the two worlds consisted of a second; a second was a lifetime.

All during the siege of Warsaw, our house continued to draw people, like an oasis. They came for many reasons: because my mother's shoulders were very broad, because we were the only people around with a heater, and because our building was one of the few that were not disturbed by the bombing. Everyone sat around our table and discussed the events of the week: young, old, *rabbanim*, businessmen, *meshugaim*. People came in and out of our lives, leaving behind only fleeting impressions, like frozen stills in a documentary film. My mother put up partitions in one of the large rooms to make separate sleeping quarters for the men and women. She fed the guests as best as she could, and she asked them no questions.

Unfortunately, Ruth Nussbaum had passed through our

revolving door of memories. My mother was fifty-nine years old now, and the bombardment was enough of a stress for her without the additional danger of keeping a German citizen under her roof. We found a family on the outskirts of town who took her in, and that was the last I saw of her.

A young couple from Galicia were among the next to seek shelter with us during the siege. They were newly married and had come to Warsaw to try to obtain papers so that they could make *aliyah* to *Eretz Yisrael,* but the bombing had interrupted their plans. Those two young people did not want to be out of each other's sight, even for a moment. Everyone said to them, "You're young — you'll make it," but the frightened looks on their faces betrayed their disbelief in fairy tales. Later, when the bombing ended, they packed their bags quickly and left, and we lost track of them.

One day there was a knock at the door. An elderly man stood there, holding a briefcase. He was short and stocky, neatly groomed, with silvery gray hair. He was obviously of aristocratic background; a Western aura surrounded him, a sense of elegant self-assurance that we seldom saw now.

He announced to my mother: "I know, Parczewer *Rebbetzin,* that you have people sleeping here in your house. I have nowhere to go, so I would like to stay with you. I'll give you as much money as you want, but you must let me stay with you. Here, among the *sefarim,* I'll feel safe."

The man spoke Yiddish with a German accent. A shiver ran through me when he told us that his name was Nussbaum —coincidentally the same name as that of the German girl who had recently left us. It was more than obvious where he had come from, but my mother never asked him his nationality, or indeed anything else about his personal life. She didn't want to know.

Mr. Nussbaum stayed with us for three weeks. It seemed that he had come to Warsaw on business and had gotten stuck in town during the bombing, but we never found out any concrete details of his background. He was a very dignified man, and he and my mother had great respect for each other. The briefcase went everywhere with him; he ate with it and slept with it. Sometimes soldiers would march through the streets in the middle of the night, their heavy boots thudding on the cobblestones, and Mr. Nussbaum would dive under the bed with his briefcase.

Each Friday he asked me to go out and buy him seven carnations, or nelkin, as he called them. He wanted them *l'kavod* Shabbos, one flower for each day of the week. The request was preposterous on two accounts: shells were still falling sporadically and fresh flowers were a luxury of the past. Where on earth would I find a florist now? But he continued to beg, putting my mother and me in a very awkward position. After all, he was our guest.

One Friday morning it was relatively quiet, and I told him I would go. I must honestly say that I probably would not have agreed to such a suicidal mission if not for my impetuous streak of independence. After a long hunt, I found a gentile store on the edge of the neighborhood. Incredibly, they had carnations for sale, and I bought seven, wondering all the time if I had let my sense of adventure get the better of me. When I walked out the door, there was a brief flurry of bombing, and the entire store fell in, collapsing on top of all the people inside.

I raced home with the carnations. When I came in, Mr. Nussbaum took them from me and kissed them. "*L'kavod* Shabbos," he said quietly, a joyous light on his face. I remembered that incident always. During the war one did not know anything about people, and yet one knew the most important things.

One day after the bombing let up, Mr. Nussbaum said to my mother, "I am going out now, and maybe I will not return." And he went the way of the young married couple — indeed, the way of so many of our guests who signed the invisible roster of our apartment and disappeared into the maelstrom. Many years later, in America, I learned that he had escaped safely to Israel.

Perhaps, as he had claimed, the *sefarim* in our house really did protect him.

The *Yamim Noraim* came upon us while the siege was still in full force, but the Jews of Warsaw were determined to celebrate Rosh Hashanah in spite of everything. My mother baked *challos* with the only flour available — rice flour, which was being peddled in the streets. The *challos* she made from it did not rise, but they were the best we had. Together with sardines, they constituted our *Yom Tov* meals.

On the morning of *Erev* Rosh Hashanah there was another break in the bombardment. We raced up to the apartment to put on our Shabbos clothing, and my mother put together a small bundle of food for me to take to my brother. Yankel had volunteered to help out at the fire department almost immediately after the invasion began, and he was now at work in a neighborhood far away from us, on the outskirts of the city.

I reached the fire station safely at about three o'clock in the afternoon and entered the courtyard of the building. I saw my brother going into the outhouse on the other side of the courtyard, and I waited nearby. The minute he came out, a bomb fell into the outhouse and blasted it into splinters.

At that moment, the bombardment renewed itself with a volcanic fury. The rocketing explosions mushroomed over the rooftops in clouds of filthy smoke, pouring debris over a city made of glass. There was not a moment's silence in that raging din. My brother rushed out to go back on duty, and I remained alone in the courtyard, with bombs raining down all around me.

The fire department had a collection of huge water barrels which were lined up against the walls of the courtyard. I found the nearest empty one and dove in, pulling the lid over my head. The splinters of the bombs crashed heavily and erupted all around me; the earth shook. I felt that the entire world had been destroyed, that there was nothing to look forward to, that I did not even exist. I had been turned into a blank, a lifeless speck in the void of the universe. During the bombing, you lived but you did not live. All accomplishment was robbed from you; you were powerless, less than nothing.

I stayed in the barrel for perhaps two or three hours, until the noise let up a bit. Sirens began to whine and cry in the heavy stillness. I lifted the lid of the barrel and stiffly, gingerly, climbed out. I saw shells lying around the building, long silver bodies with tapering noses. I counted them; there were eight. Not one had detonated. This is the truth.

That afternoon solidified my understanding of *hashgachah pratis*. The concept was now no longer a theory to me but a living ideal.

I raced home as fast as my wobbling legs would carry me. When I turned into Gensia Street, where we lived, the entire block was in flames. A canopy of fire, like a deathly *chupah*, arched over the roadway, lashing the heavens with its many tongues. I started to run. I ran down the center of that hellish aisle, running, running, running . . . I stepped over dead horses and dead bodies. A spray of glass slivers from the trembling buildings fell on my head and needled into the skin of my face and hands. All the side streets were on fire. There was hardly a sign of life anywhere, only the open jaws of destruction, swallowing everything in its path.

A few people were darting through the streets like ants, terrified, searching for anything. Others stood in the center of the flaming aisle like stone statues, riveted to their places. On Nalevki, the large adjoining street, all the *shtiblach* were burning, burning . . . as I ran through that tunnel of fire, I saw people scurry ahead of me through the gates of our building, carrying *sifrei Torah* and *sefarim*. They knew that we had a huge table in our wedding room, and they knew and trusted my mother.

As I came closer, I saw that all the surrounding houses had either collapsed into ruin or had been completely gutted by the flames. Ours was the only one still standing. I lunged through the gate of the courtyard, gasping. A neighbor of ours was standing there, and I literally fell into his arms.

"Is my mother alive?" I asked him.

"Yes — and she is so worried about you!"

The world vanished; everything dissolved in a vaporous wash of orange and black. When I came back to consciousness, I was lying across chairs in my mother's kitchen and people were picking the glass slivers out of my hair. It was already Rosh Hashanah night. Through the window, we could see my brother Yankel on the skeletal rafters of the roof next door, knocking away planks of wood so that the fire would not spread to our building.

The next day we had a Rosh HaShanah *minyan* in the *beis midrash* in our house. Everyone in the building, as well as people from the bombed-out houses around us, came. The women davened in the *chupah* hall.

In the middle of *Shemoneh Esrei*, there was an artillery barrage. The rockets were not as lethal as the bombs; they destroyed only what they hit, but they were still noisy and frightening. Three or four rockets hit our building, and the impact blew open the windows.

Not one person stepped out of the *Shemoneh Esrei*. There was not even any panic; no movement, no rustling, only the stillness of prayer. Later we learned that the rockets had all been trapped by the huge rolls of textiles that were stored in the building and never exploded.

On Yom Kippur the scene repeated itself. Our *beis midrash* was even fuller than it had been on Rosh Hashanah because so many other shuls had been destroyed. There was a continuous fusillade of rockets, but no one in the *minyan*, thank G-d, was hurt.

On the morning of *Erev* Succos, after two weeks of vehemently resisting the German invasion, the Poles capitulated. A cease-fire was declared. The Jews began to think about building *succahs*, but some were afraid, for German troops were expected to enter the city. The people in our building, however, were undaunted. In our courtyard there was a small flight of steps leading down to one of the stores. A few men improvised a *succah* by putting up some tree branches over the landing, and everyone went into that impromptu hut to make the *berachah* "*Leisheiv BaSuccah.*" There was no *lulav* or *esrog*; there was nothing to eat. That was our Yom Tov.

The news of the cease-fire seemed to lift a cloud from over the neighborhood. Some of the tenants heard the announcement over the radio and came out into the hallway to share the good news. The neighbors began to embrace and kiss each other, flooded with relief. We looked outside and saw people dancing in the streets. How premature was their joy!

Chapter Ten

We went out into the street the minute the cease-fire was announced, dazed by the sudden silence. It seemed as though the entire world had escaped annihilation by a hair's breadth and that we were the last few people on earth, like Noach and his family after the Flood. Warsaw looked like the surface of the moon, like some strange Martian planet. The black craters of buildings gaped at us on all sides; fires danced upward in a circle around us like gigantic sunflowers, reaching poisonous tentacles toward the smoking heavens.

The *kehillah* had already begun to organize rescue operations. Trucks came by and began to pick up the dead. The bodies of the victims were wrenched beyond recognition, a hand twisted stiffly this way, a foot twisted the other way; sometimes a body had no hand or foot; sometimes the workers picked up severed hands and feet and loaded them onto the trucks.

People began to trickle upward slowly out of the shelter of their basements. They looked around hesitantly, groping for reality. Their faces were incredulous, their minds enfeebled. Many of them had just lost parents, loved ones, possessions, homes. They did not behave normally. Those who still had their wits about them walked up to the lost ones and screamed: "You have to get out of this state! Snap out of it! You can't go on like this!"

Watching this numbed my soul. I did not know what to do with myself. I did not know that such things were possible. It was hard to function sanely when all around you people were no longer people. They had changed into some other form of human life, robots mechanized by fear.

After the bombing ended, the landscape of Jewish Warsaw began to metamorphose rapidly. We did not even notice how fast the pattern of our lives changed; we did not notice that we spun in eddies, drifting toward the vortex of a dark whirlpool.

A day or two after the clean-up began, on a sunny fall morning, the Germans announced that everyone in the Jewish neighborhood must come out to the sidewalks at a given hour. When we were all assembled, they came parading through the streets in all their glory. They did not shoot or hurt anyone, but the spectacle, in its own way, was as fearful and damaging as any physical abuse.

Many people have written about the diabolical strength of the German army, and it is hard to find new words to describe an old terror. I see it vividly before me, and it still makes me shake — but how can I describe to you the awesomeness of those ranks? What an evil flair they had, what power, what arrogance! They towered above us in their starched green uniforms with flashing gold buttons and gold braiding, their high-topped boots glinting in the sun. They sat atop magnificent horses whose muscles rippled beneath sleek coats, and they lifted their fluttering banners above our heads. The proud strains of a military marching band rang in our ears, announcing the coronation of a new king who would one day take over the universe.

Without lifting a finger, they ruined us. With their brilliantly timed display, they created our resignation and turned us into a scattering of flies. We knew that we would soon be crushed underfoot. The eyes of the people on the sidewalks were open and staring, wild with helplessness: they were the eyes of idiots.

We quickly began to feel the practical daily effects of the German presence. Young Jews were arrested randomly in the streets and were forced into labor gangs. One of their tasks was to erect a wall around the neighborhood. At first we did not even understand what was going on, whether the wall was intended to keep us out or to keep us in; we only saw it rise, subtly and swiftly. There was a poisonous drift in the air, a feeling of barriers closing in, a feeling that all control was slipping through our fingers.

The *kehillah* administration understood the purpose of the wall, but overnight its members had become wooden marionettes. The Germans reorganized it and formed a Judenrat, as they had done and would continue to do in countless other occupied towns. They appointed Jewish officials of their own choosing, giving them administrative responsibility in the Jewish neighborhood for law enforcement, economic management, housing, food distribution, and education; but in reality the members of the Judenrat were only the powerless leaders of a modern-day ghetto, whose major job was to heel and fetch at the command of their new German overlords.

The arrest of young Jews in the streets escalated. Any young person who ventured out of doors in those early weeks took the risk of falling into the idle hands of any local soldier looking for amusement. The captured people were loaded onto roaming trucks and sent away to work, where they performed menial tasks that were the invention of a brutal imagination.

When they came back a day or two later, they were unrecognizable. They had been beaten brutally with sticks. Many of the men did not have a white patch of skin left on their bodies, only swollen red welts with blue centers. The girls told us that they had been ordered to wash the floors of offices with their own undergarments, and then they were forced to put the soiled clothing on again. I breathed a private sigh of relief when I heard these stories, for I had been hidden in a closet when the soldiers came to search our house, and luckily they never opened the door.

Among other tasks, it was the Judenrat's responsibility to deliver quotas of people to the Germans for labor. Although the members of the Judenrat were the technical heads of the ghetto, their position was unenviable. Their backs were against the wall, and they had virtually no moral freedom — except to remove themselves from the predicament altogether. One member, a man named Rogover, chose that option. He committed suicide, unable to live with the fact that he had sent so many young people out to labor, where they were brutalized and killed. Adam Czerniakow, whom the Nazis had appointed head of the Judenrat, would later make the same choice.

In addition to forced labor, a slew of new decrees wiped the Jews out of the mainstream of city life. They were prohibited from using public transportation. They were required to wear the infamous Star of David on their clothing, and their possessions became forfeit to the Germans. They lost the protection of the law and were left at the mercy of the dozens of thieves and vagabonds created by the crisis.

Food vanished. The shelves in the stores emptied overnight; there was nothing to buy. People began to raid the bombed-out factories. We heard about a destroyed pickle factory and ran there to take cans of pickles. Then we heard about a candy factory, and we collected as many candies as we could carry home. My brother Leiby, a student in the Mirrer Yeshivah, had escaped to Latvia, and he sent us several packages of tea and hard butter during these weeks, which helped to keep us going for a while.

A few neighbors and I once spent the day in the empty potato fields on the outskirts of the city, trying to dig out some potatoes with our bare hands. The best ones were already gone; only the bulbs and roots were left, and a few very tiny potatoes, which we stretched thinly over the space of several days. Resourcefulness had always been my mother's hallmark; we used to joke that she could make *kneidlech* from snowballs. Now it was no longer a joke.

The now-active ghetto grapevine kept us apprised —sometimes accurately, sometimes not — of any developments in the food crisis. When we learned that a certain bakery would have a bread supply, we tried to stay with neighbors who lived nearby so that we could get on line in the middle of the night. We stood for hours in those lines, thousands of us, through the night and through the day, and when we reached the front, there was often no bread left. Once in a while I was lucky enough to get a loaf, only to have someone grab it from me in the street on the way home. It was an oppressive struggle not only to survive, but to maintain a sense of decency in the midst of such ruthlessness.

Sometimes on my walks I would pass the city *meshuganer*, a once-prominent member of the community who now maintained his fame by begging in the streets. He was a small man with a red beard who used to walk up and down the sidewalks even when the snow was piled high, making all kinds of bizarre announcements. He used to call out that he had gone to college with Hitler and talked to him sometimes on the phone. In the midst of his absurdity were sprinkled chips of wry truth, the sort of black humor that has come to characterize the Jewish people in their suffering:

"*Shmaltz iz billig!*" he would shout at the top of his lungs. "*Alle gevirim hubn zich oisgelost!* Fat is cheap! All the rich people have melted, just like *shmaltz!*" That was his favorite slogan, reminding us that the war had destroyed social barriers and had put rich and poor in the same sorry boat.

Somehow, during that winter of despondency, my family stumbled through. We were relatively warm at home, thanks in large part to my mother's ingenuity. One night when she couldn't sleep, she dreamed up a heating contraption in her head, just as she had once done in Siedlice. The next day she sent my brother Yankel out to find a sheet metal worker who could build it for her. This little miracle oven worked on sawdust, which Yankel collected from factories around town. We discovered that when the sawdust was moistened, it kept better and heated longer. We were even able to sell sawdust briquets for a little extra money.

Warsaw had gone black market by now. We had a great deal

of silver in the apartment, so we built a double ceiling in one of the armoires and stashed all of our valuables in the hidden compartment. From this cache, my mother sold pieces of her jewelry, little by little, to keep us going. We were lucky that we had something to sell.

Refugees began to pour into the Jewish quarter. Some of them had run away from their homes, but a large majority had been forcibly resettled. They came from other parts of Warsaw, from the surrounding villages, and later from large cities like Lodz and Kalish. We were fortunate that we did not have to resettle, for our neighborhood was later designated as the ghetto area; instead, we now played host to an assortment of desperately needy people.

Among the many refugees who came in from Lodz was an aunt of mine, Chavale Rabinowitz. Her first husband, my father's younger brother Herschel, had been the Biale *Rebbe* for six months many years earlier, before his untimely death. My aunt was now in her early sixties, a very regal woman with polished manners. Her second husband had passed away, and her two married children were no longer with her. Her son had gone to Russia, from where he would eventually travel to Israel to carry on the Biale dynasty; and her daughter Perele, an exquisitely beautiful girl who was married to the Kodenover *Rebbe,* later vanished in the Baranowitz ghetto.

My aunt contracted typhus while she was staying with us, and we did our best to take care of her. I remember how feverish she was, and how Yankel and I took her out to the balcony on a cot while the weather was still warm so that she could get some fresh air. When my mother was certain of her illness, she became afraid for my health and sent me out to Otwock, a nearby resort village. At that time the ghetto was not sealed yet, and limited traveling was still possible.

I stayed in a boarding house in Otwock for two weeks. Day-to-day life in the village was desperately normal, although food was rationed and many families had already fled to the big cities. I went to visit old friends of my parents by the name of Barnholz, a well-to-do couple who were extremely distressed by the drastic changes the war had thrust on them. As had happened to so many other families, the sudden threat to their financial security and the rationing of food had thrown them completely off balance, and they were too embarrassed to stand on the ration lines. During the two weeks that I stayed in Otwock, I brought them their rations packages several times, and they were relieved and very grateful for the help.

When I came back from the country, my aunt Chavale was no longer alive. This was a great shock to me — but probably not to my mother, who must have anticipated it some time before. Unfortunately, although she was able to spare me my aunt's passing, she could not protect me from the general scourge of death and illness which began to sweep through the ghetto. My brother Yankel, spurred by the escalating catastrophe, left the ghetto and fled to Russia, along with countless other young men whose only alternative was to stay at home and remain potential victims to forced labor roundups and deportation. Yankel was hoping to find a place to settle in Russia, and he intended to bring us over as soon as he could.

The influx of refugees into the ghetto mounted by the day, and there were not adequate facilities or resources to care for these lost people. Most of the refugees were put up in empty stores, where they were crowded together like cows. The Judenrat gave them military cots and blankets and tried to provide them with food, but there was never enough.

The Jewish youth in Warsaw had been organized almost as soon as the Judenrat was established. One of the jobs assigned to us was the daily delivery of food rations to the refugees. Our house, because of its size and spaciousness, had been requisitioned in order to set up a field kitchen, and we had not had any say in the matter. We emptied one large closet to make room for the provisions the Judenrat brought in, including huge containers of rice, oil, and sugar, and a lock was put on the closet door.

In spite of the inconvenience of no longer having total control over our apartment, I was very eager to participate in the relief effort and glad to be in the center of it. The relief committee hired me to oversee the kitchen and to cook, for which I was paid a small pittance. A neighbor from across the hall came to join our team, and she and I worked hard to stretch the food as far as it would go and to make it as tasty as possible. I remember in particular trying to spice up the onions with the few paltry supplies we were given.

Every morning at five a.m., delivery men appointed by the Judenrat arrived with three hundred kilograms of bread and several huge pots of black coffee. I was assigned to cut the bread, which had to be divided into as many slices as possible. For years afterward I had a callus on my thumb from the pressure of the knife. Along with other friends, I then went out into the neighborhood to deliver the rations.

Any survivor of that era will tell you that the winter of 1939-40 was merciless, the worst in memory. It was a burning winter, intolerable, aggravated by a lack of heating fuel and the iciness of our moods. When we awoke in the morning, the walls were coated with frost, and the blast of frigid air that greeted us when we lifted the covers would send us diving below again, clinging to the fragile warmth of our pillows. Rising was a painful chore.

When we entered the stores to bring food to the refugees, we found family members nestled together in bed to keep warm. The next day when we returned, one or more of them were often dead. Others in the room would say to us with grim practicality: "Don't give it to him. He's dead . . . give it to me."

I remember an elderly blind woman who was staying in a corner store in our building, lying on an iron bed atop a thin straw mattress. She did not have the strength to come upstairs, so my mother began to prepare extra food for me to take down to her each day. This woman insisted on washing *negel vasser* every morning. "I cannot do anything until my hands are washed," she would say. I would bring her a bucket full of frozen water, and she would say *Modeh Ani* and touch the ice. That was the best we could do.

In some cases neediness was not physical but emotional, and

this was quite pitiful to see. We knew one very wealthy older couple in Warsaw, a coal merchant and his wife, who had fallen on hard times after the invasion and had become disconsolate. We had been friendly with them since our days in Siedlice; the wife was an expert embroiderer who had made my sister Chavcia's trousseau. They began to beg us to let them sleep in our house. My mother didn't have the heart to say no. Sleeping space was already very tight, and we could not give the couple a private room, so the wife ended up sharing my bed. For me it was extremely unpleasant, but there was nothing I could say; there was a war going on.

I knew, however, that I had little to complain about in comparison to the average ghetto Jew. The misery that filled the sidewalks then was hideous, beyond description. The snow was not cleared away all winter. Monstrous, rigid white banks rose on either side of the streets, with narrow valleys in the center where the horses passed through and small depressed trails on the sidewalks. Nestled into pockets of snow against the sides of the buildings were dozens of beggars and cripples. One exposed a wounded foot or head, another the stump of an arm. They sat there in the snow all day long, begging and begging and begging.

My mother ran her own private relief effort. She kept a large kettle of water boiling constantly and sent me downstairs to the street to deliver hot water and the candies that we had collected from the bombed factory. The candies were large, oblong ones which we cut into pieces. I would go down three or four times a day, with a jug of hot water in one hand and a cup of candies in the other, to feed the cripples.

The first few times I did it, my heart went out. When you walked out into the street, you saw a vast canvas of dirty white, pockmarked with black and red spots, and then you looked closer and you saw that the black and red spots were people, and that some of them were bleeding. When you looked on that scene, you felt that you could not live. You could not watch such affliction and then go home again; you felt that you must work twenty-four hours a day to get rid of it.

But strangely, as time went on, a shell thickened around me. I became so accustomed to the sight of those human wrecks that I could walk by them as though they were no more than houses or trees, and I felt nothing. This hurt me more than the original shock of seeing them on the ground in their pain. I remember thinking that there must be something wrong with me. Surely this callousness did not happen to other people. Maybe I had lost my heart.

Perhaps the most tragic thing about the occupation, though, was not the physical havoc wreaked by the enemy, or even the hardships themselves, but rather the suspicion and mistrust that infected the Jewish community and turned it against itself. There is no doubt that this was part of the Nazis' long-range plan —and they were bitterly successful, pushing us so far over the threshold of deprivation that we no longer recognized ourselves, neither in appearance nor in deed.

The man from the Judenrat who was in charge of our public kitchen came up to me one morning during work, a severe look on his face.

"I just checked the supplies," he said. "The count is not correct — some of the provisions are missing. I think you and your mother are taking them."

The wind was completely knocked out of me. It is true, sadly, that many ghetto residents had been reduced to stealing, but to have such an accusation flung at me was beyond belief. It was worse than anything that had yet happened to us. I felt that if people could point such a terrible finger at us, we were finished.

"Listen," I said to him, "I swear to you that my mother and I are not taking a drop of anything from that closet. And I'm going to help you find whoever it is, because obviously it is someone who has access to the house."

Everything else now paled next to this mission. I began to lie awake at night, listening for every slight sound, looking for any hint of movement. It was only a night or two later that my vigilance was rewarded. I heard distinct sounds in the hallway; a door was being opened, and there was rustling and creaking.

I jumped out of bed and ran out to the hallway, only to find myself face to face with the coal merchant — the husband of the woman who was now sharing my bed.

We both froze, and our eyes met. Neither of us spoke. I went back to my bed, and he went back to his. That day, nothing was missing from the closet.

The next night I planned my strategy a little more carefully. I heard soft noises in the hall again, but this time I waited a while before making my appearance. I found the man in the foyer with a bundle over his shoulder, ready to leave the house. I was enraged.

"You are going to pay dearly for the humiliation that my mother has gone through," I whispered fiercely. "You are a man of status in the community, but my mother is the Parczewer *Rebbetzin,* and you're going to do something about it!"

"Don't say anything," he begged. "Please, don't tell anyone about this!"

"No! I'm going to make it known, because my mother's reputation and my reputation are at stake! For a little bit of food, I'm not going to let my mother's name be trampled in the mud — no matter how long you've known her!"

The man must have been seized by desperation, or perhaps he did not really believe my youthful threats, because he walked out the door with the bundle of food. I could not stop him physically. I remember thinking how incredible it was that a wealthy man had fallen so low.

The next morning I went straight to the kitchen manager. "I know who has been taking the supplies," I told him. "I don't care what you do with him, but I want my mother's name cleared."

The committee went after the coal merchant, only to be met with a flurry of repeated denials. It seemed that the incident would never be resolved conclusively — but then one day the man himself suddenly came in to see my mother. He seemed to be on the verge of tears.

"Rebbetzin," he said quietly, "*zeit mir moichel* — please forgive me. What I did was terrible, but worst of all was to let you take the blame. I haven't been able to sleep at night. Please forgive me — I was hungry."

Then he turned around and repeated his confession to other workers who were standing in the kitchen. Our nightmare was over, but it was only one of many similar incidents that took place in the ghetto, withering the self-respect of many fine people and driving the community further toward a grievous collapse.

Incredibly, in the midst of this black cesspool into which our entire world had fallen, a semblance of normal life was fabricated in the town. Day to day living had stabilized somewhat after the initial crisis of the bombing, and the Jews tried very hard to go about their business routinely.

The youth of the ghetto in particular behaved as though nothing had happened. One of my friends, a girl of seventeen or eighteen who came from a wealthy, sheltered home, announced her intention to get married. The rest of us were aghast. The idea of getting married and having a home and children under the cloud of the Invader was unthinkable. How would the couple manage? What would become of their children? The girl was unfazed by our barely stifled disapproval. Her parents gave her a full wedding, and the *chupah* took place in the courtyard of her building.

Other young people affected normalcy with an unaccustomed looseness. Some of the night clubs opened again, and here and there a movie played. Boys and girls began to mingle openly, in the offhand, careless manner of people who have decided to experience life before the world dissolves at their feet. The atmosphere in some parts of the neighborhood became tainted with a sense of rakish abandon.

Among the refugees who came to Warsaw during that time were two very prominent educators: Rabbi Yehudah Leib Orlean from Krakow, our revered teacher from the Sara Schenirer Beth Jacob Seminary, and Rabbi Eliezer Gershon Friedenson from Lodz, the man whose Jewish youth magazine had once delighted us in elementary school. Both men began to call in young people for *shiurim*. Many former Sara Schenirer students began to attend Rabbi Orlean's lectures.

There is one poignant lesson he gave that still remains with me, not only because of its relevance to our experience, but because of its relevance to all times. The topic was the *Shema*. Rabbi Orlean spoke on the *posuk* "*Lo sasuru acharei l'vavchem v'acharei eineichem* — Do not go after your hearts and after your eyes." He pointed out that we now had a shining opportunity to live this principle.

"You go out into the streets now," he said to us, "and you see that many young people are having a good time. It seems that they have no worries. But if you look deeply, you will see that their lives are empty. You have to go not by what you see, but by what your heart dictates. You should never forget where you come from. You come from the heart . . . the eyes can be blinded, but the heart still beats."

On October 2, 1940, our neighborhood was officially declared ghetto territory. All the Jews of Warsaw, along with people of Jewish origin and Jews from the provinces, were crowded into an area of approximately one thousand acres, which the Germans declared a "plague-infested" zone. Soon there were 500,000 people crushed together, surrounded by a wall ten feet high that was crowned with barbed wire. There were an average of thirteen people to a room, in addition to thousands of homeless.

The ghetto was sealed. Jews were allowed to enter and leave only with special permits and only at specific points. Very few people had the means to earn a living. Typhus raged in the buildings and on the streets. The sight of dead bodies on the sidewalks became commonplace.

Gensia Street was in the midst of what had once been the prosperous textile district, and the merchants began to come up to our apartment to ask my mother for advice. They were thinking seriously of getting out of the ghetto and wanted to know if they should try and salvage their goods. Some of these men had suitcases full of cash which would be difficult, if not impossible, to transport.

"It's not the money," my mother told them. "It's not the goods. Just make sure you don't stay here. If you have a chance to go, go — because there is no future for us here anymore."

"*Rebbetzin*," they asked, "what about you?"

"My house is full of *sifrei Torah*," she replied. "I cannot leave them here, and I cannot take them all with me. I must stay with the *sefarim*."

There were over a hundred *sifrei Torah* in our house now, in addition to thousands of *sefarim*, and my mother kept her resolve to stay with them. But she began to consider sending me away. My brother Yankel was still in Russia, and I think my mother must secretly have been dying inside at the thought of parting with her one remaining child. But the ghetto was degenerating from day to day; the life was being squeezed out of it. Maybe outside, I would have a chance.

Chapter Eleven

My brother Boruch, who was now the Munkatcher *Rebbe*, had already written to my mother several times, urging her to leave the ghetto and come to Hungary. When he saw how firmly resolved she was to remain at home, he insisted that she at least send me. Without waiting for my mother's consent, he went ahead and made all the necessary arrangements. He contacted a family named Kalb in Nowy Targ, on the Polish side of the Slovakian border. My mother knew them, and they agreed to receive me.

When I learned that my mother had already decided to send me out, I could not contain myself. I was the only one left at home now; how in the world could I leave my mother?

"Momma," I told her, "I'm not going anywhere without you."

She replied, "If Hashem *Yisbarach* left me with so many *sefarim* and He will not protect them, who am I to run away? I am nothing next to the *sefarim*; whatever happens to them will happen to me. I have lived a life already — short or long, good or bad — but you still have a life ahead of you, and I can't let you remain here because of me."

Night and day my mother pushed me to escape, and an opportunity was not long in presenting itself. There was a man named Domb, from Switzerland, who had stayed with us recently. He had a foreign passport, with which he could move about freely, both outside and within the ghetto. Mr. Domb was extremely grateful for my mother's hospitality and wanted to find some way to repay her. When he heard that she was looking for a way to send me out of the ghetto, he declared, "*Rebbetzin, ad chatzi hamalchus v'sayos* — tell me what you want me to do, and I'll do it."

My mother did not answer him at first; I think that in her heart she did not want to finalize the idea that I might actually go. But at last she accepted his offer. Mr. Domb agreed to take me out of the ghetto on his Swiss passport, having me pose as his wife. He said he would deliver me to the Kalbs' house in Nowy Targ — with one stipulation.

"I'm ready to take you," he said, "but if anyone asks me something, I won't know you."

"Mr. Domb," I asked politely, "if that's the case, what protection do I have?"

"I will take you on the rail line to Krakow," he assured me. "If a connecting train to Nowy Targ comes through in reasonable time, I will also go the second leg of the journey and take you personally to the Kalbs, so that I can tell your mother I saw you to the doorstep." But he remarked again that he would not guarantee my safety if anything went wrong.

I could not blame him totally. Traveling illegally was tantamount to suicide at this time, and I knew this was the best offer I would get, that I could expect nothing more from him. I saw, too, that my mother wanted me very much to go — and I must admit that the adventurous streak in me was willing to take the risk.

By the time I next attended one of Rabbi Friedenson's *shiurim*, some of my friends already knew of my plans.

"Why?" they asked me in mild alarm. "We're all going to stay here — at least let's stay together. Why do you want to break up the group?"

"My mother wants me to go," I answered. "She wants it so much that I have no heart to say no."

"Where will you go?" they asked.

"I don't know," I said truthfully, "but I feel that I have to go."

Rabbi Friedenson gave me a letter to a family in Nowy Targ whom I will call Dubin, only because my memory fails me. Their daughter had once attended his trade school in Lodz, and he was hoping that they could fulfill two requests: to help me out as much as they could, and to send some care packages into the ghetto. I promised him that I would do my best to deliver the letter.

There were two other important items that I took along from my house. One was a winter coat with fur lining that I cherished very much because my mother had made it for me out of my father's old *statz-peltz*. The other was the double pledge I made to her.

We had not really talked much about my future, as though my mother did not want to admit the possibility that it might not include her — or, *chas v'shalom*, that it might not exist. We had absolutely no reliable information in the ghetto about what was happening elsewhere in Europe. The Germans would come through the streets with loudspeakers and announce their victories, but most of the news we received was propaganda. The scattered rumors that we heard through unofficial channels, however, were enough to let us know that Europe was now a catastrophically dangerous place and that protection was virtually non-existent. My mother could not even prepare me properly for the trip, because she had no idea what I would find on the other side of the ghetto wall.

We were almost casual in our interaction during those last weeks before my departure. The only thing my mother kept mentioning was that she would like me to write a book someday about our experiences during the war. I heard her request, but I didn't really absorb it. I wasn't much of a writer, and I couldn't even guess where I would be a month from now, let alone think about writing a book.

On the day I left our house, I packed a small overnight bag with a change of clothing, a tube of toothpaste, a *siddur,* and a *sefer Tehillim.* My mother did not accompany me to the ghetto gate. She knew that if she came, I would not go. She waited at the top of the wide spiral staircase in our building, watching me as I descended the steps. When I got to the bottom, I looked back up for a moment and saw her way above me through the center of the spiral. She was leaning over the bannister, crying bitterly. I said to myself, "No, don't look back — don't look back, because you will not be able to leave," and in that split second before I turned my head away, my mother called down to me.

"*Kind meins,*" she said through her tears, "*tzvei zachen vill ich fun dir* — tell me that you will wear a *sheitel* when you get married, and that you will write a book."

At that time I did not see the keen judgment in my mother's requests; I did not understand why she chose these two particular items out of the many things she could have asked for. But she was my mother, and I gave her my word.

"*Mama'she,*" I called up to her, "I'll do both . . . and I hope I'll see you!"

And that's the last thing I said to her and the last glimpse I had of her. It was only a glimpse. All of it happened in a fleeting moment, and that glimpse lasted throughout my entire passage to Hungary, and it has lasted until this very day.

Mr. Domb was waiting for me outside in the street. I turned quickly and ran out to join him. I tried not to think anymore about the house, or my mother, or my life. At that moment I tried to keep my eyes ahead of me, to watch one foot follow the other, to go forward — only forward.

Several of my friends accompanied Mr. Domb and me to the ghetto gate, and I said goodbye to each of them in turn. One very dear friend presented me with a handsome volume of Yiddish poetry, bound in leather and imprinted with a beautiful array of Italian colors. I thought that I might break down and cry then, but I didn't. Mr. Domb took out his passport and presented me to the guard as his wife. There was no fanfare, no scrutiny, no mishap of any kind; it was an ordinary afternoon, and it seemed as though we were doing nothing more than going out to run errands in town. Together, we passed through the gate.

Krakow was the only city on the rail line that offered a connecting passage to Nowy Targ, a village on the Polish-Slovakian border. By the time we arrived at the station, pricks of delayed panic were beginning to jab at my heart. The building was a drab gray, a lifeless place of transience, without ornament or warmth. It announced to me that I too was now only a passerby, a wanderer without a home. I felt that somebody had pried open my fingers, one by one, and pushed me off the ledge of my mother's windowsill, casting me into a dusky, bottomless void. There was nothing at all to hold onto in that airless space — not even Mr. Domb, who would not guarantee my safety if anything went wrong. In all my life I had never felt so alone.

The scene in the Krakow train station further disheartened me. I was totally unprepared for it. An atmosphere of moral abandon hung over the place. The decency of public restraint had collapsed with the outbreak of the war, but even in the streets of Warsaw I had not felt it as strongly as I did here in the train station. It was not evident in anything that happened openly; it was more a sense of the melting down of barriers, of passage into a dim world where all the guideposts of decency had been pulled down. I was more shocked by this than by the sight of all the dead bodies I had seen on the sidewalks of the ghetto. I also felt vulnerable to attack. I was so innocent then, so sheltered; it seemed that this world of unholiness might swallow me alive, and I didn't know if I would have the strength to protect myself from its poisonous vapors.

We reached the Kalbs' house in the small town of Nowy Targ without incident, and Mr. Domb turned around to go back to Warsaw. The Jews here seemed to be living in an enclosed universe, apart from the tragedy of Nazi Poland. Although several prominent members of the Jewish community had already been deported to Buchenwald, the town functioned comfortably, closing its eyes to the terror creeping toward its boundaries. The villagers knew that Buchenwald was a concentration camp, but they did not know exactly what took place there. I think they did not want to find out.

The Kalbs, my mother's friends, were a very lovely elderly couple, but I wasn't at ease in their house. They had several grown sons who were involved in the smuggling of currency on the wartime black market, and their activities kept me on edge. I remember helping the Kalbs with their Pesach cleaning, scrubbing out cupboards and scouring floors. I was glad to be able to repay them in some way for their hospitality, but all the time I felt the discomfort of the dominant male presence in the household and the furtiveness of the boys' secret dealings. Smuggling and dealing on the black market were not crimes during the war, they were a basic means of survival; but I was fresh from home, and I didn't yet know how to approach it.

When I delivered Rabbi Friedenson's letter to the family Dubin, I found myself in much more comfortable surroundings. Here, instead of boys, there were girls — several of them. Mr. Dubin was one of the men who had been deported, and the family had not heard from him since. In spite of their distress, they received me with great warmth and invited me to stay with them for Pesach. I gratefully accepted.

Unwilling to offend the Kalbs and knowing that Mr. Kalb felt responsible for me because of the promise he had made to my brother Boruch, I clumsily fabricated an excuse. I sent a message to the Kalbs, saying that I had fallen and sprained my ankle, that I was laid up in bed and would stay with the Dubins for Pesach. I felt a prick of conscience at such whitewashing, but I was very young and very much alone, and if there was any comfort to be had, I was not about to let go of it. I certainly did not regret the wonderful Yom Tov that I spent with the Dubins.

I will never forget what this family did for me. The girls went out to the neighboring villages and brought back an assortment of staples: butter and eggs, chickens, and a goose. The *shochet* came to slaughter the birds, and we spent several days preserving the fat and putting together packages — all of which were sent to my mother in the Warsaw ghetto. Thank G-d she received the food, as well as several additional packages that we mailed later on. I am still grateful for this family's *chessed*, for their long-distance care of a woman they had never met.

I also treasured the company of young girls who were close to my age. We were filled with the naive optimism of youth and surrounded ourselves with a protective bubble of feminine dreams, shutting out the world around us long enough to share nail polish and secrets — as though no war were taking place so close to us on the earth.

One very remarkable incident took place while I was in the Dubins' house. I was standing with the girls at the window one day when a column of German soldiers passed by in the street below. Two soldiers happened to look up at the window just at that moment, and their eyes met ours. Suddenly they slipped out of the line and began to walk toward our house, and the next thing we knew there was a knock at the door.

We were terrified. Those looks they had given us could mean only one thing. There were no men with us in the apartment, and we literally grabbed each other in fright.

When the soldiers came in the front door, they stood in the parlor looking strangely unaggressive and somewhat awkward, as though our humble household were too small to contain their muscular frames.

"We didn't come here to harm you," one of them said quietly. "We haven't seen the inside of a home in a long time. We swear we will not hurt you; just let us sit here for a while."

They sat down in the parlor, and for the next hour told us story after story of their experiences in the army. They said they had been forced to join the army and to comply with the Nazis' doctrine and regimentation, and that not everyone was doing it voluntarily. Yes, they said, a great many enjoyed their task, but they had many friends who did not.

Finally they stood up. Each man took two candles out of his pocket and reached out to hand them to us. "Thank you for letting us sit," they said. "We have nothing else to give you — please take these." As they walked out the door, they were crying and we were crying. Then they raced out to catch up with their unit.

I do not know what one can make of this; I am only repeating what happened. Certainly it is not meant in any way as an acquittal of the soldiers in the German army. But to us, at that moment, it represented a thread of humanity in a world where normal human sentiment had been ground into ashes.

Before I left Nowy Targ, I was asked to speak to a small gathering of townspeople about the events in the Warsaw ghetto. I told them plainly of the horrors I had witnessed, sparing no detail. I told them about the soldiers' raids, the labor gangs, the cripples lying in the snow, the wagons full of dead passing by our windows. They were curious and secretly fearful, but their collective reaction was one of incredulity.

"That's a very nice story, young lady," they told me in effect, "but if you came here to spread panic, we're not buying it."

I'll never forget that. They deliberately cloaked themselves in a blind armor against the truth, unaccepting, refusing to prepare themselves for catastrophe. Although many of their family members were already in Buchenwald, they could not absorb the possibility of wholesale destruction.

I said to them, "I hope that I will be proved a liar, and that you will never have to live through what I did."

There was no guide available to take me over the border from Poland to Slovakia. The instructions I had were to take the bus. Now that I look back, I can't understand how I actually had the nerve to board that bus without a single piece of usable identification. Perhaps I did it simply because I had no other choice. The truth is, my entire escape was a huge gamble — but so was staying in the ghetto. The only difference was that one was an active gamble and the other was passive, and if I had a choice, I preferred to gamble by taking action.

I found a seat all the way at the back of the bus and sat down. When we were stopped at the border, the inspectors asked every single person on the bus for papers *except me*. I can't explain any of this; I know that I had not even prepared something to say in case anyone questioned me. I had the simple feeling that I would either live or die and that calculations would not make much difference, so I left it totally in the hands of Hashem *Yisbarach*.

When I arrived in the Slovakian town of Kaismark, I was met by Mendel Berger, a friend of my brother's who had been instrumental in making the arrangements for my escape. He placed me with a family named Yaeger, where I stayed for about two weeks. There I set to work crocheting myself a sweater and making a skirt — not so much out of physical need as out of the need for normal activity. While I sewed, I was lost in a private world of domesticity, where Hitler could not penetrate. I also bought myself a pair of *bata*, the Slovakian term for walking shoes.

On Shabbos, Mr. Berger came from his home and took me out for long walks in the village. During these leisurely strolls he told me about his rescue activities, and he always mentioned his great admiration for my brother. He promised he would do everything possible to help me and encouraged me to have faith. This wonderful man later made his way to America with his wife and children, but not without having paid a price; he was beaten by the Gestapo for lending aid to people and lost his hearing.

Across the courtyard from the Yaegers was a family named Goldstein, with whom I spent one Shabbos. They also had a daughter my age, and we had a wonderful time reminiscing about the Bais Yaakov schools of our childhood, dreaming about *Eretz Yisrael* and about the rosy life we were determined to have. I remember how wonderfully elastic our spirits were, how we concocted a gilded future out of dust. I had nothing then: no money, no one to turn to, no possessions but the winter coat my mother had made me. Even the book of Yiddish poems was gone — I had destroyed it soon after leaving the ghetto, fearful of being found carrying open evidence of my Jewishness. What the Goldstein girls gave me was irreplaceable. They showered me with affection, bolstering my courage and my sense of inner stability, and I was nourished from it.

Mr. Berger hired a guide to take me on foot to the next stop. At this point, I began to feel that I was being moved around on an anonymous game board; I passed in total secrecy through a series of villages whose names I did not know, staying with families of strangers, giving myself up totally to the *Ribono Shel Olam*. I was hopeful that somehow I would finally reach Hungary, and I prayed continually to go forward — only forward.

The guide brought me at four o'clock in the morning to a small, two-story apartment house and deposited me with a gentile family there. The woman of the house quickly hustled me into a tiny room that looked like a walk-in closet. The door to the room was hidden by an armoire with a false back. She must have been paid an enormous sum to risk the criminal offense of hiding a Jewish girl — and, as I later discovered, under the very noses of a platoon of German soldiers!

I stayed hidden in that tiny room for seven days. I had no idea where I was or who my hosts were, or even if I was in the right place; and I had no idea how I was supposed to get out of this village. I felt as though I were in prison. Occasionally a hand would slide through the opening in back of the armoire and deposit some food for me, most of which was fried in fats. I asked the woman of the house if she would mind simply cooking the foods in plain water, and after that she gave me boiled potatoes and eggs. There were no books or newspapers to read. I did not even have my *siddur* or my *Tehillim* anymore; I had left them behind, prompted by instinct not to carry them around any longer. I sat all day in that tiny room with nothing to do.

There was an outhouse in the courtyard, and in order to go outside I had to disguise myself in the woman's clothing and slip out as unobtrusively as possible. The first time I went out, I got one of the biggest shocks of my life. There were German soldiers everywhere I looked, camped out in the fields for miles around. Some were even in the apartment building, calling to each other from the windows of the upper floor! Apparently they had moved into the town bag and baggage and were commandeering private homes at will. I saw them cooking in their field kitchens;

I smelled the pungent odor of roasting beans, mixed with the acrid odor of cigarette smoke. Even when I was inside, the frightening sounds of their camp drifted through the walls: singing and coarse laughter, the knocking of utensils in the open air, the plaintive whine of harmonicas. If any of these men had discovered that my hostess was sheltering a Jewish girl, they would have shot her on the spot. I prayed with all my might to get out of that room alive.

One day there was a knock at the door of my hiding place, and a voice said, "There is a note for you." A slip of paper was shoved through the opening. It contained instructions: on the coming Saturday I was to take an empty pill bottle and go down a certain road, as though I were on my way to the local drugstore; in those days, one had to bring his own container to the druggist. Along the road, I was to look for a car with a specific license plate number. Someone would be standing on the left side of the car, pretending to fix it. This was my contact.

That Shabbos, I did exactly as the note instructed. With a thumping heart, doubly anxious because I was now wearing my own clothes, I made my way down the unfamiliar dirt paths toward the drugstore. The sun was shining brilliantly in a clear sky; it was so bright outside that I was sure people could see me for miles around, the illegal refugee in the battered coat. I felt that I had stepped into a huge, bottomless hole, a place where nothing made sense, where all the signs I approached seemed to go up in smoke, like mirages. I didn't know if I would make it alive to the end of the path. Strangely enough, although my heart continued to thrash inside me, my head was level. I literally steeled myself to meet the Angel of Death around the bend, prepared to die with the verses of the *Shema* on my lips.

I came to a fork in the road and saw a car parked in the grass. Just as the note had said, someone was bending down to the side of it, apparently tinkering with a tire — but the license plate number did not match.

My heart stopped. German soldiers passed by on the road, and some of them looked at me and made remarks. I could not stay any longer in this spot. What should I do? What should I do?

My first instinct was to turn around and head back to the house. It was the wrong license number; I couldn't possibly take such a chance. I took a few steps toward the car, then turned and walked a few steps in the other direction. But what if those *were* my people? What if I missed the ride? I would be stuck in a gentile village, surrounded by German soldiers, and I wasn't even sure what country I was in! I felt totally confused, as though my head were being knocked back and forth between two cymbals. If only there were some hint — anything at all that could give me a clue about what to do!

At that moment, a small gray robin hopped into the path in front of me. It began to circle me as I paced, staying unnaturally close. When I turned, it followed me like a pet cat, showing no sign of fear. I shivered involuntarily. Perhaps this bird was the clue I was looking for. I desperately needed a marker to place my trust in, and my inner voice told me that something unusual was going on — something I should not ignore. I had nothing to lose by listening to the voice.

"If this robin goes backward," I said to myself, "I'll go back to the village. If it goes the other way, I'll go with the car — but somehow I know I'll be lost."

It was a strange game to play and I knew it, but I had nothing else to fall back on. There was no time to waste. The robin hesitated for a moment and then hopped several times in the direction of the village. I am certain now that it saved my life.

Much later, I learned of a similar odd happening in my brother Leiby's life. Leiby had been arrested in Riga, Latvia, at around the same time, along with several other *bachurim* from the Mirrer Yeshivah. He spent the next five years as a "political prisoner" in a Russian jail, where he feigned idiocy in order to avoid abuse. He told me years later that a bird had flown into his cell one day and landed on his head. His cellmate, who had been under the impression all along that he was deaf and dumb, remarked, "You're going to be freed soon." The next day Leiby was released in a prisoner exchange. When he told me that story, I thought that perhaps I had not been so foolish to rely on my robin, for G-d sends us His signals in curious ways, and it is up to us to be on the lookout for them.

I began to walk back toward the village now, ambling as nonchalantly as I could. Inside, my muscles had loosened into jelly. All the houses looked alike to me. I had been in that tiny room behind the closet for a week, and I did not recognize the streets at all — but I could not afford to knock on the wrong door in an occupied town.

As I passed by the window of one house, a spark of remembrance flickered in my head. Those curtains — blue lace curtains! Those were the ones from the house I had stayed in, I was sure of it. When I entered the kitchen, the woman of the house took one look at me and passed out on the floor — and she had good reason.

When she regained consciousness, she told me that another note had come for me after I left the house, telling me that the plan had been discarded and that I should wait for further instructions. The man I had seen on the road had not been waiting for me at all; he was someone who just happened to be fixing his car! When the poor woman saw me walk through the kitchen door, she was sure that I must have been discovered by the Gestapo and that they were coming to kill her because she had taken me in. After her rush of panic subsided, she hurried me back into my room and locked the door. I waited again for several days.

Toward the end of that week, another message arrived. The instructions were the same: I was to look for a car on the path to the drugstore the following Shabbos. Once again I left the house, praying as I walked, and once again I came upon a car whose driver appeared to be fixing it. This time the license plate number matched.

The driver, it turned out, was a Slovakian doctor who had received permission to cross the border from Poland to Slovakia in order to bring back patients for treatment in his own hospital. Inside the car I saw another man wrapped almost completely in bandages, playing the part of the "patient." I gave the driver my name, and he lifted up the back seat in a flash and slid me into the trunk, leaving a small opening so that I could breathe.

When we reached the Polish border, the car was stopped by guards. I heard voices and the rustling of papers. The inspectors opened up every single compartment and bag in the car — except the trunk.

We were stopped again at the Slovakian border, and the same scene repeated itself. The guards examined every paper scrupulously, poked and pushed around inside the car, and asked dozens of questions. I lay doubled over in the trunk, not breathing, begging G-d that if I had to die, I should at least not die a terrible death.

The doors slammed shut, the engine rumbled. We were across the border.

When we had gone several miles into uninhabited territory, the doctor stopped the car and let me out of the trunk. We were among hills and trees, in the fresh Slovakian air. The car wound up the side of a cone-shaped mountain among vibrant green foliage, climbing up narrow, twisted trailways in a dizzying spiral. We were so close to the side of the mountain that it seemed we would fall off the edge into the blue abyss. I could not believe that I was out of Poland, but I did not yet feel free. Somehow I had the sensation that my journey had barely begun.

The doctor deposited me at the home of a Jewish family named Malek in Rapisk, a nondescript village in the Carpathian mountains. I stayed in this family's house for eight days. They were simple village people, very pleasant and good-hearted. They spoke both Polish and Yiddish, so we had no trouble communicating. The Maleks' youngest child, a cherubic, rosy-cheeked three-year-old, had been raised on nothing but milk. He and his brothers and sisters played happily in the grass, innocent of the terrors taking place in the world, tucked away in a nest of oblivion.

Two brothers named Stern, merchants who had professional smuggling contacts, came to the house a day or two later to discuss plans for the next leg of the journey. Apparently Mrs. Malek had already contacted a group of guides to take me to the next town, but the Sterns, both very capable and rugged young men, had other ideas.

"Why should she go with *goyim*?" they said to her. "You never know what might happen, G-d forbid, to a girl alone. We are going that way ourselves, and we have our own guides. We'll take her with us."

We then waited until the next *Motzaei Shabbos*, when the sky was a moonless and pasty black. The Stern brothers learned later on that we had narrowly avoided disaster when we started out that evening. It seemed that the smugglers hired by the Maleks had never received the message that their services were no longer required, and they had showed up not long after we left. We were extremely fortunate that they did not get us into any trouble. They could easily have disclosed us; not only had they lost their pay, but they had risked their lives needlessly by coming out in the first place. I thanked G-d that nothing had happened, for in addition to the danger of being found in the company of smugglers, I did not have a single piece of legal, or even illegal, paper — no passport, nothing.

It was very cold and silent when we left the village. The entire world, it seemed, had been suspended in time, hanging motionlessly in the cavernous black shell of an enormous paperweight. We waded on foot through the frigid air, slogging through the freshly-plowed fields at a snail's pace. The men urged me to move faster so that we could cover distance while it was still dark, but I could barely move. The mud sucked at my heels; my joints were frozen, and my tongue rattled around in my mouth like a piece of loose wood. The bitter cold and the fright combined to paralyze me. Suddenly it was not clear that I was doing the right thing. I had looked for cues all along the way, messages from G-d to help see me through, because I had nothing else to rely on; now I began to wonder if my fatigue were a cue too. It was physically so difficult to get across the field that perhaps G-d was trying to tell me that I should not go ahead. The terror of that thought slowed me down even more. After a short time I could hardly breathe. The Stern brothers literally picked me up and carried me most of the remaining distance — a walk of about two hours, through ankle-thick mud. To this day I am thankful for their dedication and their kindness. Without them, I would never have survived.

Soon we heard dogs barking, which meant we were near a settlement. The shrillness of those piercing barks in the frozen blackness petrified me. I imagined swarms of policemen lying in wait for us over the next hill. We clambered to the top of that hill, which was so slick with mud that we nearly slid down the other side.

A gate was in front of us at the foot of the hill. One of the Sterns lifted me over it, and then both brothers jumped over after me into the yard. The guides disappeared into the opaque stillness. I made out the outline of a small hut several yards away, but the dogs did not belong to it. My imagination had been overwrought; there were no sirens and no policemen.

It was about two o'clock in the morning when we knocked on the door of the hut. A gentile peasant couple let us in. The house consisted of one room with a dirt floor, the most primitive dwelling I had yet seen. There was hardly any furniture; four or five children were asleep on a single bed in the corner, and a worn wooden table and sagging bench stood wearily in the center of the room. A fire crackled in the open hearth, pouring clouds of smoke up the chimney. The smell of the cooking was suffocating.

We sat down to rest for a few minutes, but the man of the house soon became nervous.

"We cannot sit here for too long," he told us. "The children will wake up — they will want to know who the strangers are. It is best that they not see you. Small tongues wag . . ."

The Stern boys led me out to the barn in back of the house. I don't remember any other details because I fell asleep the minute my head touched the straw. I had never slept so deeply in my entire life. The Sterns disappeared and did not come to wake me up until noon the next day.

"Hurry," they said, "we're going into Kashow — into Hungary."

The peasant had hired a covered wagon for us, along with a driver. He stuffed the three of us into the back like herrings and covered us with layers of coarse blankets. I lay there crumpled up amongst the prickly straw, my coat starched with dry mud. After several hours of rumbling and rocking, the driver pulled up in the courtyard of a church and let us out.

The Stern brothers were familiar with Kashow and took me to the home of a family named Reich, who were expecting me. I had made it to Hungary.

I remember the very first thing Mrs. Reich said after greeting me. She looked at me with a disturbed expression and said forthrightly: "You know why Hitler came? Because you are wearing nail polish."

The remark knocked me off my feet. I was so exhausted by the agonizing travels of the past several weeks that it caught me completely off guard. I was too dizzy even to consider its import. Although I had not thought about it much, polishing my nails had become something of an outlet for me. For the ten minutes that I spent on it, I was not a fugitive, alone in a wilderness with the weight of life-and-death decisions on my back; I was a young girl again, my mother's daughter. Polished nails were an esthetic touch that nourished my femininity and kept me hoping for better days; I certainly did not think of it as a sin. Now that I look back, though, I see Mrs. Reich's statement in a different light, and I understand what she meant. Perhaps, in her own way, she was not wrong. At the time, though, I was too disoriented to respond.

I asked for a coarse brush to take the mud off my coat and went out into the back yard.

As I was brushing my coat, I looked out of the corner of my eye, and my heart leaped into my throat. Coming up the pathway to the house was Volvy Friedman.

The brush slipped out of my hand and clattered to the ground. It was fantastic, dreamlike, that the very first person I should meet on the soil of Hungary was one of the oldest and most frequent faces from our table in Warsaw! A breath of relief rushed through me. If familiar people were alive in the world, perhaps there was still hope. After mountains and fields, the heavy tramping of Nazi boots, the muddy darkness of endless and nameless villages, after being so long a stranger in strange places, I allowed myself to think that perhaps things would turn out all right.

Volvy and I talked for a short time in the yard. His perpetual itinerary through the yeshivos of Europe had now brought him back to Munkatch, his hometown, where he had close ties and many friends, and my brother had sent him out to bring me home. I could not help mentioning that although my hosts were pleasant people, I did not feel comfortable here, and Volvy promised to put me up at his aunt's house.

The aunt, Sara Rivka Weiss, was a lovely person, and her family could not do enough for me. They told me that there was a train leaving for Munkatch at four in the morning and arranged to have Volvy meet me at the station. In the meantime, I lay down to take a rest and fell into a deep, dreamless sleep.

When Mrs. Weiss came to wake me up in the middle of the night, I was so exhausted that I could not even be roused. After a few attempts, she gave up; she told me later that she didn't have the heart to wake me. I slept until twelve noon without picking my head up off the pillow, and then took the next train out.

Volvy, in the meantime, had boarded the earlier train in the dim predawn hours, assuming that he would find me in another car, according to plan. When he did not, he got off the train in

Munkatch and waited in the station until the next one showed up. For the second time in two days, I was surprised to see a familiar face where I least expected it, somehow providing me with an anchor in a world that had lost its balance; and for the second time in two days, I regained my footing.

Soon we were in my brother's home. I was in Hungary, together with my family, completely beyond the grasp of the ghetto.

Why did I not feel safe?

Chapter Twelve

Munkatch was a town about the size of Siedlice, with a diverse Jewish population. The war itself was not fully present when I arrived here in the fall of 1941, but there was a strong undertow of apprehension. Political talk was on everyone's tongue, and the Hungarian police, called gendarmes, were on every corner.

The almost deliberately casual daily life of the city's streets belied the advancing hurricane. Many people of Polish citizenship had already been deported from the country, and the pollution of anti-Semitism was thick in the air. When I came to my brother's house, it was nearly empty because the furniture had been seized by the local government as tax collateral. It was not difficult to see that this had very little to do with tax laws and everything to do with my brother's position as rabbi of the largest Chassidic following in Munkatch. Even after he had paid the extravagant sum demanded of him, the furniture was not returned. As yet there had been no violence, but many other subtle indicators pointed toward the onrushing black clouds from the north.

The Alter Munkatcher Rebbe, the Minchas Elazar, zt"l, with some of his followers. The Rebbe is in the middle, holding the walking stick; to his right is the Lubliner Rav zt"l, and at the far left is Chaim Ber Greenwald, zt"l, the Rebbe's devoted gabbai.

Not long after I arrived, I received a letter from the Dubins in Nowy Targ, telling me that the Germans were now occupying their town. The people who had blamed me only a short time ago for "spreading panic" were now discovering the truth for themselves. A ghetto had been established in Nowy Targ, but the mail was still going through. I wondered how long it would be before the hurricane swept onto Hungarian soil.

I was inexpressibly happy and relieved to be among my family again. My sister-in-law, Frimele, whom I had never gotten to know very well, received me warmly. I had brought absolutely nothing with me except what I was wearing, and she immediately ran out and bought fabric to have some clothes made for me. She also purchased a new pair of shoes and a coat for me.

Frimele was young, only a few years older than me, and very lovely. Slim and dark, with black, almond-shaped eyes, she was the adored only child of the previous Munkatcher *Rebbe*, Rabbi Chaim Elazar Spira, *zt"l*, by his second marriage. She had three

Chapter Twelve / 139

Reb Boruch after he assumed his position as the Munkatcher Rebbe.

With my brother's three children in Munkatch.

small sons and was living comfortably in a house that had been built for the *Rebbe*.

Frimele was already quite ill when I came to Munkatch. I was aware that she was not well, but I was very naive then and had no idea what was wrong with her. Although she had plenty of household help, the proper medical attention was apparently not available. Her mother, the *alte* Munkatcher *Rebbetzin*, somehow had to accept the fact that her precious only daughter was infected with a serious disease, and the family, tragically, was forced to cope with Frimele's illness by hoping it would disappear.

I stayed in Munkatch for nearly a year, never quite adjusting to the drastic change in lifestyle. The Jews here lived in a much less sophisticated environment than the one in which I had grown up. My brother Boruch, who had become the new *rebbe* at the young age of twenty-one, suffered from the imbalance as well. Although he was very much respected in the community, his traditions were new and strange to them. Our own family had thrived in a home where general education, though of course secondary, was valued and encouraged, and as a result Reb

Boruch personified a more polished approach to the world, not only in his learning but in his interactions with people. The *chassidim* were somewhat wary of his long pants and tie tack, which were a bit too Western for their taste, and they were extremely intrigued by the fact that he hired a private tutor for me so that I could continue my *Limudei Kodesh* studies, a practice unheard of among Munkatcher daughters. Nevertheless, in spite of this difference in style, they admired him greatly and lavished their loyalty upon him.

Some of the *chassidim* tried to suggest *shidduchim* for me, but although I was already at the ripe old age of twenty-one, I did not want to think about it. I could not commit myself to anyone in the midst of a war; it seemed irresponsible to me to bring children into such a dangerous world. The Munkatchers, however, had not seen what I had seen in the Warsaw ghetto, and the Jewish continuum was inviolable to them. In fact, Volvy Friedman became engaged and got married during that year to a girl from Salish. He was twenty-five, and his father, a staunch Munkatcher, was adamant that he get on with his life.

I prayed with all my heart that these people would never have reason to fear Hitler, but I could not rid myself of my own worries. I did not sleep at my brother's house at night for fear of getting him into trouble; he too was a Polish citizen, and it would not do to draw attention to the fact that he had a sister in town who was a refugee, who did not know the language, and who did not have a single legal document. Instead I stayed at the home of Rabbi Kahn, one of my brother's devoted *chassidim*.

I was very comfortable in the Kahns' house. The family had seven lovely children and a beautifully organized, punctual household. The children had a well-practiced morning routine, washing in order of their age for breakfast, *bentching* together, and then filing out for *cheder*. I was given a pleasant room hung with crocheted curtains and large, attractive needlepoint tapestries that Mrs. Kahn had made herself. Rabbi Kahn took the enormous risk of housing me in spite of the potential

This is me on a visit to Strobiczow during my stay in Munkatch.

danger of sheltering an illegal alien for no other reason than that he loved the *Rebbe* dearly, and I was very grateful to him.

Volvy Friedman had tried to ease my situation by procuring Hungarian papers for me under the name of Rochel Landau. But even though I now had papers, the feeling of uneasiness persisted. Policemen were everywhere. They roamed the streets, keeping close watch on the comings and goings of all visitors to the town. Everyone was suspect. Occasionally the gendarmes would knock on doors and go through a family's papers or search the house for people in hiding.

Somehow, one always tends to insulate himself by thinking that "it will only happen to other people," but this pleasant illusion burst for me one day. Without warning, the gendarmes showed up at my brother's house one afternoon while I was helping out with the children. In panic, I grabbed the two youngest, both of whom were babies, and raced to the storage room at the back of the house with the maid. We heard footsteps in the foyer, then loud voices and commotion. My heart beat heavily against the wall of my chest, pounding so hard that it hurt.

The footsteps came closer. Suddenly there was banging on the storage room door. They knocked and knocked and knocked, and I held my breath, praying. By some strange twist of good fortune and in spite of my own fright, neither of the children let out so much as a whimper. After a time, the knocking stopped and the footsteps receded. The tumult died down outside, but the four of us stayed in the storage room until nightfall, petrified. I was desperate to find out if my sister-in-law was all right but much too scared to open the door.

That evening, Volvy Friedman came to the house and found us huddled in a corner, stiff with anxiety and weariness. I came out of the storage room to find that my brother was gone. His citizenship had been discovered, and he had been forced into the roundup of Polish citizens who would now be deported back to their homeland. But the news was even worse — my four-year-old nephew Herschele was gone too. He had run down the road after his father, and the policemen had grabbed him and taken him along.

My sister-in-law was beside herself. The gendarmes had left her alone, thank G-d, because she was lying in bed ill, but the combined effects of her sickness and the shock of her husband's arrest overwhelmed her. She collapsed and had to be rushed to the hospital. I was left alone in the house with the two young boys and the maid, but this was the least of my worries. Perhaps the roundup was not over yet: there was still me — I was also a Polish citizen, but worse than that, I was an illegal one. By this time, although I was not aware of it, the police had already heard that the *Rebbe* had a sister in town, and they were looking for me.

I took the infant to the hospital every single day so that Frimele could nurse him. She insisted on this, even though she was so ill. After a few hours, the maid would come to pick up the baby, and I would remain for a while to keep my sister-in-law company. It was an awful time, a long stretch of unrelieved anxiety. Frimele lay weakly in bed in an emotional limbo, with no idea where her husband had vanished, or even if he were still alive. The *alte Rebbetzin*, too, had been traumatized by her son-in-law's arrest, and she did not have the strength to comfort her daughter. Frimele had no one to lean on at that time except me.

One day when I arrived at the hospital room, I found her feverish, too exhausted to nurse. She held the baby, and I lay

Chapter Twelve / 143

down in the empty bed to rest for a while. I had almost drifted off into a restless slumber when I felt an odd push inside me, as though someone were jabbing at my ribs, prodding upward. I sat up sharply — or, to be more accurate, I was pushed up off the bed by this force, which seemed almost demonic. I had the urgent sensation that I must get out of this place immediately, and I was very frightened.

"Frimele," I said, "*ich muz gain* — I have to go."

Frimele had often teased me about my restlessness, but now she panicked. "Why? Why do you have to run all the time?" she cried anxiously. "Please — stay a little longer!"

Poor Frimele; she depended very much on my company, and now she especially needed it. The streets were in an uproar over all the people who had been deported, and she did not know where to look for security. But the hand pushed desperately against my rib cage.

"I don't know why I have to go," I told her, "but I *must* go."

I hurried down the corridor and out the front entrance to the huge courtyard that ran the length of the hospital. Three men were coming in as I was leaving, and we passed each other in the gateway. Later I learned that they were policemen in plainclothes. They had gone straight to Frimele's room and had shown her a photograph of me; where they had obtained it is still a mystery. Frimele told them she did not know who I was, and they did not press her any further.

As I was rushing home, I met an acquaintance in the street, one of my brother's friends.

"Don't go to the *Rebbe's* house," he warned me breathlessly. "Go to the Pearlsteins' bunker — fast!"

The Pearlsteins had a son who had been called to the draft. They had told the army officials that he was dead and had been hiding him in the bunker underneath their house ever since. They quickly pulled me into the house without asking questions and locked the door. I stayed with the Pearlsteins for about a week, sharing a bed with their daughter Rivka and never venturing near an open window. Every time we heard boots

With Rivka Pearlstein (right) in front of her house.

thumping in the streets, I would quickly climb through the entrance to the bunker, which was beneath Rivka's bed. After a week of climbing up and down the steps to the bunker, I began to feel suffocated.

I couldn't stand it anymore. How much longer could this game of hide-and-seek continue? How much longer could I stay in a locked house, not knowing what was happening to my family, not knowing what would hit me if I opened up the front door? Staying in Munkatch suddenly no longer seemed a viable option. My false papers were only a marginal protection, and my continued presence in the town was a threat to my whole family. I did not want to abandon my sister-in-law, but it seemed to me that I was endangering her more by staying.

One day when the Pearlsteins were not in the front room, I slipped out the door. I cannot honestly say what I planned to do just then, or even if I had a plan at all. At that moment, Volvy Friedman was coming up the walk to check in on me, as he had promised my brother he would.

"Where are you going?" he asked in alarm.

"I'm going to register," I said point-blankly. "I'll tell them who I am, and I'll join my brother. There's no use in my remaining here."

"Are you crazy?" he shouted in a fierce whisper. "Don't be foolish! Do you think they're going to send you exactly where they sent your brother?"

I stood on the walk, my head spinning, feeling that a huge chasm had opened up below my feet. It was a familiar feeling; I had had it once before, half a year ago, when I stood in the road

Chapter Twelve / 145

on the way to the village drugstore in some unknown town and thought to myself, "What should I do? What should I do?" — the same sensation that had possessed me until a small gray robin walked into my path.

While I stood there frozenly, Volvy hailed a horse and carriage and made me get inside with him. He had the driver take us around town for the rest of the afternoon while he talked to me about all kinds of things — some important, some not —trying to divert me from my objective. Toward the end of the afternoon, he directed the carriage driver back to the Pearlsteins' house.

"You're not going anywhere," he told me firmly. "You're going to stay here." By then I was too exhausted to argue.

During the next few weeks, the gendarmes came to the house several times, and each time we would pull back the opening to the bunker so that I could dive into the basement. Once, Rivka had barely rolled the carpet back over the opening when they barged into the bedroom. In all my life, I never said as much *Tehillim* as I said in that basement.

During this time, although I did not know it then, the *alte* Munkatcher *Rebbetzin* was toiling ceaselessly to bring my brother back from Poland. It is impossible to know how she managed to make so many high-placed contacts. She talked to army officials, to the police, to the government, to the foreign consulate; she was afraid of no one and she left no stone unturned. She did not eat, sleep, or in fact do anything else until she located her son-in-law. And, most miraculous of all, she did bring him back — six months later.

She learned that the *Rebbe* was being held in the Polish town of Yagolnice. Thank G-d, he had not been imprisoned or sent to a concentration camp, but — as for any other Jew in Eastern Europe — his fate was only a matter of time, for all the ghettos were eventually to be liquidated. The *Rebbetzin* contacted a Jewish Hungarian soldier by the name of Avrohom Mann, who was able to pass across the border because of his military status. She promised him that if he returned her son-in-law safely, she would give him a prized pair of heirloom candlesticks that had belonged to her *zeide*, the Komarner *Rebbe*. Although this may sound like small compensation now, it was a considerable sacrifice in a time when every family treasure was beyond value.

Mann got in touch with a doctor who agreed to disguise the *Rebbe* as an invalid and bring him back to Hungary. Herschele, my nephew, was hidden at the bottom of the car, covered with blankets. The two of them returned home safely, and Mann received his candlesticks. When he met me, he joked, "If I had known that the *Rebbe* had an unmarried sister, I would have asked for her hand instead!"

My brother returned from Poland not much the worse for wear, thank G-d. He had spent his time in the Yagolnice ghetto learning, speaking to the people, and above all, looking for a way to get out.

During those six months, he was on the receiving end of two remarkable chains of Divine Providence, each of which had been initiated years earlier. The first was begun by my own father, who had always been very involved in helping young *bachurim* evade the Polish draft. In those days, life for a Jew in the armies of Europe was a life of desolation. Not only was a Jewish soldier subject to rabid anti-Semitism, but any possibility of remaining *shomer mitzvos* was virtually eclipsed. The son of one of the people whom my father had helped was living in the Yagolnice ghetto when the *Rebbe* arrived, and he quickly extended a helping hand. This son said to the *Rebbe*, "Perhaps my father was saved from the army in order that I should be here to take you in."

The second incident was even more miraculous, and its roots were much older. My brother did not speak much to us about his exile in Poland, but this story was later told to us by my brother's son, Rabbi Yitzchak Yaakov Rabinowitz, who is now the Dinover *Rebbe*.

The story goes back about two hundred years to Reb Moishe Leib Erblich, a renowned Chassidic *rebbe* from Sassov, Poland. Reb Moishe Leib once passed through the town of Yagolnice when the Jewish community there was in its infancy. The Jews were about to construct a cemetery, and they asked the *Rebbe* if he would agree to write in his will that he be buried there one day. They knew that the merit of a *tzaddik* buried in their midst would provide spiritual protection for the entire community.

Reb Moishe Leib, for reasons of his own, said that he could not agree. He did promise, however, that his one and only son, Reb Shmelke, would be buried in the Yagolnice cemetery, and the Jews were satisfied. Reb Shmelke was a direct ancestor of ours; my grandfather from Strizhev, whose house I had played in when I was a little girl, was a grandson of Reb Shmelke's, and he himself was named Moishe Leib after Reb Shmelke's father.

In accordance with the promise, Reb Shmelke was indeed buried in the Yagolnice cemetery after he passed away. He had a daughter named Baila, a widow with no children, who had moved home to Sassov after her husband's death. This daughter desired very much to buy a burial plot next to her father in Yagolnice. At that time the Jews of Poland were extremely poor, and food was hard to come by. For three or four years, Baila sold her supper in order to save the money for the burial plot, which she was finally able to purchase.

Some time later, because of an error which was never untangled, the *chevra kadisha* of Yagolnice sold Baila's plot to someone else. She did not find out about it immediately because she was living in Sassov, but when the news reached her she became hysterical. The burial plot next to her revered father, for which she had literally gone hungry for so many years, was the only thing of real value she had in the world. Not knowing the circumstances and unable to reverse them, Baila, in her outrage, condemned the entire city of Yagolnice, declaring that it should burn down. And that is exactly what happened: many years later, in 1864, most of the city's wooden buildings burned to the ground. The catastrophe was recorded in the files of the city hall.

Yagolnice was a small, provincial town, whose inhabitants — gentile as well as Jewish — were of a spiritual turn of mind. They all knew the story of Baila's dispute with the cemetery officials, and they interpreted the disaster as a direct retribution for the sale of the burial plot. Even the gentiles viewed the sale as a sin and the fire as a punishment, and that is how the incident remained in the town's anecdotal history.

When my brother was left by the Germans in the Yagolnice ghetto in June of 1941, one of the first things he did was to ask the townspeople to take him to the cemetery. He knew that his great-great-grandfather was buried there, and he wanted to offer a prayer not only for himself but for the entire population of the ghetto, which was in imminent danger of liquidation. The Jews of Yagolnice quickly heard that the Munkatcher *Rebbe* was going to offer a public prayer at the grave of Reb Shmelke, *z"tl*, and a large crowd gathered at the cemetery.

It is said that the *Rebbe* became very emotional during his talk and that many in the crowd were crying. "My great-great-grandfather, Reb Shmelke of blessed memory, never lived here in Yagolnice and never was a *rebbe* here," he said. "So why was he buried here? . . . Because the *Ribono Shel Olam* knew that his great-great-grandson would be brought to this town and would need a place to pour his heart out . . ."

The gentile community heard about the gathering at the cemetery, and it became the talk of the town. Everyone knew that the descendant of the great rabbi buried in the cemetery had come to pray there.

Eventually, my brother received deportation orders. He was to be transported deeper into Poland, which would have made the prospect of an escape even more remote. Rabbi Nosson Rosenzweig, the rabbi of Yagolnice, enlisted the community's support in my brother's cause — but the most powerful assistance came from the most unlikely corner. The priest of Yagolnice's one church held a sermon the following Sunday, and its message was extraordinary.

"Everyone here is aware of the history of the rabbi who is buried in the Jewish cemetery," he said. "It is well known that the town once suffered a catastrophic fire because honor was not properly accorded to the rabbi's daughter. Now his great-great-grandson is in town, and if we do not do our best to protect him, a further calamity may befall us. I am going to make sure personally that this rabbi is hidden from the Germans — and anyone who divulges my plan will be excommunicated from the church."

The priest kept his word, and not one person in the gentile community disclosed him, although they would have been rewarded handsomely by the Germans for doing so. Reb Boruch remained in hiding in Yagolnice for several months until the *alte Rebbetzin* was able to arrange his rescue. The *Rebbe* and his son were smuggled first to the town of Tluste and from there back to Munkatch.

And so my brother returned unscathed from the jaws of the Polish Holocaust. But the episode did not end happily. The **Rebbe** was able to resume a normal life, but his little son had changed.

The child was restless and nervous; he lost interest in learning and misbehaved frequently. Herschele was the first grandchild on his mother's side of the family and had always been showered with love. Although he was not harmed in Poland, my brother was so distraught and so consumed with his search to escape that he could not adequately care for his son, and the loss of attention in those months clearly showed.

But there was much worse news during my stay in Munkatch. It was not actually news to me then, only a strong intuition, but it was every bit as dreadful. I remember the day: it was the fourth of Av, 1942. I woke up with an awful feeling that morning, a wave of inner horror. I was certain that something drastic had happened to my mother, and I cried inconsolably from morning till night. I did not know what it was, but I knew beyond a shadow of a doubt that it was disastrous. I felt that I must go to her, that I should be with her, and I didn't know how. The turmoil nearly strangled me.

I did not find out until much later that my mother had died of typhoid fever in the ghetto on that day. No doubt she had contracted it from Chavale Rabinowitz, the aunt from Lodz who had stayed in our house before the ghetto was sealed. To this day, I feel that she died *al Kiddush Hashem* in her unwillingness to abandon the *sifrei Torah* and *sefarim* in the apartment. To this day, I cannot forgive myself for not being there with her before she died, however irrational this feeling may be. But at the same time, I feel that I was privileged. G-d gave me the benefit of those bitter, unaccountable tears on the day of her passing. My bond with my mother was so strong and so close that He did not spare me the pain of losing her. And even though I did not know with certainty what had happened on that day, I am grateful now in retrospect that I had the opportunity to mourn for her.

Mr. Domb, the Swiss gentleman who escorted me to Nowy Targ when I left the ghetto, was in Warsaw when my mother passed away. It was he who took care of her when she became ill and who made all the funeral arrangements, for my brother Yankel was still in Russia and would not return until 1943. Mr. Domb sent us a postcard in Munkatch relaying the bad news, but no one told me about it. Reb Boruch sat *shivah* in the *beis midrash* so that I would not find out. I did not learn of my mother's death for several months and never sat *shivah* for her myself.

My brother had not been long at home when he decided that it would be best for the family to leave Munkatch altogether. He wanted to go to Budapest, where he had a wider and more sophisticated network of supporters, people who were informed about the war and who would be better able to help him out.

The *alte Rebbetzin* and I went up to Budapest along with a few of the *chassidim* to begin looking for an apartment. Many of my brother's supporters immediately came to our aid, including one very pleasant couple named Roth, with whom we stayed. This visit was like deja vu for me; many years earlier I had gone through very much the same motions, leaving a small town for a big one, shedding the old life for a new one. I had become accustomed by now to living in a blindfold, trusting myself completely to the hands of G-d. He had taken care of me so closely and in such an open way many times before, and I felt sure that He was with me. I wanted to go forward — only forward.

Chapter Thirteen

The year that I spent in Budapest was a spinning wheel of hopes and fears. Our lives revolved constantly, changing color and pattern from day to day, spilling steadily toward the brink of that ominous, unseen cliff. We were never safe, only buying time; we lived with a superficial nonchalance, one step ahead of panic.

Budapest was a very colorful, lively city. In style it was similar to Krakow, full of ornate buildings, with the taste of an aristocratic past lingering over it. We were fortunate once again to find an apartment in a stately old house at 9 Ou Street. Unfortunately its facilities were no more modern than its appearance. We did not have hot water, but this was not a time to think about inconveniences. We were very thankful to have a roof over our heads.

For my brother, the move, at least temporarily, was a wise one. The Munkatcher following in the city was large, and there were quite a number of influential and secularly educated people who were able to set up a protective string of contacts for him. The anonymity of a large town was in his

Mr. Fried, the house bachur, with my brother's children in Budapest

favor, and he soon became very involved in clandestine rescue activities.

Reb Boruch's *chassidim* put him in touch with a Hungarian countess who turned out to be, certainly, one of the *chassidei umos ha'olam*, or righteous gentiles. Apparently she had contact with foreign diplomats in Budapest, and with her help he was able to arrange visas for many Jews to escape to Brazil, Australia, and other distant countries. Refugees of every type and nationality passed through our doors, and it is to the *Rebbe's* credit that so many of them eluded Hitler's net.

This benevolent countess lived in Buda, across the river from us. She did not want anyone coming up to her apartment during the daytime, so we used to cross the river at twelve or one o'clock at night. Ephraim Fried, the *Rebbe's* devoted house *bachur*, and I always went along on these nocturnal visits. The outings were not safe for any of us, to say the least, but I was too nervous to stay at home. We had no telephone service and no other reliable means of communication, and I felt more secure staying close to my brother and knowing what was happening to him.

We never met the countess herself. Someone would escort my brother up to her quarters while Mr. Fried and I waited downstairs in the street. Sometimes the *Rebbe* would not come down until four o'clock in the morning. He would heave a sigh of relief when he saw us and say, "*Baruch Hashem* — fifty people." He knew what it felt like to be held prisoner and was overjoyed to have the opportunity to save others from a similar — or worse — fate. Years later, when I was already in *Eretz Yisrael*, there were many people who came up to me and said, "Thanks to your brother, I am here." I always felt a swelling of pride when I heard those words.

Both for his lifesaving efforts and for his wonderful leadership abilities, the *Rebbe* was greatly loved and respected in Budapest. He had wide financial support from his *chassidim* and the invaluable assistance of Ephraim Fried. Although he was able to accomplish a great deal in Budapest, he was constantly aware that the war was nipping at his heels, and he talked often about moving on — perhaps, with G-d's help, to *Eretz Yisrael*.

I was the only member of the entourage who had come to Budapest on false papers. As in Munkatch, it was still too risky for me to stay in my brother's apartment, so I slept most of the time at the home of the Marines, another of the many wonderful families who took me in on my seemingly endless itinerary. Mr. Marine was involved in the manufacture of false documents, and he took great risks to help the escaped Jews.

One prominent refugee who stayed at the Marines' house at the same time was the current Bobover *Rebbe's* sister, Gicha, with whom I became very friendly. I can say without hesitation that although I would never want to repeat a single moment of my life during the war, I am grateful at the same time for the many special people whose paths I was privileged to cross during my flight. Gicha was among them.

Daily life, became, if anything, much more strenuous in Budapest. Because of the *Rebbe's* position and relief activities, there was still a constant flow of people through the house, a phenomenon that seemed to brand our family — thank G-d —wherever we went; but it meant that much more cooking and cleaning, along with the attendant lack of privacy. This was probably my first real glimpse into my mother's wisdom, for now I finally understood why she had given us so many household responsibilities when we were growing up. The experience now proved invaluable.

My brother began to depend heavily on me for emotional support as well. We talked frequently during this time and drew very close. He did not show his doubts to anyone else, but I saw that he felt very lost and apprehensive in this big city and very uncertain of his future. This was the first time since we had been reunited that he began to ask me detailed questions about what had happened in Poland, and he was realistic enough to see that the ripples of the German onslaught were steadily widening. He began to think more and more seriously about finding a way to get to *Eretz Yisrael*. There was one particular episode which lent that dream urgency.

There were no concentration camps in Hungary as yet, but the Hungarian authorities had established a labor force, into which they randomly conscripted able-bodied men. In order to avoid being drafted into a *munkotabor,* or labor unit, the *Rebbe* went to a sympathetic doctor who induced a temporary hip displacement, so that he walked with a limp and needed a cane. The *Rebbe* asked in particular for a treatment affecting the leg, having been inspired by his morning *tefillos*. That day was a Wednesday, and he had earlier said the *Shir Shel Yom*, which contained the verse "If I said, 'My foot falters,' Your kindness, Hashem, supported me" (*Tehillim* 94:18). He used these words as a guideline, deciding that if he would let his "foot falter," the *Ribono Shel Olam* would come to his aid.

When he received the labor summons and reported, he was indeed excused due to his disability — but he was ordered instead to a local camp, where he was given lighter work. He was confined in the camp, but at least he was not far from home. Naturally he could not eat the *treif* food given out there, but because he was close by, I was able to smuggle food into the camp every day. Recently I met someone who was imprisoned with him at that time, and he recalled how my brother spoke and thought constantly about his Torah studies.

Chapter Thirteen / 155

One day I actually saw my brother through the bars that surrounded the compound. Only those thin bars separated us, and yet I was acutely aware of the difference they made between freedom and bondage. A sharp pain went through my heart; my brother was right in front of me, and yet I could do nothing to help him. I pushed the contents of my package through the closely placed bars, and he hastily stuffed them into his pockets. Then a guard spotted us and began running toward me.

I fled in terror, the guard close behind me. As I sped by a tall building, a janitor, apparently one of kind heart, reached out and pulled me in. He took me downstairs and hid me in the boiler room. I heard the sounds of a search going on above me, the footsteps, voices, and banging, but once again I was not discovered. When I had stayed in the boiler room a safe amount of time, I left the building. After that I was much less foolhardy, slipping my packages through the bars only when I was certain that no one was watching.

On Chanukah the *Rebbe's* captors gave him a one-day furlough, and he came home to light the *menorah*. Many of his *chassidim* came to watch and listen — and weep — as he recited the *berachos*. Reb Boruch spent the evening at home and returned to the camp the next day. Eventually he was freed, but that episode left *Eretz Yisrael* an even stronger target in his mind. There was no telling when the Hungarians might decide again to exercise their authority, placing him in a trap from which he might not, *chas v'shalom*, escape.

My sister-in-law was expecting again, and her illness drained all her energy. Her three children were all under the age of seven, and she simply did not have the strength to take care of them. Clothing was constantly lying around the apartment, and there was no regular schedule. I saw that if anything was going to get done, I would have to do it. Before I knew it, I was in charge of the household, managing by trial and error. Being responsible for three small children was a completely new experience for me. As the youngest child in my own family, I had never taken care of

My sister-in-law Frimele (center) in Budapest

younger siblings and really had no idea what a juggling act motherhood was. I was amazed to discover how much time it took to do the laundry alone.

Frimele went into labor right after *Kiddush* on the first night of Pesach and left for Varos Moyer, a large private hospital, where she soon gave birth to a baby boy. She pleaded with me to come with her into the labor room; and that is how it came about that I was the first person to hold her little son, Yaakov Yitzchak, who later grew up to be the Dinover *Rebbe* in America. From the first cry of his life, this child became like my own son, and I was very involved in his upbringing.

The *bris* was a memorable occasion. I stayed in the hospital with Frimele and did not see it, but reports came in to us by the dozens. A restaurant named Stern's catered the *simchah*, reportedly putting out 5,000 individual portions of carp for the guests. The *Rebbe* spoke for a good three hours at the Kozhnitzer *shul*, with thousands of *chassidim* in attendance. I heard that the streets were solid with people and that everyone was hanging on his words. It was not difficult for me to imagine this. My brother had always been an exceptional speaker, with a refined and commanding presence and a radiant way of articulating his ideas. Here in Budapest, before he was thirty years old, he reached the pinnacle of his leadership.

His new son, unfortunately, was often sickly and required delicate care. I had to mix a special formula for him, and needless to say, I felt quite clumsy when it came to such matters. I remember that Mr. Fried and I once had to run across town with the baby on a Shabbos afternoon to find a doctor; but over time the need for such vigilance subsided, and with Hashem's help I was able to nurse him back to health.

My nephew Yaakov Yitzchak, wearing a sweater that I knitted for him.

I often stayed up with the baby at night, rocking him back and forth in the carriage, because I didn't want to disturb my sister-in-law. Sometimes I was so exhausted that I would tie one end of a string to the carriage and the other end to my arm, so that the carriage would rock if I merely shook my hand. Even when he was older, he used to ask me to rock him.

Besides child care, there was one other item for which I had received no preparation at home, and that was because there had never been a need for it. I still shudder when I think of this episode.

We had come to Budapest with almost no furniture. Reb Boruch had never been able to retrieve his own furniture, which had been taken from him long ago in Munkatch as a tax appropriation. When we arrived in town, someone had told us about a place where the discarded furniture of visiting dignitaries was sold very inexpensively. My brother found a set of magnificent antique pieces at the warehouse which were in nearly perfect condition, and as an added benefit, they fit the rooms in our apartment beautifully. There was only one problem: they had been in storage for a long time, and the seams had become infested with tiny tenants. Reb Boruch did not know this, of course, when he bought them.

I once stayed overnight in my brother's house. The apartment happened to be full of guests then, so I slept on one of the new couches — or rather, I tried to sleep, which is a very hard thing to do when you are being attacked by bedbugs. What I had yet to learn is that bedbugs travel.

A *chassid* came to the house one evening not long afterward, and I showed him to his room. A little while later, he came out in his robe. My first impression was that the robe was polka-dotted. Then I took a second look, and I saw that the polka dots were falling to the floor — by the dozens. All I can say is that I have never seen an expression, neither before nor after, like the one on that man's face.

"This cannot go on," I thought to myself, half in aggravation and half in embarrassment. It was bad enough to endure the bedbugs ourselves without the additional humiliation of subjecting the guests to them!

I called an exterminator, and we moved out for three days while they bombed the entire apartment. I remember sweeping away piles and piles of bugs, thousands of bugs. When I closed my eyes, I saw bugs . . . when I ate, I saw bugs. It was the worst experience of our life in Budapest, worse even than the political tension, and it was especially stressful for me because the burden was entirely on my shoulders.

Thoughts of getting to *Eretz Yisrael* never left my brother's mind. This was my aim too; I felt in my heart that all these cities were only stepping stones to a final stop, a place where my soul would find rest. I knew, too, that I had family waiting for me in the Holy Land.

In fact, it was my sister Devorah who managed to get sponsorship certificates for Reb Boruch's family. Her husband, Jacob Landau, was very influential in the Israeli branch of Poalei Agudas Yisrael, and he promised to send the certificates to us within the next few months. We would then be cleared to make *aliyah*, but only two obstacles remained: how to get out of Hungary, which was legally impossible with the war on, and the *alte Rebbetzin's* disapproval.

The latter was a very difficult problem. The *Rebbetzin* did not want to leave the country. She was only in her mid-fifties and was strong enough, thank G-d, to travel, but it seemed ludicrous to her to abandon the country of her birth and the place where her husband was buried. She, like so many others, could not accept the possibility that the Nazis might actually reach Hungary or that the Jews here were in any danger, so the idea of uprooting and leaving her home, or allowing her children to leave it, seemed preposterous to her — a gamble on air.

I had seen this pattern everywhere I went, from the Jews of the Warsaw ghetto who had not believed that Hitler could want to do anything more than degrade them, to the Jews of Nowy Targ, who had accused me of spreading panic with my stories of the ghetto. The concept of a Final Solution, of a scourge that would follow them like a poisonous fungus to every corner of the continent, was not an admissible notion.

Volvy Friedman came to see me one day with a message from the *alte Rebbetzin*.

"She feels that you have a lot of influence over your brother," he told me. "She asked me to ask you to convince him not to go."

I understood the reason for the indirect message; the *alte Rebbetzin* knew that Volvy Friedman was a long-standing friend of our family and that he knew me well. She was hoping that he would be able to persuade me. But I already knew what I had to do. I did not mean any disrespect to the *Rebbetzin,* but this was an emergency, and there was no place for compromise.

"*Herr* Friedman," I told him, "please tell the *Rebbetzin* that I have come from *Gehinnom*. Six souls are at stake, and I will do everything in my power to try and save them — even if it means sacrificing myself."

My brother, thankfully, was astute. He sensed the danger, and his long talks with me about the events in Poland had convinced him that there was no other escape for us. It was an extremely difficult decision for him to make, for it meant upheaval for him too; but at last he committed himself to it, in spite of his mother-in-law's objections.

We began to make very quiet preparations to go to *Eretz Yisrael*, for we did not want to cause the *Rebbetzin* any distress before it was absolutely necessary. I started to take the children out for occasional walks, and while we were out I would stop at the tailor's to order cotton outfits for them, because I knew we would be going to a hotter climate. Mr. Fried, the house *bachur*, purchased a brown hat and a more modern set of street clothes for my brother, who had arranged to leave Hungary under a false identity and could not afford to appear *Chassidish*. Fried pulled all of these packages up through the window with string, and we tried our best to stash them away quickly so as not to cause any anxiety to the *alte Rebbetzin*.

It was difficult enough to plan an escape without the additional headache of my illegality. I was still living under my assumed name of Rochel Landau with the papers that Volvy Friedman had acquired for me in Munkatch, but I never felt comfortable with them. The police were constantly on the lookout for false documents, and one day they turned up at my brother's apartment while I was there, just as they had done in Munkatch. I had escaped their notice for so many months that I had become somewhat complacent about my long run of good luck. Now, in a flash, I found myself trapped.

One of the policemen addressed me in Hungarian, and I thought I was lost. I had prepared something to say in case I was ever questioned, but the one Hungarian expression that I desperately needed right now — the one that meant "I am a nanny to the children" — was such a tongue-twister that I could barely get the words out of my mouth.

"Don't worry," the gendarme said to me with a sinister nonchalance. "It doesn't matter if you don't know Hungarian. We'll send you to a place where you don't *have* to know Hungarian."

For some inexplicable reason, he did not arrest me. To this day I don't understand it. All I could think of then was that perhaps Reb Shayale Czechower's *berachah* was still going strong; perhaps G-d had granted me some kind of projection that made people look favorably upon me. I really don't know. All I know is that I was saved from disaster by a hair's breadth on more than one occasion, and this was one of them.

The next day I set about learning Hungarian with ferocity. I must admit that in all my years of schooling I had never exhibited such a fierce determination! I talked to Mr. Fried day and night and became reasonably fluent in a very short time. Perhaps it is true, as they say, that necessity is the mother of invention, and I had never needed a language as I needed it now.

One day I went into a trimming shop and requested a few items in my new tongue. The clerk smiled at me strangely and let me stand there while he attended to another customer. Then a second person walked in, and he took care of her too. After standing there for twenty minutes or so, I became suspicious. For all I knew, he had detected my very unauthentic accent and was holding me until he could call the police. I took my chances.

"Excuse me, sir," I ventured, "but why are you taking care of other people when I was here first?"

"Because I enjoy listening to your Hungarian!" he replied with a twinkle in his eye. I breathed a sigh of relief — not only because there was no danger, but because there was still amusement to be had in this bleak world of ours.

By this time, we were preparing to leave Budapest openly. With the tasks at hand, it was no longer possible to hide our plans from the *Rebbetzin*. My brother had a huge library of thousands of *seforim* which had to be boxed. I went to a carpenter to order crates, and Mr. Fried and my brother and I stayed up through the nights packing the *sefarim*. The *Rebbetzin* saw by now that her son-in-law was very determined to leave the country and that there was nothing she could do to keep him back.

Then disaster struck — a disaster more devastating than anything that had yet happened to me. Our Palestine certificates finally arrived in the mail, and mine was not in the envelope. I had no certificate.

The enormity of the error was more than I could grasp then. I could not go to *Eretz Yisrael* with my brother. I would be left alone in Budapest with nothing to my name — not even an identity.

I tried very hard to rationalize it to myself. Surely it was for the best; maybe I was being saved from some worse ending. Maybe the certificate had been misplaced or had fallen into the wrong hands — or maybe it had even been stolen. Certainly this was an act of *hashgachah pratis*. Maybe if I had tried to leave Budapest, the border guards would have discovered that my citizenship papers were false, and I might have landed in jail —or worse, G-d forbid. I gave myself a hundred and one reasons, but I never let my brother see even a hint of my distress.

The *Rebbe* was distraught beyond words, but I would not think of allowing him to stay behind on my account. Frimele was expecting her fifth child, and there was no way I would allow my brother to endanger six and a half lives for my sake. I continued to help with the packing as though nothing had happened, once more throwing myself on G-d's mercy. This wasn't the first time in my life that I had no idea what I was going to do, and somehow I knew it wouldn't be the last. But somewhere, deep in the recesses of my heart, I told myself that I would one day reach the Holy Land and kiss its soil, no matter what I had to do to get there, no matter how long I had to wait; and that thought comforted me.

In the winter of 1943, the moving company finally came. Mr. Fried and I, along with dozens of friends and *chassidim*, accompanied the *Rebbe* and his family to the border city of Chopp to see them off. My brother's *chassidim* were very distressed to see him go, especially because there was no Nazi presence in Hungary yet and there seemed no reason for the flight; but they accepted his judgment.

I don't have words to describe that leave-taking. Even now when I think about it, I am too agitated to discuss it. I was thrilled that my brother and his family were finally on their way to the Holy Land, but I was not sure I would ever see them again. My brother, for his part, was extremely anxious about my welfare. A wealthy friend of his had promised to take me in, but he still felt that he was leaving me adrift. There was nothing to say, nothing to do; he had to go and I had to stay.

When the train was out of sight, I took a deep breath and looked for G-d. There was no one else to help me now.

Chapter Fourteen

Before moving to my new quarters, I returned to my brother's apartment to take care of a few last things. Most of the furniture had been sold already, and the apartment was almost bare. One couch had been moved into the kitchen, and the *Rebbetzin* was sitting on it when I came up. She told me that she wanted to return to Munkatch, where her husband, the *alter* Munkatcher *Rebbe,* was buried. I knelt beside her and took her hand.

"Rebbetzin," I said, "I've seen *Gehinnom.* I know that in a big city you can protect yourself better than in a small city, because there everyone knows who you are. In Budapest you can lose yourself in the crowd. Please don't go back. I'll take care of you; please stay here."

But the politics of war played no part in her logic. She had already lost her daughter and son-in-law, and she did not want to be left alone, friendless, in a place she considered a jungle. She packed a few belongings and went to stay, for the meantime, with another family, and later she left town. She did not actually make it back to Munkatch but went instead to a town called Neirethauz, where she had friends.

I received a letter from her not long after she had left, asking that I please go back into my brother's apartment and send her some of the clothing she had left behind, as well as some food. Twice the packages went through; the third one came back marked "Unreceived," and the food had been removed from it.

The last communication I had received from the *Rebbetzin* was a postcard, in which she informed me that the Germans had come to Nierethauz. She wrote: "Now I realize what a special son-in-law I have. He saw what was coming and was able to save his own family and so many other people. You did not listen to me — and now I want to say *'Yasher koach.'* " The *Rebbetzin* was taken away shortly afterward, and she died in a concentration camp. She had already been deported by the time the third package arrived.

As soon as I had distributed or disposed of the remaining items in the apartment, I went to stay with my brother's *chassid*, whom I will call Kapowitz. I had no money at this point and no idea where I would go from here. As it turned out, I had to make up my mind more quickly than I expected.

One evening, about two weeks after I had moved in, I was sitting in the parlor of the Kapowitzes' beautifully furnished apartment when my host came home from work.

"*Fraulein* Peska," he said to me, "I just heard that the Germans are coming into town. You have to leave my house."

He said it just like that: no explanations, no apologies. This man, as I have mentioned, was quite wealthy and a distinguished member of the community, and he surmised — no doubt correctly — that the Germans would come after people like him first. He could not afford to have any extra strikes against him by housing an illegal alien. I figured all of this out within a few seconds, but it did nothing to numb my amazement. Kapowitz had no intention of letting me stay in the house overnight, and the hour of the Jewish curfew had already passed. He did not give me any money, and he did not tell me where to go. He was a coward.

I thought: G-d brought me to this point and He will not leave me. Somehow I will get out of this. But the very first thing is that I must get a roof over my head.

Within half an hour I found myself out in the street after dark, holding a bag with a few essentials in it. There was not a soul to be seen on those eerie sidewalks; only fools ventured out after the curfew. Where on earth could I go?

I thought of the Roths, the family with whom we had stayed when we came up from Munkatch to look for an apartment. I had just enough change to get on the crosstown train, but I was petrified. It was pitch black outside. The gate to the courtyard of every apartment building closed at ten o'clock during the war, and the watchmen kept tabs on everyone who came and went. You could not get past any of these gates without identification. The hand that had once pushed me off the bed in my sister-in-law's hospital room began to nudge against my ribs again. Get up and go, it said — and I obeyed it.

When I arrived at the Roths' building, the gatekeeper recognized me because I had been up to visit the family on several occasions. Strangely, he let me in without asking any questions. When the Roths opened their front door, I passed out. The terror of the deserted sidewalks had been awful enough, but the disappointment of being turned out on the street weighed so heavily in my heart that I could not carry the load.

This was the bleak beginning of my solitary sojourn in Budapest. Somehow I managed . . . somehow I always managed. One or another of my brother's *chassidim* always seemed to have a few dollars for me when I was most desperate, and Mr. Fried constantly kept an eye on me.

I had to do a bit of hopping during those last few weeks of my stay in Budapest, but I thanked G-d every night that I was not sleeping in the street. For a short time I rented a room with a woman who lived near the Dahein synagogue. She was not

Shomer Shabbos, however, and I could not use her kitchen, which made things very inconvenient. I then moved in with the Shorberg family, who had been very devoted *chassidim* of my brother.

Mr. Shorberg, a man known for his great generosity and hospitality, had been suffering from a long-term illness. When I arrived, he had just taken a turn for the worse. The family was large, and I think they were glad to have an additional helping hand. I didn't mind; I was no longer a novice at household tasks, and I was very happy to be kept busy.

There was another refugee my age staying in the house at that time, a very fine, *frum* girl from Pressburg named Malka Reizel Frankel, and we did quite a bit of work together in the kitchen. It is very remarkable to me now, looking back, to think of the odd ways in which the war threw people across each other's paths, tangling up the roads so that they recrossed even many years later. Malka Reizel was destined after the war to marry my nephew Raphael Horowitz, the son of my half-brother, Reb Chaim Shlomo Horowitz. The young married couple escaped the war only to meet a tragic end; when they were on their way to America at the end of 1947, their plane crashed on European soil, killing them both. Their infant was caught in a tree and discovered the next morning by a farmer, who turned him over to the members of the local Jewish community. Reb Chaim Shlomo and his wife were traced and notified, and their orphaned grandchild was returned to them. The baby eventually did come to America with his grandparents, there to carry on another branch of our family.

But of course, this was all in the future; Malka Reizel and I had no idea then that we would one day be related. We did not have very long to become acquainted, for Mr. Shorberg passed away on a Shabbos only about three weeks after I arrived. I was glad to be there to keep Mrs. Shorberg company during the *shivah*, but afterward the family was bound up in its own emotional trials and I no longer felt comfortable staying in the house. Mr. Fried helped me find an apartment whose owners were not occupying it at the time, and I stayed there by myself until I left Budapest.

Ironically, although the refugees lived between worlds in the shadowy arena of the underground, that was a very interesting and rich period. The two kosher restaurants in town, Stern's and Nissel's, became meeting places for all the displaced and illegal Jews in town. The owners had nothing to serve us except a little wine and whatever scraps were available, but they opened their doors because we came. Many of the people who sat around the tables there became prominent figures in the post-war Jewish world — *rabbanim*, professionals, and community activists. Among them were *HaRav* Sheah Vorhand and Herschel Halberstam, a friend of our family who later became a rabbi in Los Angeles. I remember many evenings when these fine people sat together in the restaurants discussing philosophy, trying to nourish themselves with ideas in place of food, actively grinding out a foothold of faith in a world that was fast disintegrating around them. There was a tremendous sense of respect among them, a mature appreciation of each other that is not often found in our own times.

When I look back on those days, I think about how very dear and precious one's youth is. It is a time when the spirit is still elastic, when optimism can thrive in the darkest pit. I don't remember that we ever sat down and cried over our bitter lot — and we had reason to cry. We were all very upbeat then, and we did the best we could to give each other *chizuk*. We told ourselves that as long as the day was here and bombs were not falling and we could *daven* and make a *berachah*, we still had something. We encouraged each other not to fall into despair but to live to the fullest and thank G-d for it — and ask for more.

At that time, there was really nothing left to eat except an item we called *shtop* liver, one of the national foods of Hungary. This liver was halachically problematic because the geese from which the livers were taken were force-fed, and it was known that sometimes their esophagi broke. It wasn't exactly *treif*, but it wasn't *glatt*, and my family had never eaten it at home.

I remember going to Reb Yonasan Steif, *zt"l*, the *Rav* of the Budapest *kehillah*, to ask for a *heter*. He granted me one immediately, but the next day when I came to the restaurant, all the liver was gone! My friends and I laughed about it; and the truth is, I had to thank G-d for that too — that we could sit at a bare table in an empty restaurant, homeless, and still laugh.

Volvy Friedman occasionally looked in on me. His wife and child had gone home to her parents in Salish when the Germans entered Budapest, and he had not heard from them since. I asked him what he planned to do.

"I'm staying here," he said.

"Why?" I asked in surprise. Every refugee I knew was looking for a way to get out of Budapest.

"She only went for a visit; soon she'll return. We'll be safer here in the city."

"Your place is with your family," I told him, thinking of what had happened in Warsaw. "Hitler will come to the big cities too, just like he came to us. You'll see. You have no idea what's going to happen tomorrow, and you should never have any reason to question your conscience about whether you did the right thing or not. You should be with them."

It was an odd turning of the tables; Volvy had acted as my informal guardian for so many months now, and here I was giving him advice. Yet I felt very strongly about this matter and did not regret my words.

"You really think I should go?" he asked after a long silence.

"Yes."

And he did. Much later he told me that he was glad he had gone, because he was still able to see his wife and child before they were deported.

The subject of leaving had become an urgent matter for everyone. The Germans were on the streets of Budapest, and I could not afford to drift in a no-man's-land any longer. I was doing no more than spinning my wheels here, waiting for the Nazis, G-d forbid, to catch up with me.

An opportunity to leave quickly arose. I was still in contact with the Shorberg family, and one of their married sons was beginning to prepare for an escape to Czechoslovakia. He offered to take me along. I thought about it at length, but as badly as I wanted to get out of Hungary, I was extremely uncomfortable with the idea of returning to a place I had already left. My brother had helped dozens of people to get out of Czechoslovakia; to me, it seemed ridiculous and unwise to go back to a place from which people were escaping. When the Shorbergs pressed me, I told them, "*A koze geit tzurik, a mentsch geit forvarts* — a goat goes backward, a person goes forward. My aim is to go forward, not back where I came from."

The family kept insisting, and for a while I wavered. It was impossible to know what the right decision was, or even if there were such a thing as a "right decision"; Hitler was faster than we were. Mrs. Shorberg, assuming that I would come to my senses and take the opportunity, invited me over and baked some cookies for me to take on the trip.

"They're not to be eaten," she told me. "They're meant to be watched twenty-four hours a day, and they shouldn't go out of your sight."

Although I had had a great deal of experience — too much for a person my age — I was still very naive in some ways. I had no idea what she was talking about. Cookies were cookies, as far as I was concerned. I had never heard of a cookie that wasn't meant to be eaten.

A messenger came to my apartment a day or two later. It was *Erev* Shavuos. A passage to Czechoslovakia had been organized for the Shorbergs' son, daughter-in-law, and their baby, and I had been included in the plan. The messenger had come to inform me of the arrangements.

"I haven't decided yet if I'm going," I said.

"Think about it," he replied, "and I'll come for you tomorrow morning."

On Shavuos morning, as promised, he stood on the steps. This was clearly a case of *pikuach nefesh*, and the Shorbergs were planning to get on the transport even though it was *Yom Tov*.

"Are you coming?" he asked.

"No," I said. I really couldn't give a clear reason, even to myself, except for my own stubbornness.

"Then give me the cookies," the messenger said.

What a fuss, I thought, over a bunch of cookies! As I handed him the package, one cookie fell out and broke on the step — and a golden coin rolled out of it. No wonder the cookies were "not meant to be eaten"! I had a fleeting, nauseating vision of a cookie breaking apart on the floor of the train I had almost boarded, and of the gendarmes coming to arrest me for carrying contraband.

I never said anything about it either to the messenger or to the Shorbergs. People were frightened out of their wits in those days, and sometimes they did things to protect themselves that they would never have done under normal circumstances. Mrs. Shorberg knew that because I was a young girl, the officials would probably not bother too much with me. But her son and daughter-in-law had several pieces of luggage, and there was always the chance that their things might be searched. She was only trying to protect her children, but I was glad that I had decided not to go.

Two days later I was even more grateful to Hashem *Yisbarach* for the intuition He had granted me. We heard that the entire train to Czechoslovakia had been bombarded, and not one person had survived.

The next offer I had to leave Hungary was from my mother's son, Chaim Shlomo Horowitz, who lived in Temisvar, Romania. He wired me to come out to him, but there was no way of getting papers and no money to buy them. I was not altogether disappointed, for Romania was in the north, the direction from which I had come. I simply did not want to go backward. If I went anyplace, it would be further south.

Then I heard about a transport that was being organized to go — of all places — to Palestine. The negotiations were headed by Rudolph Kastner, a Zionist leader and journalist in Budapest. Two other people who were heavily involved in this project were

Mr. Phillip (Pinchas) Freudiger, the previous head of the Budapest Orthodox *kehillah*, and his brother-in-law Mr. Blau, both of whom were very active politically. I stayed in constant contact with both of them, and they assured me a place on the transport, even promising to look out for me personally. The Satmar *Rebbe* was rumored to be one of the passengers, as well as several other dignitaries. People paid stout sums for a place on the list; some sold everything they had, gambling on a miracle.

I had no inkling whatsoever of the politics behind the transport, and as far as I know, neither did most of the other people on the list. All we knew was what they told us: we would be stopping in Germany on our way to Palestine, but only briefly; then we would proceed to Istanbul, and from there to Palestine. The Jewish committee was probably hoping against hope that the Hungarians would cooperate with them and that they really would be able to sidetrack us to Turkey. All the people who boarded that train really believed they would make it to *Eretz Yisrael*.

I remember with gratitude four special acts of kindness that marked my departure from Hungary that spring. The first was the Pesach I spent with the Kiviazhder *Rebbe* and his wife, distant relatives of mine who welcomed me warmly into their home. During the first *seder*, the air-raid siren sounded, signaling the first bombardment of Budapest, and we were forced to spend several hours in the basement. In spite of this frightening intrusion and the escalating panic in the city, the *Rebbe* and his wife did their best to make the *Yom Tov* a pleasant one for me.

I received the second *chessed* when I went up to say goodbye to my brother's *gabbai*, Chaim Ber Greenwald, and his wife. Chaim Ber was one of three *gabbaim* who had managed the *Rebbe's* affairs; the other two were brothers, Moishe and Shloime Goldstein, very devoted men who acted respectively as business manager and spokesman for the *Rebbe*. Of all three, Chaim Ber Greenwald was considered a fixture in the Munkatcher entourage. He was now an elderly man who had been a loyal servant of the *alter* Munkatcher *Rebbe*, and he had attached himself with equal diligence to my brother, leaving his home and following us to Budapest when we moved. He and his wife really had no identity of their own; their lives revolved around the *Rebbe's hoif,* his "court." Of the entire establishment that Reb Boruch had inherited when he came into the Munkatcher *rabbanus,* this couple was among the most cherished legacies.

Chaim Ber's wife was affectionately called Baila Nany, *"nany"* being the Hungarian word for aunt. That day she said to me, "Peska, you are going away; let's bake some cookies for you to take along."

The word "cookies" struck a sour note with me — but this batch bore no resemblance to its unlucky predecessor. The plain sugar cookies that Baila Nany made for me were not meant to be watched, but to be eaten — and they seemed to last forever. They sustained me on the long train ride out of Hungary and for quite some time afterward, remaining dry even in the rain. The girls who were with me laughed and joked about my "magic" cookies.

Later that evening I went to see Mr. Blau, one of the arrangers of the transport. He informed me that all the passengers would be gathering at six o'clock on Friday morning in a courtyard on Andrashe Street, and he advised me to stay in the neighborhood the night before so that I would not be late getting to the assembly point.

The next day I went back to Nissel's restaurant to say goodbye to some of my friends. We sat around one of those still-bare tables, reminiscing about the events of the last few months and wondering aloud if we would ever see each other again. Sheah Vorhand told me to come to his apartment building, which was not far from Andrashe Street, on Thursday, promising to find a family for me to stay with overnight.

Herschel Halberstam, one of the many refugees in our circle, was there too, and he proffered the third *chessed* of my departure from Budapest. He took me aside and handed me an American twenty-dollar bill.

"Here," he said, "take this. American money will go further

than European currency, especially on the black market, and you never know when you might need it. If we're both alive and you see me again, you'll pay me back — just don't give me any interest!"

"You know what?" I said. "I'll take it." I later sewed the bill into my belt, where it stayed for nearly a year; and I did indeed pay Herschel Halberstam back — without interest.

On Thursday night I packed a few belongings and left my apartment. I was running late, and this was the second time in Budapest that I found myself alone on the street after curfew. It was past eleven when I arrived at the address Sheah Vorhand had given me — only to find four separate doors at the entrance! No names were on them. To ring the wrong doorbell at this hour of the night, with no papers and no passport, would have been about as reckless as handing myself over to the police.

Sometimes I wonder now if I was a foolish child or a brave gambler, because instead of turning around and heading back, I held my breath, picked a door at random, and knocked. I listened carefully to that little voice inside me that had given me guidance so often in the past, and I felt sure that it pushed my hand in the right direction. I am still thanking G-d today that I knocked on the right door. Sheah Vorhand was so shocked to see me that he trembled visibly with relief. He was certain I had been caught.

Then it was *my* turn to be shocked. Standing in back of Sheah was a familiar face — none other than one of the two Stern brothers who had taken me across the frozen fields to Hungary over two years ago! Apparently he was still involved in rescue work and was glad to lend me a hand again. "We did it together once before," he said to me kindly, "and should we not do it again?"

That evening was the fourth *chessed* I received on my way out of Budapest. Somehow, no matter how bad things got, there was always some sort of protection that came through, some friend who came to my aid at the last minute. Sheah Vorhand's sister Iby, who lived nearby, came in soon after I arrived and brought supper for the three of us. I still think about how wonderful that supper was because it was so hard to get any decent food then, even in the restaurants. Then they took me to the home of a couple in the building, where I spent the night.

I inscribed that evening, especially the incident of the doors, in my mental register of the open cycle of *hashgachah pratis* that I had seen in the past three years. It felt almost as though a gentle, invisible monitor was lodged in my brain, pushing the right buttons, making the right decisions — because it wasn't me. I never had any idea why I did the things I did or why I merited the protection of so many strangers. I did not let myself think about it too much, and I certainly did not let myself think about how long the blessing would last.

Chapter Fifteen

The next morning was Friday, August 15. It was a dismal day, raining and chilly. When I came to the big iron gate at the courtyard on Andrashe Street, the first thing I saw were small groups of people huddled together in each corner of the tall iron fence. They were trying to do what people do naturally in public: create a private space around themselves, an area they could call their own. It seemed to me that everybody in that courtyard belonged to a group of some kind. I had nobody . . . no relation, no friend, no one to whom I could attach myself. I felt acutely lost and so frightened.

There was a miserable confusion in the courtyard, a mess of anxious faces and nervous hands. About three thousand people were crammed into that small area, sitting on top of each other, on top of soggy luggage, holding their children in their laps. The rain was coming down in torrents, falling so hard that it seemed the entire world was crying for us. There was nothing to hide behind, no eaves to shelter us. We were soaked through — our clothes, our lives, our future, our past; everything was drenched, hanging from us in limp tatters.

Just as I crossed through the gate, the gendarmes began spraying bullets randomly into the air in order to scare people. I had only been there a moment or two when one of those flying bullets went through a man's foot. It shocked me so strongly that I almost jumped out of my shoes. That was my welcome to Andrashe Street.

My head rang with opposing voices.

"What are you getting yourself into?" one voice shouted. "You're just going from one *Gehinnom* to another!" And the other voice countered: "But thousands of other people are going too. Why am I different or better than they? There's nothing else to do . . . I can't just sit here and wait for the Germans to come get me — I have to try to escape; I have to do *something*!" My mother had been accustomed to saying that G-d should "shield us with His right hand," and I now offered the same prayer.

We were all loaded onto horse-drawn wagons and driven to the outskirts of the city. The iron wheels of the wagons bumped along rough dirt pathways, bouncing us up and down on the wooden planks. We stopped in the middle of an open field. Train tracks ran through that flat, muddy expanse, and a cattle train was waiting for us. It had large freight cars with no passenger seats — the type of train that the war has made famous. Many people in the crowd became agitated at the sight of the train; they saw it instinctively as a symbol of malignancy, something foreboding and perhaps inescapable. But we had been promised that we were going to Palestine. We didn't know what else to do except board.

I knew very few people on the transport. Most of them were among the elite of Budapest, the most distinguished element. Aside from Mr. Blau, the only faces I recognized were those of Rabbi Deutsch and his family, lovely people who had hosted me often, and the four Kapowitz brothers, all of whom had been very friendly with my brother. One of them was the man who had evicted me from his house without notice. I crossed his path several times during the trip and tried to behave as though nothing had happened. This was not a time to hold grudges. For my brother's sake I did my best to be civil to him and to maintain a relationship with the rest of his family. My gut feeling was that it was important now to be civil to everybody, to glue ourselves together as a unit. We had no other allies.

The most important friend I made on this journey was the Satmar *Rebbetzin*. By the grace of G-d, I climbed into the same wagon as she. The *Rebbetzin* was in her thirties at that time, a second wife to the Satmar *Rebbe* and much younger than he. She never had children of her own, and her life was given over to others. I remember clearly how much more concerned she was for the *Rebbe* and for those around her than she was for herself. She recognized me from Budapest and took me under her wing immediately. I came to value not only her compassion but her keen, practical way of thinking, and it was the beginning of a long and wonderful friendship.

That night, as the train rocked forward through the humid midnight air, we found places on the floor and went to sleep on our rucksacks. I awoke at about five in the morning, while it was still dark outside, and found my head at the feet of the Satmar *Rebbe*. He was sitting on a bench *davening* in his *tallis* and *tefillin*. Quickly, I drew away from him.

"Don't move away, *kind*," he whispered softly. "Remain here and go back to sleep."

And that was how I met the Satmar *Rebbe*. Those were the kindest words I heard during the entire trip, and they were not the last I was to hear from him. His calm faith and warm sense of humor would bolster all of us in the days to come. I was fortunate to have climbed into the right car.

We traveled onward for the better part of that day. The compartments were stuffy and airless, and the lice swarmed mercilessly around us. There were no windows and no toilets, but we were more fortunate than most other transports, for they let us out into the fields from time to time to take care of our needs. During the first of these stops, one of the officials announced that we were going to stop in Bergen-Belsen before going on to Istanbul.

A panic erupted. People began to scream that we were going to Bergen-Belsen; rumors flew that the Jewish management was also nonplussed. Most of us really didn't know what was going on in the concentration camps. We had heard about them and we knew that people worked there, but we didn't know to what extent. We tried to convince ourselves that the stop was only a formality and that we would go on to Turkey, but it was impossible to know what to think. While we were standing there in that muddy field, under a driving rain, a number of people came over to ask me what I thought. One of them was Mr. Kapowitz.

"*Fraulein* Peska, what do you say?" he asked. "Should we stay? Should we leave?"

"I am going on," I told him. "My aim is to go forward, not back — and Hashem *Yisbarach* will help." And if He chose not to help, *chas v'shalom*, then I would be no worse off. I thought of what my mother had always said: *Anah mipanechah evrach*? There was no place to run and hide. G-d was everywhere and could help us anywhere.

Those people who had left family or friends behind in the city decided not to take the chance. We were still in walking distance of Budapest, and they decided to sneak out and run back. Although there were German officials aboard the transport, it was not as strictly supervised as those in Germany and Poland; some of the Hungarian gendarmes themselves were confused about what was going on, so the security was not as tight as it should have been. The defectors were able to dodge among rolling dunes and ditches in the field, and they disappeared. I have no idea what became of them.

The fierce rain let up after a while, but it continued to drizzle for several days. A cold mist enveloped us and clung to our hair and our clothing. Swollen purple clouds hovered over us, shielding us obstinately from the sun. I have no idea what towns we passed; we saw only sporadic houses and very few people. They had carefully chosen back routes for the transport, desolate stretches where no one would see us. I kept telling myself: I'm going forward. I'm going forward.

The second major stop was in the Austrian town of Linz. This is the one town whose name I remember, because of what happened there. I cannot forget it even if I try.

We were led off the trains and taken to a huge, empty warehouse. The guards announced that we would be deloused. They divided the men and women into separate cagelike enclosures and ordered us to take off our clothes and throw them into a pile. I wondered if I had heard right. When I saw thousands of terror-stricken women taking off all their clothing, I thought I must have lost my mind. It was outrageous, like a scene from the depraved fantasies of the Satan himself. Then all the people who wore glasses were told to take them off and throw them into a separate pile.

They led us to showers, men and women in separate groups. Female guards watched the men shower, and male guards watched the women. There was not a person among us who made it through those next few minutes unscathed. You had to activate every mental defense you possessed in order not to buckle; you had to believe that the guards did not exist, and that the women standing right next to you did not exist. A few hours ago we had thought of Israel, and now I saw that we had no right to dream of anything, or even to imagine what might happen in the next minute. We did not have the right to do anything except to pretend, individually, that each one of us was alone and that the thousands of people around us were figments of a delirious imagination.

Afterwards they cut off our hair. They cut it brutally, with mechanical shears. My hair was shoulder length, and it wasn't gorgeous hair, but it was *mine*. Losing it made me feel even more naked than not having any clothes on. They had no right to take my hair. They had no right to take away whatever it was that made me a human being.

I kept asking myself: Is this happening? Who are these people near me? What have they done with my hair? Two days ago we had been sitting in houses with furniture, talking to friends, eating with forks and knives. We did not have the slightest idea what was really taking place in the war, that a hunt was in progress to suck the last Jew out of every crevice and throw them to the dogs.

The Germans had sport with the children too. They had been drinking beer on the train and kept throwing the caps out the windows. They now sent the young boys to pick up the caps from the ground, allowing them to bring back only one at a time. With a simple command, they turned the children into mechanical toys.

In the meantime they herded us, naked, into a huge cage that stood in the center of that open hall. The cage was enormous, nearly as large as a house; it was made out of chicken wire and was enclosed on all sides, even on top. I cannot put into words how we felt in that cage. Many others have written about the humiliation that the Jews suffered during the war, but words are not powerful enough to talk about it. We did not have words then, and I do not have them now.

Partly we were shocked at the extent of the brutality. But much worse was the realization that they wanted not only our lives but our humanity. We became lower than animals in that cage. People looked at each other, and some tried not to look at each other, and tears rolled down their faces. I really thought I would go crazy. I felt totally homeless; I didn't know to whom I belonged, or to what species I belonged. We stood there in that wire cage, with people staring in at us as though we were a curious side-show at the circus. Many of us wished for death and would gladly have welcomed it.

After a while the Germans chased us out to retrieve our clothing from the pile. Three thousand people had thrown their garments into the pile, and we were now ordered to find our own things. The soldiers stood around and watched in amusement as swarms of naked people scrambled in the heap, like ants on an anthill.

Next to the pile of clothing was the pile of hair they had shaved from us. Did you ever see haystacks in a field — towering haystacks that seem to reach the sky? That's what the pile of hair looked like. And next to it was a pile of eyeglasses, hundreds and hundreds of pairs. We were told to find our own glasses too. Somehow we managed to separate the items and to get dressed, but it took an entire night.

The next day the train trip continued. We didn't know then that we were traveling on special tracks that had been built directly to Bergen-Belsen. We saw no signs along the way, and we never really had any idea where we were going. We passed tranquil farmhouses that were scattered sparsely over the countryside and dirt roads that seemed to lead nowhere. I barely looked at the surroundings; I was very busy keeping myself alive from minute to minute, watching my next step, trying to go further, further, further, just to push on.

In the late afternoon we arrived in the town of Hanover, in Germany. It was still overcast outside, with a drizzling mist; those purple clouds seemed to have followed us all the way from Hungary. We were chased down from the wagons with shouts — *"Raus! Raus!* Out! Out!" — and with rifles, and with dogs. These were the same rifles and dogs that had been hunting our brothers in Poland and in Germany for the past four years, but we had known almost nothing of it. To us this was a new terror, a monster arisen from the deep.

We were marched forward and soon found ourselves passing along a tall wire fence. A sign above us read, "Welcome to Bergen-Belsen." Behind the wire fence we saw a vast, flat compound with regular rows of barracks set up in neat geometric formations. We walked and walked, passing unit after unit of these colorless buildings. When we were almost at the last one, we heard some noise behind the fence and turned to look. Standing on the other side, at some distance, we saw a group of live skeletons.

I don't know of any other way to describe them. They were bundles of bones, covered with a dry, scaling skin. Their cheekbones protruded and their ears jutted out grotesquely from the sides of their shrunken heads; they had no eyes, only deep black holes. They wore uniforms that looked like striped pajamas. On top of their shirts the yellow star glittered palely, and beneath it was stitched the Dutch word "Jud."

We were led inside the camp to an open square where long tables were set up. Clerks sat neatly at regular intervals behind the tables, with typewriters in front of them. We were told to form single-file lines to the tables. I looked for faces that I knew and tried to edge closer to those people. In particular I clung to Herbert Kapowitz, one of the four Kapowitz brothers. He was a slight man with a short white beard, and I knew him to be a very sincere person. I got behind him in line, and we inched forward slowly.

"*Fraulein* Peska," he said to me after a moment, "don't worry. You give me your name and dates, and I will register for you. Find a place to sit down. I will take care of everything for you."

I went to the side for a while and sat down on my knapsack. The endless lines of forlorn people dragged forward toward the clerks, like bottles on a slow-moving conveyor belt. I was very tired and very worn out, especially since I was wearing heeled shoes; flats were not popular for women at that time. Thankfully it was still warm outside, and I was not too uncomfortable.

Suddenly, I felt a jab inside. It was the hand again — that same prescient, invisible hand that had picked me up off the hospital bed in Munkatch. The hand did not signal danger now, only urgency. I simply had the feeling that I should register on my own.

Herbert Kapowitz was already close to the front of the line. I got to my feet and made my way through the crowd.

"*Herr* Kapowitz," I said, "I'm going to take care of my papers myself. But thank you anyway."

I got into line behind him and was soon standing before the clerk. She asked me my name, and my date and place of birth. I answered truthfully on all counts; but when she asked for my citizenship, I said, "I am Hungarian." I don't know why I said it. There was no logical reason to say it, for as far as anyone could see, we were all in the same boat. But those were the words that came out of my mouth. The clerk wrote down what I said and asked me no other questions.

We were ordered into what is now known as the classic German *appel*, or roll call: a column with five people in each row. One of the German commanders stood in front of us and gave a speech. He told us that we were a privileged group and would not have to work, as did all the other prisoners in Bergen-Belsen, but that we must obey orders without hesitation.

What orders? we thought. Surely the *appel* was a one-time event; surely this whole strange interlude was temporary, and we would soon get out and continue our journey. Our stomachs told us otherwise, but we were not prepared to listen to any deeper instincts right now. This was just a technical snafu. Somebody would straighten it out and we would go on our way. We would go on our way.

Chapter Sixteen

The women and men were divided into separate groups and assigned to barracks. Small children stayed with either parent; older children were split up according to their sex. All of our jewelry and valuables were taken away, but we were allowed to keep a change of clothing and whatever small items we could carry. I held onto the ring my mother had given me when I turned twelve, a plain gold ring with a single pearl. Aside from the American twenty-dollar bill sewn into my belt, it was the most precious thing I had.

The barracks were wooden and medieval. Two long, even rows of dark bunk beds lined the walls, with a narrow passage down the center. The beds were attached to posts which held up the roof. There was only one window in each barracks, at the far end; otherwise, they were totally enclosed. The floor was lined with wooden planks.

Black coffee and bread were distributed amongst us, and we were assigned to bunks. Each of us received a blanket. Although I was disoriented, I did not feel totally lost, for it seemed that everybody wanted to take care of me. I was amazed at the outpouring of concern; Reb Shayale Czechower's *berachah* had not deserted me yet. I was also very relieved to find a few people I knew in my barracks. Among them were Mrs. Deutsch and her daughters, sweet girls who had tried to teach me English at home in Budapest. I quickly attached myself to them.

I was assigned to the top row of bunks. Directly beneath me was a woman in her mid-forties, and at my side was a young girl whom I had seen on the transport but did not know by name. The lights went out at exactly ten o'clock.

When I drew the blanket over myself, I was flooded with nausea. We had heard many rumors about the concentration camps, but no one had told us that they were making blankets out of human hair — Jewish hair. Those hairs tickled my arms and gave me goose bumps, and every time they touched my face, I felt like throwing up. I couldn't stand it. To this day, when I'm asleep and my own hair brushes against my face, I wake up in terror, flinging it away.

After a while, I settled my rucksack under my head and tried to relax. I was about to drift off into an uneasy slumber when I heard muffled sobbing and sighing. It was the girl right next to me — the girl whose name I didn't know yet.

I put out my hand and gently touched her.

"Let me be your friend," I whispered to her. "Talk to me."

The girl picked her head up. I could tell that she was about my age and that she was very lovely, even though her face was puffy and streaming with tears. After taking a minute to collect herself, she began to talk.

"My name is Lilly Gottesman," she whispered hoarsely in Hungarian. "I came to Budapest and left all my family behind . . . I heard there were jobs available in the city hospital in Buda, and I went to work there. There were two other boys working there also, one named Berkovi* and one named Kuper.* They

---

*Not their real names.

told me they were trying to get on this transport to go to Palestine, and that they would help me get on it too . . ."

Lilly paused for a moment to catch her breath. "The man named Kuper was deformed. Something was the matter with him; he wasn't exactly straight somehow. He took me aside one day in the hospital and assured me that he would get me on the transport —and then he asked me to marry him. I never actually promised, but I gave him the impression that I would. The Germans were in town and I had to get out — I didn't know what else to say. What am I going to do now? I can't marry that man — he is not for me, and I am not for him. But I let him think that I would marry him! Both those boys are here now in the group. How can I face them?"

I was touched — and amazed. Only a person of extraordinary integrity would be shedding bitter tears over a promise made in desperation when there were much greater things to cry about. I knew who those two boys were, and I knew that this poor girl had enough to bear right now without the additional burden of needless guilt. I tried to think quickly of some practical advice to make her feel better, thankful that I was able to converse fluently in Hungarian.

"Listen," I whispered, "you're not going to marry him tomorrow. We don't know if there's even going to *be* a tomorrow! You have no right to cry about something you can't even predict. You didn't really give him your word of honor — you meant, 'Maybe; if everybody lives and we get out of here, then we'll decide.' So there is no promise as such.

"And secondly, I'll help you out with those boys; I know you are worried because you don't want to seem ungrateful. They will need help here, because there is no one to do anything for them. We will help them out and you will remain on decent terms with them — but just forget that you ever said anything about getting married."

As it turned out, Lilly Gottesman was an extremely fine, *frum* girl who came from a good family. Once I understood her better, I saw that I had guessed correctly about the source of her distress.

She was *erlich*, a person of firm principle, and to her a promise was a promise. It took some time for all of us to discover that our logic must take a different track in a world where all ordinary logic had been suspended. We had to find entirely new ways of coping, ways that preserved every extra drop of our physical and emotional energy.

Lilly took my advice and was able to relax somewhat. In the long run it was very fortunate that we met that night, because our friendship deepened into a rare and precious bond. Lilly and I shared everything. If one of us needed something, the other gave up a portion of food to get it. I was to see many cases in the camp where a mother would siphon off portions of her children's rations to stave off her own hunger, but that never happened to Lilly and me. We were armed with one of the most important defenses a prisoner could have in the camps, and it is a friendship that is still very dear to my heart.

We found out the next day that there had been no technical "glitch." This was not a temporary delay; we were prisoners, guinea pigs whom the Germans used to indulge their passion for routine. We remained in Bergen-Belsen for over nine months.

Our day began at five-thirty a.m. At six we had to assemble for the *appel*. We lined up in a long column with five people in each row, and we were counted meticulously. The German women who counted us wore leather jackets and high, white leather boots, and they ate ham and cheese sandwiches in front of us. They carried billy clubs, and sometimes they would pick on people at random. They would say, "You didn't do this right" or "You didn't do that right," and they would beat our women with the clubs.

In sun, rain, snow, and sleet, every day of the week, we stood *appel*. Sometimes we stood for an hour, sometimes for three hours, sometimes for five. Then we were chased out to a shower hall to wash ourselves. The water was nearly frozen in the winter, and you could see people's bodies vibrating from the cold. We got used to it, though, and after a few weeks people no longer shivered. It is amazing what a person can get used to. After the shower, there was no water to be had for the rest of the day.

Then we returned to our barracks to eat "breakfast." The meal consisted of something called black coffee, which was actually coffee sediment mixed with water. We received a thin, diluted soup at one o'clock in the afternoon; supper consisted of more of the same. Once a week we were given a loaf of bread mixed with sawdust, which was hard as rock and nearly impossible to chew. Along with it came some sort of sausage or cheese, and occasionally a pat of margarine or jam. Once a month we also received some cigarettes.

Except for those people who had been assigned specific duties, our time was our own after the *appel*. On Shabbos, those with work assignments tried to do as little as possible. This was the first time since I was three years old that I was not able to light candles on Friday night. I promised myself that if I ever got out of there, I would light an extra two candles to make up for all the missed weeks. Some people said *Tehillim* by heart on Shabbos, but otherwise it was hard to tell it apart from any other day of the week.

Time became random and meaningless, the hours and days running into each other in a gray swill of nothingness. We had no distractions, nothing to read or to keep our minds occupied. It was during those months that I was forced to look for inner occupation, to learn how to be satisfied with my own thoughts. I think that is the reason I can still be alone today and not be very lonely.

Once a month they put out big tubs full of warm water, and we were able to wash our clothing. We were not allowed to bathe in this water, however. They gave us soap for the clothing — the famous soap whose source we could only guess at then — but it never worked because it made no lather.

We were also deloused once a month. Our clothes were heated in the crematoria to kill the bugs, and in the meantime we went into the showers. The guards followed the same practice as in Linz: women officials watched the men shower, and men watched the women. The men stood around us, making vulgar and offensive remarks about us. On the one hand, we felt degraded beyond words; on the other hand, we felt that we still had G-d's image in us, and that even without our clothing we were as far above these animals as the heavens from the earth. When we reached that level of thinking, we were able to ignore the guards.

When we came out of the showers and put our clothes back on, they were still so hot from the fires that anyone who had a metal buckle or button on his garment was burned. The burns sometimes were so severe that they lasted for weeks.

The Germans were also masters of the art of psychological deprivation. They split families into pieces, with devastating results. Although the men and women were allowed to see each other during the daytime, the nighttime separations filled people with insecurity and despair. No one knew what to expect; husbands and wives went to sleep at night not knowing if they would find each other alive in the morning. Guards were posted during the night to make sure that no spouses broke the curfew to visit each other. An electric wire fence surrounded us, with four tall watchtowers which sent out huge searchlight beams across the camp after dark. We knew we could be discovered and shot at any moment.

And yet, with all this, we did not have any idea how lucky we were in that camp. During all the time that we spent there, we were kept in a *sonder* camp, a separate, privileged unit reserved for the people from the Hungarian transport. The Germans, I think, were still hoping to exchange us for the supplies they needed so badly now that their fortunes were falling, but as I have said before, I never completely understood the political angle. Most of us did not work. We were not beaten as often or as brutally as the prisoners in the main camp, and perhaps we received a bit more food. But we did not know that we were lucky. All we knew was that we were hungry and alone; that *Eretz Yisrael* was a quixotic dream; that we had no future. Our days were as repetitive and bland as an unending asphalt highway, eternally gray and numb. We had no idea then that monotony was not something to complain about during the Holocaust.

Three weeks after our arrival in Bergen-Belsen, there was a selection during the morning *appel*. We had heard many rumors about selections, and we had smelled the sickening odors from across the fence — but we had not seen any visual proof, and so we chose not to believe.

Mengele himself, the demonic executioner of Auschwitz, came to preside over this special occasion. How ordinary he looked: a short man, well-groomed but of undistinguished appearance, carrying a riding crop and wearing the shiny, high-topped boots that were *de rigueur* for German officials. The Germans were attentive to every little detail, scrupulously careful to make us feel degraded in any way possible. Mengele and all the members of his entourage were dressed smartly in fur-lined jackets, for it was very early in the morning and still chilly outside. They passed leisurely up and down the ranks, watching us shiver in our haphazard outfits and clumsy homemade shoes, silently savoring our misery.

As it turned out, this was not a selection for death but for release. The Germans had agreed to send a group of three hundred prisoners to Switzerland in exchange for supplies. But to the freed people, it made no difference, for the doctor of Auschwitz had only sentenced them to a living death. In his selection he forced apart husbands and wives, parents and children, brothers and sisters, in the nonchalant fashion for which he has become notorious. Waves of hysteria rifled through the column; many of these people would rather have died on the spot than be separated from their families. Some would later be reunited after the war ended, but any sort of future held no meaning for them now. Their freedom was a tragedy.

That was the only selection we went through during our time in Bergen-Belsen, but again, we did not understand how much better our lot was than that of the average concentration camp prisoner. When one is in distress, it makes no difference to him how much pain others endure.

Although death did not hunt us, we suffered terribly from sickness in the camp. Dozens of people contracted typhoid fever, and there was no real medical care. We had an infirmary of sorts, but healing was not its main function.

One of my friends once caught pneumonia, and I remember what her breathing sounded like: it was a grotesque rasping, like the engine of a train which is just starting up. I added that breathing to my aural memory of the war, along with the airplanes, the whistling plummet of the bombs, and the cracking of the hail on our roof during the invasion of Warsaw. When my friend died, the workers came with a wagon, threw her body up on top of the waste barrels, and took her away. Her mother and sister remained in the camp. The sister tried to commit suicide by throwing herself against the electric wire fence, but someone pulled her away in time.

I had volunteered to help out in the infirmary. There was a pregnant woman who had come with us on the transport, and I was with her when she gave birth. I wanted very badly to give her something when her son was born — but what in the world was there to give? I had nothing — except my bread. After much thought, I finally sliced off a piece of my loaf and spread a drop of margarine on it. Then I went hunting in the barracks until I found someone who still had a spoonful of jam from the allotment we were given once in two weeks. I spread a dollop of jam on the bread and poked it around with my knife until it spelled "Mazel Tov" in Hebrew, and I brought it to her. An extra slice of bread with margarine and jam was an extravagant bonus in camp, something not to be believed; but even more welcome were the good wishes behind it, and the woman was thrilled to receive it.

The next day someone took a pillow and smothered her baby to death. I was in the building and knew what had happened, but I didn't know who had done it. The German officials themselves never came into the infirmary because of the fear of contagion, but they had lackeys who carried out their orders. One of the infirmary workers came to the mother afterward and said, "The child is dead. A pillow fell on its head and it suffocated." The doctor who worked in the infirmary was one of us, but he had no control over the proceedings there. That poor young mother sobbed until her body was convulsed with a dry racking; I thought she would die of crying.

I used to wonder constantly how much worse it could possibly be in the main camp. We were not allowed any contact with the other prisoners, and we didn't really know what was taking place on the other side of the fence. But we did receive news from the outside — the only authentic reports we had of the inner workings of the death camps. Letters were occasionally smuggled in to our men from prisoners in other camps, and they were circulated amongst us. I have no idea how those letters got through; maybe they were brought in by workers or delivery men who were bribed. They came from Treblinka, from Plaszow, from Buchenwald, from Birkenau, from Dachau. Each contained a long list of names of prisoners, both old and new.

We used to cluster together around a candle in the dead of night, or sometimes around the one or two flashlights that were available, and read the names. Many of our people would involuntarily cry out when they recognized friends and relatives on the lists. Those cries were so horrible, so full of ruinous pain, that they must surely have gone straight to the *Kisei HaKavod*, G-d's Heavenly Throne. I knew no one on the lists, but the reports in the letters were chilling enough. The prisoners wrote of their misery; of their tattoos; of their labor. They told us that even in the snow they had to go out to work, whether they had shoes or not, or the Germans would shoot. We had not even been tattooed, and we began to understand how truly fortunate we were.

"Maybe it's not all lost; maybe we will still be saved," we told ourselves, and the blood came back into the faces of some. There was only one time during those nine months when I actually saw the reality of the rumors played out before me — only once, but once was enough. It was on the night of Tisha B'Av. They had given us pea soup in the afternoon, an unusual treat, but we were still not wise enough to know that any unaccustomed delicacy must be treated with suspicion. The soup was undercooked and perhaps contaminated. A few hours later everyone was either vomiting or suffering from diarrhea.

There was a tiny latrine in our barracks, and I crept into it that night, feeling nauseated. Suddenly I heard *kolos*, the crying and calling of voices. They were thin and frantic voices and seemed to come from a faraway place — from the world of dreams. For a few moments I did not know if I was asleep or awake.

The voices held a hideous attraction for me. I had to see where they came from. I had to know if they were real — if *I* was real. There was a small window above my head in the latrine. I was too short to reach it and sick to my stomach, and I don't know how I dragged myself up there; all I knew was that I had to see those voices.

I looked out into the navy blue fog of the midnight sky. A crowd of people were being led across the compound to the crematoria. As they came closer, the voices got louder. Some were screaming *Shema Yisrael*, others were saying goodbye to each other.

"I hope I'll see you!" brothers shouted to their sisters. "I hope you'll survive! . . ."

And the mothers called out names: *"Moishe, bist de du? Faige, bist de du?* — Moishe, are you here? Faige, are you here?"

And hands went up, and clawing fingers went up, and the people pressed against each other and trembled. And laced among the voices was the voice of the Holocaust: "Why? Why? *Far vus kimt es mir?* Why is this happening to me?"

Gevald, gevald . . .

Their hands reached to the skies, their voices reached to the heavens. They tore at themselves and clung to each other, jerking, stumbling in the dark, a knot of doomed humanity.

It was unbearable. I couldn't listen, but I couldn't tear myself away. I hung onto the windowsill and watched as they receded in spasms into the darkness. I couldn't listen anymore, yet still I hung on. The night swallowed them, and their voices became faint again, dissolving once more into the realm of dreams. I promised myself that if I ever got out of there, the two extra candles that I would light each Shabbos would be in memory of those voices.

The next morning we were awakened at six as usual and stood *appel*, as on any other day. But it was not like other days. It was Tishah B'Av. A towering flood of fire was gushing upward from the crematoria, adding more souls to the thousands claimed through the centuries by this day of affliction. The smell of death lunged at my nostrils. I knew that smell from the Warsaw ghetto; it had often assailed us after the invasion, every time we passed a burned-out house where people had been trapped inside. The smell kept me up at night for weeks on end. It stayed in my hair and clothing, and it poisoned my heart.

I talked to myself constantly, trying to give myself comfort. I had friends here, and yet I had nobody. In the depths of the struggle, it was every person for himself. And so I tried to be for myself, to nourish my own soul; and G-d helped me.

We had one other occasional reminder of the ghastly machine that ran twenty-four hours a day across the fence from us. Sometimes we caught glimpses of the Jewish prisoners from Holland, our closest neighbors in the next compound. We still looked like human beings, but they did not.

These were the men we had seen when we first entered the camp, the ones who looked like misshapen cardboard figures. In the camps we called such people *"musselmen,"* the term for any person who was walking on his last legs. You could count every bone in those men's bodies. It was as though someone had taken a bunch of laboratory skeletons and stretched dried, yellow parchment over them. All the Dutchmen had the same black, sunken eyes, lifeless holes that seemed to have been drilled right through their skulls. Their heads were shaven and their faces were all alike; it was difficult to tell them apart. At night when I went to sleep, I used to see the image of those lightless holes in front of me, so black and so deep that they would not let me sleep.

And yet the Dutchmen had faith. Sometimes when no one was looking, we used to sneak out to the fence and talk to them, although it was dangerous to do so. They still believed that they were going to get out and have a life again someday, and we were embarrassed in front of them.

The Dutchmen had a *Chumash*, a *shofar*, and a *machzor* for the *Yamim Noraim*. It is impossible to know how they kept these things in Bergen-Belsen. Perhaps it was in the merit of their profound faith in the *Ribono Shel Olam*. I had thought that we were "rich" in comparison to them, with our pocket knives and our thread and combs; but when I heard what they had, I knew they were somehow richer.

The man with the *shofar* lent it to the Satmar *Rebbe* for Rosh Hashanah, and we actually had a *minyan* in his barracks. The Germans must have had a greater economical stake in our preservation than we imagined, for they maintained their hands-off stance and did not interfere with our worship. The *Rebbe's* barracks was turned into a *shul,* and one side was partitioned for the women. About two hundred people from the transport came to *daven* on Rosh Hashanah.

One of our men had undertaken to copy over pages from the Dutchmen's *machzor*. Of course, he could not copy the entire *davening*, but he copied enough parts so that most people who were interested had at least a few of the main *tefillos*. The women only stood and listened — but how glorious it was to stand there! Inside ourselves we prayed. Our hearts swelled as we spoke to G-d, threatening to burst, and still we prayed, more and more. We prayed until we ourselves were the prayer.

On Yom Kippur we assembled again, and the *Rebbe* spoke at length before *Kol Nidrei*. He spoke in Yiddish, and I can still see the people standing in that wooden room, listening and crying. People discussed his words for days afterward, and you could see from their faces that they were heartened. Some said that the talk had been strong enough to see them through to the end of the ordeal. I knew in my heart that I had been privileged, here in the cesspool of the German machine, before the gates of Hell, to hear words of *chizuk* from a great *tzaddik* that would not have meant the same to me under any other circumstances. I no longer remember what the *Rebbe* said, but I remember what he meant, and this has remained with me always.

Chapter Seventeen

Hunger is one of the main threads of every Holocaust survivor's memory. Even for us, who did not suffer as greatly as the rest, the topic of food consumed our days and nights. I had to wait only one night in Bergen-Belsen until it took over my life completely. On the day after our arrival, an official had come in to make a series of announcements about procedures and duties. Suddenly he called out, "*Fraulein* Peska Rabinowitz!"

Shaken, I stepped forward.

"You will be the server for this group. Each day when the food comes, you will be responsible for distributing it in this barracks."

I have no idea why I was picked; there was nothing to set me apart from the other women. This was not the last time I was to be chosen out of the blue for special duties, but in this case I found myself in an extremely unenviable position. The food distributor, both in the ghetto and in the concentration camps, was one of the most maligned people during the war. He or she was the focus of everyone's frustrations. If the food was not divided into exactly equal portions, the distributor was in danger of abuse.

I quickly realized what I was up against when someone thrust a tape measure into my hand and demanded that I measure each slice of bread precisely. The loaves were as hard as rocks. Everyone watched carefully to make sure that my knife would not waver, that not one extra quarter of an ounce should go to the next person. I was always afraid that my hand might slip and that someone might do something terrible to me.

I saw with my own eyes what happened in other barracks; sometimes people lost their heads and brutalized the server. They were hungry, and a few days' experience had taught them not to trust any distributor. This was exactly as the Nazis intended; they wanted to make us our own enemies, and in too many cases they succeeded. There was never quite enough food for the entire group. The men who hauled the barrels — our own men — inevitably ate from them, so that by the time I received my barrel, it was only three-quarters full. If the soup was too thick, it didn't stretch to everyone, and if it was too thin, people complained. The food distribution never took less than an hour because of all these problems, and the sessions were nerve-wracking. Many times I gave away my own portion and shared Lilly's so that people would not be angry with me. I knew I could not last long with such a burden on my shoulders, and one day I took a gamble.

"Listen," I announced, "I have an idea. I think somebody should make a list of all the people in the barracks, from A to Z. One day we will distribute the food from A to M, the next day from N to Z, and we will keep changing it, so that in case there is not enough food, it won't always be the people at the end of the alphabet who get hurt." I asked for a volunteer to read out the names, hoping to establish myself as a mere worker and not as a policy maker. Luckily, someone volunteered, and my plan worked. The women in my group respected the fact that I tried to be fair, and they did not harm me. Reb Shayale's *berachah* was still on my head, thank G-d.

In addition to the daily trial of distribution, the food presented me with one of the most serious decisions of my life. I had decided from my first day in Bergen-Belsen that I would not eat *treif*. I didn't know how naive this was, and when I look back, I think that maybe I was more stupid than brave. But I made up my mind to hold out as long as I could. There were about three hundred people among us who had made the same pledge. In two days, there were two hundred people, and by the third day there were even fewer. Three weeks later there were only five of us —including the Satmar *Rebbe* and *Rebbetzin*, and me.

When I first arrived, I still had the "miracle" cookies that Baila Nany Greenwald had baked for me in Budapest, the cookies that stayed dry in the rain and that seemed to multiply like the *mon*. I lived on those cookies for three weeks in the camp. Once in a fortnight the Germans gave out salami and *skvargl*, a kind of unrefined, coarse cheese that was coated with a slimy film. I always tried to exchange the salami for the cheese; other than that and the weekly loaf of bread, there was nothing to eat.

Because we were in a *sonder* camp, the *Rebbe* was fortunate enough to receive his own rations, but he had to put up a tremendous fight for the privilege. Every day the *Rebbetzin* went to the gate with a pot, and the kitchen workers brought her back a little rice or potatoes, and that's what the two of them ate. For a few weeks our provisions lasted, but after that we were really put to the test. My cookies ran out, and the *Rebbe* saw that even with the rice and potatoes he was quickly losing strength.

Finally we came up with the idea that since we were in a *sonder* camp, we might be able to arrange to have the chunks of meat extracted from the soup. Some of us, boys from the *Hashomer Hatzair* group, had been drafted into kitchen duty, and the boys agreed to do what they could. From then on, when they delivered the barrels, one of them was marked with a K. A portion of the soup was still missing as always, but at least there was no visible meat floating in it. And that's how it turned out that because of the few of us who held out, everybody who wanted to was now able to have kosher food — or at least what we could call "kosher" in the concentration camp. Of course, there was never any way to know with certainty what was in the broth, but it was still a considerable achievement, and it was the best we could do.

No one in our group discussed what they were eating or not eating with anyone else. When it came to food, we respected each other's privacy; food was survival, and we did not point fingers at anyone. We did not know that in the death camps prisoners ate anything they could get their hands on, and that we would have appeared to them as foolish heroes. But the Hungarians in particular were very sensitive to this issue because their troubles had been thrust upon them so suddenly. They had not lived for years in a ghetto, as I had, and they had not known any real deprivation. Within a week, the world had been pulled out from under their feet. They found themselves trapped between two walls: their utter desperation and their lingering embarrassment at the idea of eating *tarfus*. And so they suffered and did not talk about it.

Hunger was the reason I undertook my most dangerous enterprise in Bergen-Belsen. One of the Dutchmen in the adjoining compound was my accomplice. During a chance meeting at the fence, he offered to trade me bread for the cigarettes he knew we received. I marveled at this: here we were, desperate for bread, and the Dutchmen, who had less to eat than we did, were ready to give up their bread for cigarettes! Now I understand it much better than I did then. For a prisoner, a cigarette was a symbol of independence, of the leisure pleasures of normalcy. For the short time that it lasted, it shut out the brutal world around him, and the Dutchman was willing to risk his life for those few moments of respite.

He promised that if I met him again that night at twelve, he would make the exchange with me. At that hour, he explained, the searchlight moved so that it was not pointed in our direction. I had a luminous dial on my watch, and I kept it close to my face that night so that I could keep track of the time. True to his word, the Dutchman was at the fence at midnight. I do not remember anything about him except that he looked exactly like the others;

his face was a prisoner's face, its cheekbones dangerously hollow, its head shaven, its ears disproportionately large. He scratched a hole in the ground below the fence with his fingers and pushed a few slices of bread through. Then I slid him the cigarettes. I kept one slice of the bread for myself and gave out the rest to the women in my barracks.

These midnight transactions went on regularly for several weeks, maybe as long as two months. I think now that I was crazy for doing it. If the searchlight had landed on us for even a split second, we would have met a brutal end. But I was crazy for doing many things. I was young and headstrong, still possessed of that rash streak of independence that had once sent me out beneath a hail of bombs to look for seven carnations in the Warsaw ghetto. I am not sure exactly why I took such risks; perhaps it gave me a sense of confidence to be able to help people. I do know that Reb Shayale's *berachah* had not weakened with time, because the *kapo* saw what was going on and never said a word.

One night when I came to the fence, there was no bread. I didn't know this until it was too late; the Dutchman grabbed the cigarettes I pushed through the hole and ran off. The searchlight came on and began to rove the grounds, casting ghoulish shadows over the frozen compound. I got down on my hands and knees and groped my way back to the barracks, and the light followed me, tripping in and out around my hands and feet. When I was safe in my bunk, I gave myself the biggest *mussar shmuess* I had ever received — but even while I berated myself, I did not regret what I had done. For two months, a few people had had extra bread.

In spite of all our efforts and perseverance, we still hungered. There was simply not enough nourishment to keep a person of average height and weight from deteriorating, even with the soup. I remember with a pungent clarity the few occasions on which we received something different to eat. A couple of times during the year they gave us a soup made from grape stems, and twice we received a shipment of vitamins and onions from the Red Cross. The onions were the best food I have ever eaten in my life. Their sharp taste burned in our mouths and jolted us out of our lethargy, like the jangling of an electric shock. Our lives were so bland, almost trance-like, with nothing to ripple its colorless surface; and the onions, for the moment, reawakened our senses and sent the blood coursing again through our veins.

Many years later, my friend Lilly mentioned to me that I was pained by the hunger more than many of the others. "You don't realize how hungry you were," she said to me. "Somehow, when I ate, it was enough to tide me over. But you were never satisfied, always hungry . . ."

I was supposed to receive an extra portion of soup for being a server, but in all the time that I was in the camp, I received it only two or three times because the kitchen workers took part of our rations. Sometimes I also lost portions of my bread to the bedbugs. These miserable creatures had a grotesque method of attacking their prey, which I remembered well from Budapest. They would climb up to the ceiling, aim for your face, and drop down on you from the air. Believe it or not, this did not trouble me as much as the disgusting thought that they might touch my bread, and I always tried to find a scrap of cloth or paper to cover it up.

But then, when the bread was hidden away and you knew it was safe — that's when the real trial began. That bread, a black loaf that was as hard as a brick, was given out only once a week. I quickly became initiated into one of the classic dilemmas of the Holocaust prisoner: should I quiet my hunger now, or save a little bit for tomorrow?

"Shall I?" I used to ask myself as I lay on my bunk each night. "Shall I not? Shall I?"

Once I could not resist. With tears in my eyes, I ate the bread — but I was lucky, because I had a genuine friend. When Lilly found out the next day what had happened, she said without hesitation, "Don't worry, I still have a piece of bread. We'll share it."

Others in the camp admired us deeply for our friendship, especially because we shared food. Giving away food had quickly become a deed of outstanding courage, as well as an outrageous exhibition of naivete. We had become, *l'havdil*, almost like the people of Sodom — we, the Jews, *rachamonim b'nei rachmanim*, the very personification of compassion. The Nazis did it to us; they killed our kindness. For some people this was much more painful than the lack of food.

Lilly and I kept each other alive through those difficult months. I am sure now that it was in my parents' *z'chus* that I was able to see even marginally beyond my own needs, a task which required great fortitude in the camps. The *ahavas Yisrael* that I had seen in my home was profound. My parents were always giving — attention, food, money, shelter, love. I kept thinking about the times my mother had sent roasted turkeys to people who had never had a turkey on the table in their lives. My parents' blessing, thank G-d, was still alive in me.

I was thankful also, ironically enough, that I had already seen trouble. My family had been through financial hardship, and we had lived in the Warsaw ghetto. Those who had suffered adversity were much better off, for their situation now was just a little worse than what they were used to. The rich people, on the other hand, were miserable. They could not cope; some of them became nearly deranged. It was bitter to them that they had to stand in line for a piece of bread or a little soup, that all their energy was consumed in the acquisition and preservation of that food, and that their sole satisfaction in life now was that they had received a slightly better portion on a particular day. They spoke often of suicide.

We lived one day at a time. Those of us who had a little more emotional stamina tried to look out for the less fortunate. The day after we arrived, in fact, we began to round up the children who had come alone on the transport and to care for them as best we could. This always took up several hours of the day and kept us too busy to think about ourselves. We also tried to provide our own services within the group. One man, for instance, was a cobbler by trade, and he would repair shoes in exchange for food or milk.

Lilly and I could both sew, and later on, when the weather turned colder, people began to come to us with "orders." We were not given any sweaters or coats for the winter, and we tried to improvise with what we had. Those parents who had extra clothing asked us to cut them up and make pants for their children, and they paid us with milk. We collected whatever tools we could find — a pair of scissors, a needle, a bit of thread — and we created crude hats and shawls and muffs. What we lacked in materials we made up for with our imagination. It is very interesting how inventive one can become when the situation demands it. All sorts of mechanical and emotional abilities came welling to the surface, a fountain of primitive talent. Sometimes these things preoccupied us so much that we did not even have time to be afraid.

I also remember the pair of shoes that I manufactured for myself. I had realized quickly that I would not last three days in the high-heeled shoes I was wearing when I arrived. I pulled out a piece of loose wood from one of the bunks, placed my feet on it, and traced around them with a pencil stub. I had a small pocket knife, and for a few days, day and night, all I did was carve. When these crude soles were finished, Lilly traded a portion of her milk to get me a few nails. I cut the belt of my dress into strips, placed them in a crisscross fashion on the wooden platform, and nailed them down. These were my shoes. I was lucky; others did not have it so good.

All the while, the words my mother had once said to me in my youth reverberated in my head: "Learn how to work, because you never know when you will need skills." How wise she had been —and how thankful I was that she would never discover where those skills were being put to use!

The next thing I did was to put up a bit of civilization. I found another loose two-by-four in the barracks and hung it on the wall over my bed, using a leftover strip of my belt for loopholes. On this tiny shelf I kept whatever small trinkets I still had: a comb and a mirror, my little pocket knife, and a bit of toothpaste, which I used sparingly. People called it the "salon" of the camp. That shelf and its contents represented home to me.

Whenever we had time on our hands, we spent it wrapping ourselves in a world of fantasy. We gathered in small groups, and we told stories, and we sang. We tried to pretend that we were not in a concentration camp but in a camp of joy. We cooked such extravagant gourmet meals in our heads that the greatest chefs in Europe would have been unable to duplicate them. The competition was stiff. "My recipe is better than yours," we would say to each other in semi-truthful jest. "Just wait until we get out; then I'll show you how to make it, and you'll appreciate me!"

It was immensely gratifying to discover the wonderful power of our minds, to find that we could actually nourish ourselves with mental images. It gave us a desperately needed sense of control. Someplace, somewhere in the corners of our hearts, we really hoped we would survive, and so we cooked and cooked in preparation for that glorious day.

I also remember the wonderful birthday party that my friends made me for my twenty-third birthday. I donated two slices of bread for the occasion, and the others brought their precious savings of jam and margarine. I took my knife and cut the bread into a decorative arrangement, making sure there would be enough pieces for everyone. The rest of the birthday meal we created in our imaginations, and we sang and reminisced. To this day my friends remember that party.

There was a very interesting group of people with us in Bergen-Belsen. I tried to remain on friendly terms with everybody, but I was especially close to the Satmar *Rebbetzin*. Lilly, too, became friendly with her. The *Rebbetzin* was not in my barracks, but we used to meet every day. I would walk with her to the compound gate, where she received the *Rebbe's* special allotment of food. I remember how tolerant and understanding she was, because I used to smoke on our walks. I had started smoking out of nervousness in the ghetto, along with so many other young people, but the *Rebbetzin* never said a word about it. We had many discussions, sometimes about politics, sometimes about the unique issues of a *rebbeshe* household. I enjoyed the very sharp and practical outlook on life and often shared my deepest feelings with her.

There was a wonderful couple from Yugoslavia, Dr. and Mrs. Charles Schwartz, who became very involved with the children in the camp. He was an excellent doctor, and in fact he was once called out to perform a serious operation on one of the Nazi officials. His wife became an informal social worker in the camp. She kept an eye on the children who had no family, some of whom were as young as eight or nine years old. She also organized the young adults in the group and assigned each of us to a family who needed help. We did whatever we could for their kids; we washed their clothing, combed the lice out of their hair, and took them to the infirmary if they caught cold. Among those children were Devorah Halberstam, now Spira, and her young siblings, who were related to us. The younger children were very fragile and needed special attention. Lilly and I did everything we could to make them comfortable, and sometimes I told them stories about their parents, whom I remembered well.

The Schwartzes were really the primary caretakers of the children during our stay in Bergen-Belsen. I think of them with great admiration because it was no simple matter in the concentration camp to extend oneself for others. It demanded a profound psychological generosity, the ability to transcend the boundaries of one's own struggle for survival and to give other people encouragement against every logical likelihood — against reality.

Another person whom I would certainly label a heroine was Charlotte Blau, the wife of one of the men who had helped arrange the transport. She was a highly intelligent, aristocratic woman, but even more importantly, she was very pious and giving. Her love of people was so deeply ingrained that even in Bergen-Belsen she went out looking for people who needed help. She was very friendly to me and loved to dispense motherly advice, which I greatly appreciated because I was so much alone. We were fortunate enough to meet again after the war.

I also "adopted" two families. In addition to the Deutsches, whom I had sought out immediately upon our arrival, there was the Neuman family. Mr. and Mrs. Neuman were a prominent, wealthy couple from Budapest who had come with all their children on the transport. They were extremely devoted to each other, and the separation of the men and women devastated them. You could see the suffering on their faces.

I remember lying awake one night and hearing muffled voices nearby. After listening for a few minutes, I realized they belonged to the Neumans. Mr. Neuman had somehow sneaked past the guards and crept into the barracks to visit his wife and children. It was a tremendous risk; many prisoners, sadly, informed on each other to the *kapos* in exchange for better treatment, and Mr. Neuman's lot might have worsened severely if anyone else had seen him. I remember the great relief with which he greeted his wife, and how he kissed each of his children. Mrs. Neuman must have known that I was awake because when she got up the next morning, she thanked me profusely for not reporting her.

I wish I could say that it was so easy to get along with everybody, but the war had a paradoxical effect on people. It brought out the best in some and the worst in others. When I think of the best, I think of the Satmar *Rebbetzin* and the Schwartzes; I also think of an elderly woman named Mrs. Rand who slept near the door. She was the mother of one of the arrangers of the transport. Every morning when I went out to distribute the coffee, I used to see this tall, gray-haired lady tugging part of her dress up over her head and saying *"Modeh Ani"* quietly to herself. Mrs. Rand was not a religious woman and had never worn a *sheitel* in her life, but somehow in Bergen-Belsen, that priceless diamond pinpoint of Jewishness, the *"pintele Yid,"* had awakened in her. She really did not know how to *daven*, but she knew how to say *Modeh Ani* and sensed that she should cover her head when she said it. I felt moved every time I passed her.

The trauma of imprisonment and deprivation, however, had the opposite effect on most people, in some cases completely disorienting them. Many people lost their natural personalities, and it was very difficult to live in such close quarters with them. One of them was the woman who bunked below me. She was in her mid-forties, and I am sure that in her regular life she had been a lovely person. In Bergen-Belsen she was like a rolling wave: a wave of kindness, a wave of meanness, a wave of kindness, a wave of meanness. One day I was an angel to her because I helped her out, and the next day she would tell me that I shouldn't have been born.

It wasn't her fault; she had come directly from a rich, comfortable family life to the pit of a Nazi prison, and on top of that she had no idea where her husband was. Still, it shocked me the first time she screamed at me. My father's deep affection had left a soft spot in my heart, and I was easily hurt by harsh words.

This woman complained constantly that it annoyed her when I passed her climbing down from the upper bunk.

"If it bothers you," I offered, "let's change. I'll sleep downstairs, and you sleep on top."

"You don't mean it," she snapped nervously. "You're just talking like this."

"No; try me out."

"I'm not going on top. I can't climb up and down."

"Then you have to bear with me," I said as gently as I could. "I'm not doing it to spite you, I'm doing it out of necessity. I can't sleep on the floor."

So we would leave it for a while; and then out of the blue, when I was on my way down, she would suddenly burst out, "No! You cannot come down now!"

I felt sorry for her. She was a good person who had raised a good family, and in fact her son is now a prominent *rosh yeshivah*. She simply didn't have the strength for this. I tried to be friendly to her in spite of the aggravation, and eventually she came to respect me. That was one of my greatest rewards in the concentration camp.

Another person whom the war left the worse for wear was Mr. Kapowitz — the same Mr. Kapowitz who had sent me out of his home on the night the Germans entered Budapest. In spite of that frightful evening, I had maintained a cordial relationship with him in the camp, out of respect for my brother. Mr. Kapowitz, I am sorry to say, had not changed a bit.

One day we heard that there was going to be an inspection in the barracks. A few minutes after the news reached us, Kapowitz came running into our bunk with a box.

"*Fraulein* Peska," he said urgently, "please take this and hold it for me."

My natural instinct was not to refuse a request if I could help it, and before I knew it, he was gone. I quickly slid the box underneath one of the lower-level bunks, and then I began to think. Why was this man trusting me with something that was obviously valuable? Perhaps he knew that I would return it to him, while others might not. Somehow, this whole situation rang a bell; it reminded me of the time I had been given a bag of cookies that were "not meant to be eaten" . . .

I bent down and lifted the lid of the box. Inside was a cache of Hawaiian cigars — pure contraband. Heaven only knows where they had come from. I was afraid to think of what might happen to me if I were found in the barracks with that loot.

I tucked the box beneath my dress as inconspicuously as I could and ambled casually to the next building. I found Kapowitz and handed him his merchandise. When I got back to my barracks five minutes later, the Germans were already inside. If I had waited another minute, I would have been caught.

Mr. Kapowitz never apologized to me, but I forgave him long ago. I tried to put myself in his shoes. He was an intelligent man, but like so many other people, he couldn't cope well enough to see beyond his own immediate needs. One had to forgive during the war — and one still has to forgive, because the Jewish people were up against trials that were beyond all sensibility, and they were completely unnerved.

The trials came in all shapes and sizes. The very fact that men and women were permitted to meet during the daytime posed problems. For families it was a lifesaver; for many of the young single people it was a vicious enticement, especially for the more modern element. They reasoned that they had no tomorrow and were therefore entitled to squeeze out of life whatever it had to offer; their behavior was loose in every respect.

To be alone without supervision and to hang on to one's convictions in such a desperate situation was a herculean task, no matter what background one came from. It was very easy to get lost in the current. I am relieved to say, though, that this lure did not trap me. I was full of life then and many people tried to befriend me, but I chose my company very carefully. Some of the young people called me a snob, but I was glad that they had a name for me and kept their distance.

I tried hard always to remember where I had come from. Just as Yosef *HaTzaddik* was saved from temptation by the image of his father's face, which hung perpetually before him, so too I saw my father's image; it followed me lovingly in the darkness and guided my every action. I thank G-d every day that I am able to look back now without regrets and that I came with a clear conscience from the depths.

Our release from Bergen-Belsen was a sudden and unexpected surprise. One morning after the *appel,* the *kapo* announced that we should pack up and be ready to leave at a given time. That's all — there was nothing else. We were freed *"k'heref ayin,"* in the blink of an eye. Only later did we learn that negotiations concerning our fate had been conducted in Switzerland and that we were released upon payment of an additional bribe to the Nazis.

The salvation, however, was not a complete one. There was one group of people who were not allowed on the transport — those of Polish birth. They were left behind, relegated to the eventual fate of all the prisoners of Bergen-Belsen. When I learned this, I could hardly believe my ears. I was here, in the freed group, only because nine months earlier, when I had stood in front of the clerk at the entrance to Bergen-Belsen, I had said that I was Hungarian. I remembered how strange those words had sounded coming from my mouth, so unprompted and illogical. And yet they were not senseless at all — for they were prompted by G-d.

We were released on the twelfth of December, the twenty-first of Kislev, 1944. It is a date which the Satmar *chassidim* still observe as the day their *Rebbe* was freed. Our exit was as dreamlike, as surreal as our entrance had been the previous year. We trudged on foot back to Hanover across a barren winter landscape, following the same route we had used coming in. We chattered in our soiled, ragged outfits, watching the film replay itself backward in slow motion: the same grayness, the same stinging rain, the same empty field. I even had the two precious possessions I had brought in with me the previous year: the pearl ring my mother, *a"h,* had given me, and Herschel Halberstam's twenty-dollar bill. Everything was the same, except that the train this time was a regular passenger train, for the Germans could certainly not afford to have us show up in Switzerland in cattle cars.

I tried to tell myself that we were going to freedom, but the notion did not penetrate my frozen skull. We are going forward, I said to myself again and again. Forward, forward, only forward . . .

When we were on the train, some sort of canned lard was distributed. I knew that it was pig's lard and passed my can to someone else. No bread was given, and strategically so; about twenty people became sick and some eventually died from that canned lard, more than had died of illness during the entire year in Bergen-Belsen. Their stomachs, unaccustomed to heavy food, were unable to digest fats, and their intestines rebelled. How very predictable of the Nazis to bring us down even after they had freed us.

Chapter Eighteen

The train ride to Switzerland lasted two days. The landscape around us changed so drastically that at first we could not place ourselves in the picture. The white-capped mountains in the distance whose peaks dipped into the clouds could not be more than a flat canvas, like the ones my sisters had painted in their youth; the evergreens that swirled past us were only to view, not to touch. And yet slowly we began to see that these things were ours, that we could breathe the air and claim the free world as our own. The fallen planet lay behind us.

We arrived in Switzerland on December 14, 1944. A relief delegation from Montreux and other nearby Jewish communities was waiting for us in the train station with packages of food and other necessities. The first person among them to step out and greet us was Yitzchak Sternbuch. He and his wife Recha were one of the great relief teams of World War II.*

We were housed for the time being in a large, empty hall that

---

*See *Heroine of Rescue*, ArtScroll, 1984.

The Satmar Rebbe with visitors in Switzerland.

had been cleared for the refugees. One of the Jewish social workers came in to announce that they would be glad to send telegrams to anyone who had a relative's address, but that they could not afford to pay for them.

Now was the perfect opportunity to make use of the twenty-dollar bill I had carried since leaving Budapest. I ripped open the lining of my belt and gave it to the woman, along with my sister Devorah's address in Israel, which I had memorized long ago. The social worker promised to bring me change, but she never returned. No doubt my face was lost to her in the chaos of that motley gathering, and she couldn't find me afterward. But I do not begrudge the money. The satisfaction that my family knew I was alive was worth every penny; just the thought that I had a sister and two brothers waiting for me someplace in the world gave me peace inside.

The Satmar *Rebbe* and *Rebbetzin* were taken to Geneva, where the Swiss *chassidim* put them up in a lovely house. The rest of us were taken to Caux, a village in the mountains not far from Montreux, where there was a substantial Jewish community. We were housed in two hotels, the Regina and the Esplanade, both of which had been requisitioned for the Jewish relief effort.

Slowly, we started to come to ourselves. It would be nearly a year until everyone in our group found places and dispersed to new lives. In the meantime, we edged back into the current of ordinary life at our own slow pace, in the tranquil air of the Swiss mountains.

The village of Caux was breathtakingly beautiful, a collection of scenes from a fairy tale. Mountains swept down steeply around us to a scattering of whimsically shaped blue lakes, and the air was nearly intoxicating. Horses and buggies clip-clopped placidly along the gentle earthen pathways of the village. It was as peaceful here as it had been violent in the war-torn provinces. In fact, the quiet was so loud that it was difficult at first to adjust. The Swiss Jews led an ordered, even life; the war had left them unshaken.

Lilly and I remained close friends all the time we were in Switzerland. We both stayed in the Regina hotel but in separate rooms. I was placed by myself in a small, cozy attic room which had two snug L-shaped beds. I also became the lucky caretaker of an alcohol burner, which I could use to heat water or milk whenever I pleased. After a day or two, one of the relief workers came to ask me if I would mind taking another girl into the room with me, and I agreed. Her name was Naomi; I knew her superficially because she had stayed in an adjoining barracks in Bergen-Belsen. She was a very attractive girl, tall and slim, from a very fine, *frum* family. Her two brothers had also come on the transport and were dorming in Caux.

Naomi and I were both pleased with the arrangement. We got along well, but at the same time we gave each other space to recover. When a young man from the transport began to take Naomi out, I said nothing and did not interfere. Each of us was dealing with private emotional pain, and we tried to respect each other's distance.

The relief organizers asked those of us who felt well enough to help out with various tasks, and once again I was appointed to the kitchen. I don't know why it was always me! Maybe there was something homey about my appearance that people instinctively associated with a kitchen; I have no idea. The community was very kind to us even though its resources were limited, and I was glad to be able to do my part.

Food was in short supply because the war was still on, but we would not have known the difference. The food we were given was normal food, and we could not have asked for more. The first meal I had in Switzerland consisted of boiled potatoes and sardines — a meal fit for a queen. My friends and I couldn't believe that sardines still existed, and we began to improvise all sorts of inventive ways to coordinate them with the potatoes. The greatest philosophers of the century never discussed anything more seriously than we discussed those sardines.

Having food itself, however, was not enough to restore our health. Our digestive tracts were so corroded by all the months of hunger and illness that eating was actually a dangerous undertaking if one did not monitor it carefully. For a while we had no control over our bowels. I was horrified when this first happened; it was as awful as anything we had suffered in Bergen-Belsen. Our bodies had had no fats in them for such a long time that they were unequipped to handle meat or any foods containing oils, passing them on so quickly that sometimes we didn't even feel it. The doctors who came around to check on us said that there was nothing to do but wait until our intestines were strengthened and to be very careful what we ate in the meantime.

The war trailed us in other ways as well. The Germans had added a substance to our food in the concentration camp that altered our body functions, and we were frightened to death that we would never be able to have children. There is no way to describe the intense psychological pain we suffered because of this — and no words for the relief we felt when we saw and heard about women who married and gave birth to healthy children after the liberation.

When the fright of that ordeal had subsided somewhat, I developed a middle-ear infection. I think we were physically so vulnerable then that we simply could not fight off even the mildest of germs. The ear infection was a new form of pain, and I was so sick that the Satmar *Rebbetzin* came from Geneva to see me. She sent me immediately to the local hospital, and one of the doctors from our group came and drained several large clots of pus from both ears, which greatly relieved the pain. The *Rebbetzin* and my friend Lilly came to the hospital to see me every day, always bringing cookies or perfume or some other small gift. I think the attention did even more for me than the treatment.

The backwash of Bergen-Belsen continued to linger, lapping up over our feet when we least expected it; the war seemed determined not to let go of us. One day I climbed the steps to my attic room and found the door locked. I knocked and knocked, but no one answered. Finally, I went down to the hotel office and asked if they had a key.

The clerk came back up with me to open the door, and there was Naomi, lying in her bed — dead. On the floor were the empty wrappers of the alcohol tablets we used to fuel the burner; apparently she had swallowed them. She had left a note for me on the nightstand, apologizing for the trouble she had caused me by moving into the room and keeping such late hours, and she asked that I take a pair of blue, Swiss-made pajamas that she had just bought. I kept those pajamas for a long time, but I could never bring myself to wear them.

Naomi's brothers came to ask me what had happened, but I really did not have much to tell them. Naomi had been very quiet and kept mostly to herself, and I never knew what she was going through. To me, she is a symbol of the haunting of the Holocaust, a victim of one of the myriad ghosts who played on our psyches and on our hearts for decades after the war and gave us no rest.

Although we were all struggling with private demons, we developed a wonderful knack for making believe that nothing had happened. We were determined not to waste our precious freedom by staying indoors and nursing our aches and pains. By the time we had been in Caux a few weeks, we had developed a network of friendships in the neighborhood and were fending nicely for ourselves.

Every two weeks or so, a few other girls and I went into Montreux, where we ate at a community kitchen run by the local Jewish relief committee. Rabbi Eliyahu Botchko, the rabbi of the Montreux Jewish community and *Rosh Yeshivah* of the only yeshivah then functioning in Switzerland, used to come into the kitchen to visit us and see how we were doing. He was a very pleasant man, tall and thin, with a trimmed beard, dark eyes, and a black top hat. Once he invited us to his home. We had known beforehand that his wife was no longer alive, but the minute we stepped into the house, we saw the evidence all around us: the house was badly in need of cleaning.

"Girls," we said to each other with a wink, "let's do something about it!" and we got to work immediately. We scoured the pots, dusted all the furniture, and put the house back together as best we could. We joked as we worked and enjoyed ourselves thoroughly. Rabbi Botchko, needless to say, was very appreciative, but not as much as we; we were grateful for every opportunity to repay the kindnesses that the community had showered upon us.

In addition to my kitchen duties in Caux, I was also appointed head of the clean-up committee in our hotel. Three girls worked under me, but I had the luckiest job — I was assigned to take care of the rooms of the Swiss army captain who was supervising the refugee operation. Captain Schucebeli was a very pleasant gentleman, and I really extended myself to keep his room in ship-shape order, sometimes even bringing in fresh flowers for the table. Apparently, the last person in charge of the room had done a less-than-satisfactory job, because the captain was so pleased that he sometimes used to give me chocolates — an unheard-of luxury during the war.

In the meantime, we were all looking around for people who would be willing to sign our release forms. We were not free to pick up and take off on our own unless someone agreed to take responsibility for us. The relief committee made extensive contacts for us, trying to find distant relatives or friends who would sponsor us. I had not heard from my sister or brothers in *Eretz Yisrael* yet, but somehow I had the feeling that Devorah had received my telegram and knew I was alive. I was aware that securing entry papers to a new country was a very involved and lengthy process, but I felt sure that eventually they would come through. In the meantime, I was not concerned. I was among Jews and I had what I needed.

One day Captain Schucebeli called me into the office.

"*Fraulein* Rabinowitz, you may leave," he told me. "Your release has been requested by a Mr. Yosef Gottesman from Zurich. He will see to it that you are placed, and you will no longer be a ward of the state. You are free to go."

I was dumbfounded. "Gottesman? I don't know anyone by that name. How does he know me?"

As it turned out, Yosef Gottesman — no relation to my friend Lilly — was a cousin of my mother's. When the lists of the refugees' names were posted in the Jewish administrative offices of the surrounding communities, he had recognized my name and put in a request to release me.

I was thrilled. I was also shocked; I had not expected to have an arrangement made for me so soon. Then I had a flash of inspiration. Maybe my ticket to freedom was really somebody else's ticket.

"If there is any possibility," I said to the captain, "I would like my release papers to be given to my friend Lilly Gottesman instead." I reasoned that if somebody had recognized my name on the list and knew I was alive, I would manage. Eventually someone would come after me. But Lilly had no one; not one person beyond the arena of the war even knew that she existed.

The captain looked at me incredulously. All he could say was "*Zints zi ferikt* — are you nuts?" He knew that no refugee in his right mind would actually pass up the opportunity to begin a normal life, especially since the wait for another release could last

Mr. and Mrs. Grunfeld in Zurich.

indefinitely. When the captain saw that I was serious, he told me that it was possible to exchange a release assignment, but the problem was that Yosef Gottesman did not know Lilly and would not want to take responsibility for her. He suggested that she be sent temporarily to a refugee youth camp called Heiden, a transition point for young people who were awaiting placement. I called Lilly in, and the three of us made the arrangements together. Lilly packed her things and went off to St. Gallen, where the camp was located, promising to stay in touch with me.

My faith in the eventual resolution of my fortune paid off. Two months later, Yosef Gottesman sent me a second set of papers. This time I was ready to return to the turf of ordinary citizenship.

The Gottesmans were living in a tiny apartment in Zurich and could not take me in themselves. When I arrived, Mr. Gottesman placed me with a lovely family named Grunfeld. The Grunfelds had opened their doors to teenagers and young adults who had just come from the concentration camps. In addition to their own several children, there were two other refugees staying with them when I came. Food was still being rationed; we received two slices of bread with margarine and coffee in the morning, cereal and an apple for lunch, very simple suppers, and no meat. But it didn't matter, because we were no longer hungry, thank G-d. I was free — living in a regular house, sleeping on a bed with a mattress, surrounded by a family! It was here in Zurich that I finally began to get my bearings and to think of myself not as a homeless person spit out by the war, but as a young woman with a future.

Chapter Eighteen / 221

I began to work as a finisher for a small local dress manufacturer. I received only a token salary, but it kept me occupied during the day and gave me a sense of independence. I had also written to the Polish government-in-exile in London, reporting my status as a Polish refugee, and after a month or so they began to send me a stipend from their relief funds. When the first check came, I went on a long-overdue "binge." I bought myself a coat, a pair of shoes, and a hat, relieved at last to have a fashionable covering for the unsightly crop of curls on my head. My hair had still not grown in fully from the time of the shaving in Linz, and although it was a decent length by today's standards, it was very odd-looking at that time.

In Zurich I cultivated another asset that had always been a vital lifeline for me: friends. All along, I had been blessed with the hospitality of one wonderful family after another, and my good fortune continued to stand by me. Among the special families I met who were heavily involved in the relief effort were the Sternbergs, the Kovalskys, the Buchingers, the Bollags, the Mayerovitzes, and of course, the Sternbuchs. In Zurich, I often spent Shabbosos with three additional families: the Eises, the Rubinfelds, and the Wagshals. These were all well-to-do families who worked tirelessly to make the refugees feel comfortable. Mrs. Wagshal in particular liked me very much. One Shabbos she opened up her china closet and took out a small silver basket with a matching tong that was meant to hold sugar cubes.

"You know," she said to me, "you are going to get married one day, and I want you to take this for *drusha geshank*." I have that beautiful little silver basket to this day, and I cherish it very dearly.

I was extremely fortunate that my family's reputation had preceded me. Because of this I received invitations from many people I had never met. The family Mayerovitz from Lugano invited me to stay with them for a while and treated me royally, taking me on tours of the historical sites in Lugano. We even went mountain-climbing outside the city, hiking up the sides of the majestic hills I had admired from afar. I stayed in touch with

Mrs. Peshy Wagshal in Zurich.

the Mayerovitzes long after coming to America and shared many family *simchos* with them.

Another family whom I remember with affection are the Kovalskys, *chassidim* who had connections to my family from before the war. They took me out to buy fabric, and I spent a few days in their home sewing some needed items of clothing for myself. The Kovalskys were in contact with relatives and friends in *Eretz Yisrael*, and they had received information about my family that I did not know yet myself. I remember that I was just beginning to cut out the pieces of a white silk blouse when *Rebbetzin* Kovalsky asked me gently if I had heard anything about my sister-in-law Frimele.

"No," I said quickly, but the foreboding tone of the question sent such a tremor through my system that I lost control of the scissors and cut right through the lapel of the blouse. I felt the blood draining from my face. *Rebbetzin* Kovalsky must have sensed that it was best not to pursue the matter, and I was relieved. I didn't want to talk, or even think, about anything that might be wrong.

Dr. Yaakov Griffel, a well-known attorney, geologist, and Agudah activist who was very involved in the relief effort, happened to be in Switzerland at that time, and he came to bring me regards from Devorah. But Griffel said nothing about my brother Boruch and his wife, and that sting of apprehension pricked me once more. Like a person who has awakened from surgery and asks with dread what has happened to him, I began to press Dr. Griffel. He was reluctant to talk, but after I had repeated

Chapter Eighteen / 223

The Satmar Rebbetzin.

The Rebbetzin in front of her house in Geneva with one of the Gross children.

my question at least a dozen times, he saw that he would have to answer.

"What can I say?" he finally replied. "Your sister-in-law is on vacation . . . on *Har HaZeisim*."

I had no idea what that meant, but the other little voice inside reminded me that I really didn't want to know. When the Kovalskys asked me later what I had discussed with Yankel Griffel, I told them naively, "He said that my sister-in-law went for a vacation on *Har HaZeisim*," and the matter was dropped. I could not afford to involve myself with any more tragedy right now, and so I tabled the incident and turned my thoughts to happier things.

The Satmar *Rebbetzin* called me up around that time and asked me to come visit her in Geneva. When I arrived, I found the *Rebbe* and his wife living in a very comfortable home; the *chassidim* had set them up and provided them with everything they needed. The house was now full of guests, as it had been before the war, and it radiated with the *"balabatishkeit"* of old times. There was only one difference: the *Rebbetzin* could no longer cope with it. Although she was still a young woman, the

My dear friend Lilly Gottesman.

management of an active rabbinic household was too big a handful for her after the struggles of Bergen-Belsen. She had not had time to make a transition, to recover from her own inner sadness. I did not know what to do for her; travel permits were being issued on a very limited basis, and I could not stay in her house indefinitely.

The answer soon presented itself. My good friend Lilly Gottesman had been writing to me from the youth camp in St. Gallen where Captain Schucebeli had sent her. She was very unhappy there. The other young people in the camp were of a more modern element, and Lilly felt very uncomfortable. She came from a very simple, *frum* family, and her own sensitivities for *Yiddishkeit* had deepened greatly during the war. She told me that she was eating only dairy foods in the camp and that she did not have any friends. That's when it struck me that she and the Satmar *Rebbetzin* would make a perfect match — the *Rebbetzin* needed help, and Lilly needed a home. We were able to arrange papers for Lilly once again, and the partnership proved to be a great success. Lilly and the *Rebbetzin* suited each other well; their needs were perfectly complementary, and they soon grew quite close.

In the meantime, my sister Devorah had finally written to me from *Eretz Yisrael*. The mail crept through channels at a snail's pace, and this was the only letter I received from her during all my months in Switzerland. Her husband, after painstaking effort, had finally been able to obtain an entry visa for me through his connections in the Agudah, and Devorah said that the papers would be arriving soon. I had asked them if they could get a visa for Lilly too, but Devorah said it was impossible. The immigration quota for Palestine had been filled.

One day during lunchtime, I came home from the seamstress's shop where I was working and turned on the radio. I couldn't believe my ears. The broadcaster was in the midst of announcing that a cease-fire had been declared and that the war was over. It was the seventh of May, 1945.

I didn't know what to do with myself. I felt crushed between laughter and tears, and could only stand there rooted to the carpet, dazed with disbelief. After a few minutes, when the news had penetrated, I began to scream so loudly that Mrs. Grunfeld came running in.

"What happened?" she cried.

"The war's over!" I shouted. "It's over!"

We danced in the hallway and cried tears of joy. I was so overwhelmed that I couldn't go back to work that day. I had to sit and digest the thought that the fighting was over. Hitler's iron band of malice had finally snapped. We had been sprung free from our cages in a split second, so weightless that we were catapulted into the deep blue of the heavens, where the rush of clear air made us lightheaded.

Very soon after this joyous news, my visa to *Eretz Yisrael* arrived. Many people from our original group in Bergen-Belsen, including the Satmar *Rebbe* and *Rebbetzin,* had also been able to obtain Palestine certificates through various sources. A transport was arranged for us out of Geneva that would take us to the French port of Cherbourg, from there to Italy, and then across the Mediterranean to Tel Aviv. I had dreamt of the Holy Land ever since my days in Munkatch, when my first opportunity had gone up in smoke. I prayed now that the dream would not elude me again and that I would be able to bend down and kiss the soil of *Eretz Yisrael,* as I had once promised myself I would.

Only one thorn marred the euphoria of these wonderful plans — my dear friend Lilly would be left behind. The *Rebbetzin* had made arrangements for her to stay with the Grosses in Geneva, a very fine, wealthy family with young children, who would provide well for her. Nevertheless, she was inconsolable.

On the day we left, Lilly was so distressed that she fainted on the steps of the *Rebbetzin's* house. When she came to, we both cried. She hugged me and hugged me, as though she could not let go; it seems that she is still hugging me now. Lilly had no family and no direction; her future was a blank page. I did the best I could to comfort her, but I knew that my words were meager. The *Rebbetzin* also gave her a beautiful *berachah*, but it did not make our parting any less painful.

We did not know then that our story would have an unusually happy ending. There was a young man in Geneva named Mr. Walter, a person of excellent character who tutored the children of several wealthy families in town. I had met him myself in the *Rebbetzin's* home during my previous visits to Geneva. In the course of conversation with him, Volvy Friedman's name had come up, and Walter mentioned that Volvy was his cousin. I remember thinking what a small world it was.

It seems that Walter had taken a liking to Lilly when he first met her on his tutoring rounds. When I was already in *Eretz Yisrael*, Lilly wrote to tell me that Walter was interested in marrying her. I wrote back immediately, telling her not to hesitate, that Walter was an extremely fine person and that I thought very highly of him. It was gratifying to be able to provide a little push for such a wonderful match. Lilly's later correspondence set my mind completely at ease. She spoke about how good Walter was to her, how considerate he was of her needs; he had even bought her a winter coat, a gesture of great kindness in the frozen aftermath of the Holocaust. Lilly continued to write and give me news of her life; she and Walter later settled in America and were blessed with eight children. Of course, I had no way of knowing that Lilly, through her marriage to Walter, would eventually become my cousin — a very pleasing turn of events in a very precious friendship.

In terms of my own future, I had not given much thought to getting married. I was now twenty-four years old, an "advanced" age in the European Jewish world. Of course, no one had counted on the interruption of the war, but facts were still facts. Prospective matches had been arranged for me in Warsaw and later in Munkatch and in Budapest, but to me the idea of committing myself and bringing children into a ravaged world had seemed neither healthy nor realistic.

The Satmar *Rebbetzin*, too, had tried her hand on me in Geneva, but she did not know what a stubborn young woman I was. I simply was not ready yet to head into the next chapter of my life. Thank goodness she and I were on such good terms that I was able to joke and laugh with her about it, but it was not an easy matter to refuse a match from the Satmar *Rebbetzin* herself.

The problem was that I no longer had an excuse. I was on safe ground, beyond the periphery of the war, free to begin a new life. So what was holding me back?

I sat down one day and gave the matter some serious thought. I had always tried to be very honest with myself about my feelings, and finally I had to admit that the block I had encountered was a considerable one; it went by the name of Volvy Friedman. Volvy had even expressed a subtle interest in me at one point in Munkatch, but I had made it clear that I had no intention of marrying anyone while the war was still on. Under pressure from his parents to begin a home, Volvy had turned his sights around and married his wife.

I began to think about how comfortable and safe I had always felt when he was around, how relieved I had been to see his face during some of the most anxious moments of my flight through Europe. I hadn't thought about it in a conscious way at the time; it had just seemed natural to have him there, a person who had been so close to my family, someone on whom I knew I could rely totally. I felt it was brazen to entertain such thoughts now. I didn't even know if Volvy were alive, or if his wife and child had survived the war. But some deep-seated instinct told me that I would not be able to get on with my life until I found out.

There was a very pleasant young man named Fishel Scarp who had courted me briefly in Zurich. One day we were walking in the park, and in a discreet, modest way, he made his intentions known. I gently refused.

"Why not?" he asked.

Suddenly I felt prompted to make a clean breast of things. "You know," I told him, "there is someone I met at home a long time ago — and I think I would not like to make any decision until I find out what happened to him."

"What is his name?" Fishel asked gently.

"Volvy Friedman."

Fishel said the name sounded familiar; he thought that he might once have attended yeshivah with Volvy. He was very respectful of my feelings, and although he was clearly disappointed, he did not press me any further.

I did not think of either of them again until I was settled on the train out of Switzerland. The conductor came through our compartment calling, *"Fraulein* Rabinowitz! Is there a *Fraulein* Rabinowitz here?"

I was afraid to answer, irrationally afraid of all the terrible things that could go wrong. The haunting wartime fear of being discovered overpowered me, and I sat stiffly in my seat, staring out the window. The conductor left the car, but after a few minutes he returned and called my name again.

"There she is," someone said. My heart leapt into my throat.

The conductor came over and handed me a telegram. It was from Fishel Scarp. He wanted to inform me that Volvy Friedman was alive and that he was running a Displaced Persons' camp in Bregenz, Austria. There was no other information.

I tucked the telegram into my knapsack and sat back in my seat, flooded with mixed emotions. Most of all, I was astonished and touched by Fishel Scarp's kindness. He had been generous enough to try and make possible for another what he could not have for himself.

So Volvy was alive; but the thought of turning back never crossed my mind. It was time once again to go forward — only forward.

Chapter Nineteen

At the end of May we came to Rome. It seemed to me that I had been halfway across the world by now. Every bone in my body ached with fatigue, and I wished with all my heart that I would wake up one morning and discover that the entire past six years had been nothing more than a bad dream.

As we got down onto the station platform, another train was coming in. It was full of German soldiers, prisoners of war. I gathered the saliva in my mouth and I spat in their faces as hard as I could. It was a small but satisfying revenge for me, and my soul felt lighter afterward. The German soldiers said nothing and showed no reaction. It was almost as though they knew it was coming to them.

It felt strange to be walking leisurely along the sun-bathed streets of Rome, like tourists without a care in the world. In spite of its bitterly anti-Semitic history, the city was beautiful. I remember going on a walking tour with some of the other people from the transport, strolling with an unaccustomed ease among the elegant stone fountains in one of the central piazzas and wondering if I had merely exchanged my nightmare for a pleasant dream.

We were put up for a little over a week in the nearby town of Bari, where we stayed in an empty school building. There was absolutely nothing in the room except benches and a few coarse straw mattresses. I slept on a bench with my knapsack beneath my head and covered myself as best as I could with one hand, for there were no blankets. It was chilly, but we didn't feel the cold; we were too exhausted to feel anything, too weary even to pity ourselves. We fell asleep quickly and slept soundly through the night. Thank G-d that night went by, and then a day, and then another day . . . we pushed ourselves ahead, gathering a little strength at each moment to take the next step.

The Satmar *Rebbe* and *Rebbetzin* had been taken in by a *frum* family in town named Steinberg, and after a few nights in the school building I went to stay with their hosts. Although the war had left its mark on the Jews of Italy, it seemed to have passed over the heads of the Bari community. The Steinberg family was living comfortably in a spacious house with high, European-style ceilings. They did everything in their power to make me feel welcome. Mrs. Steinberg and one of her daughters indulged me by taking me shopping to some of the most exclusive stores in Bari. They bought me a beautiful cashmere sweater set and a number of pieces of fabric. One piece was of exquisite green silk with a delicate bird pattern on it.

"You'll get married one day," they said to me, just as Mrs. Wagshal had said in Zurich when she gave me the sugar bowl, "and you'll need a trousseau. Make something out of this — and remember that it came from us." I had rarely seen such rich cuts of cloth, and I had certainly never received gifts of such extravagance. But at that point in my life, a little luxury and a little spoiling were exactly what I needed. Just the touch of that watery tumble of green silk made me feel feminine and whole again, and hopeful of the future.

In September we finally arrived in Tel Aviv. I held the Satmar *Rebbetzin's* hand as we descended from the ship. The first thing I thought of was the promise I had once made to myself in Budapest, and I bent down and kissed the ground of the Holy Land. I could hardly absorb the idea that I had set myself a goal beyond all reason, and that Hashem had enabled me to attain it. I had never felt such deep stirring, such a profound sense of a cycle of *hashgachah* being completed. It was totally unnatural that we were in *Eretz Yisrael*; it was something that was never supposed to happen. I had merited an extraordinary blessing, and I did not know what to do to thank the *Ribono Shel Olam*.

We entered the immigration center in Atlit, a suburb of Tel Aviv, where we had to remain in quarantine for several weeks. There was also a ton of legal paperwork to be done. My brother Reb Boruch sent a few of his friends to greet me. He and my brother-in-law, Jacob Landau, both had contacts in the government and promised to try to secure my release early.

The first night in the immigration center, Dovid Barnholz came to visit me, bringing me packages and regards from Devorah, Boruch, and Lazer. Barnholz was a long-time friend of my parents, and he was also related to us; his sister Chanale was married to the Biale *Rebbe*, Chavale Rabinowitz's son. In fact, when my mother had sent me out from the Warsaw ghetto to Otwock during my aunt's illness, it was Dovid's parents to whom I had delivered rations packages. I was now able to give him greatly belated regards from them. Neither of us knew yet that they were no longer alive.

Dovid Barnholz — or Baranhor, as he called himself now in *Eretz Yisrael* — was a married man of forty then, and he was very involved in the *Haganah*. He and I sat out on a bench in the immigration compound for many hours that night, and I found myself pouring out everything that had happened to me during the war. We talked and talked, until it seemed that six years of toxins had drained from my blood. For all the months in Switzerland I had let the feelings ride, but suddenly I found it a wonderful catharsis to talk about my experiences with a dear family friend who really seemed to understand me, even though he himself had not been through it. We talked about the future too, a place as bright and promising as the past was black.

I remember admiring the beautiful sky above *Eretz Yisrael* as we talked, so different from any sky I had seen yet. It was much cleaner and purer, and also much faster; it took only a few minutes for the night to descend, a flicker from light to darkness. Perhaps, I thought, our *geulah* as a people would come so quickly, but in reverse, from darkness to light, and the memories of our mired past would remain as no more than a painful flicker in the recesses of our souls . . .

Reb Boruch sent people in daily to check on me and to press for my release. I remember that when I went to bring the Satmar *Rebbe* his breakfast one morning, he joked good-naturedly, "I see that you have pull here. The people are busier with you than with the *Rebbe*!" And in fact, I was released before he was.

My sister was waiting for me on her porch on Rechov Fierberg when I finally arrived. I didn't recognize her. She was about thirty-six then, but she had aged beyond her years.

Devorah had been living a burdened life. Although she had eluded the war, I think her conscience had weighed heavily on her all these years, knowing that she had left Poland against my mother's wishes. The fire of old, undimmed, still burned in her green eyes, but I could only imagine what terrible conflict such intensity must have cost her: a battle between her ardent devotion to her family and her zealous desire to leave the *golus*. Devorah had always had keen foresight. She had seen, perhaps better than any of us, what Hitler's rise to power portended, and she had gotten out in time. But she had ached for us and worried about us for all the years of the war, with such anxiety that it had turned her hair white.

On top of that, she had had to deal with the most recent tragedy in our family. In the past, Devorah had often opened startling and poignant windows for me into the lives of our family, and now that role had fallen to her again. I could no longer avoid the news I had been dreading to hear: my sister-in-law Frimele, Reb Boruch's wife, was dead.

Frimele had been pregnant when she and my brother left Budapest in 1943. She had given birth to a little girl, after four boys, in Istanbul. When they arrived in Tel Aviv, her illness took a turn for the worse; the fifth child was too much of a strain on her system. She finally collapsed and had to be rushed to the hospital. The baby was taken away from her immediately.

For three months, Devorah told me, my brother had not gotten undressed, prepared at any moment to be called to the hospital. Devorah had found them an apartment on the street where she lived, and she took over their household. In addition to her own two daughters, one about nine and the other a baby, she now became mother, cook, and housekeeper to her nephews and niece. She would not have done otherwise; she did not think twice about devoting herself completely to Reb Boruch's family, but it wasn't easy. Her apartment was very small, there was no diaper service in those days, and money was scarce.

When Frimele passed away, the children were dispersed. The baby was placed in a children's home, and the two younger boys were taken in by a family named Friedman. Only the two oldest children, Dovid and Chaim Elazar, who were about ten and twelve at that time, remained at home with their father. This is how I found them when I arrived: a family dissolved into fragments, ruined by death and separation.

When I first came to my brother's house, the devastation that I saw was unspeakable. I remembered his household from Budapest; what a glory it had been then, what an assembly of people, what a cycle of comings and goings! All day long, the life of the spirit had flourished there. Now there was nothing. My brother was isolated, empty; he was not the same man anymore. He sat at the table learning quietly by himself, and the spark had gone out of him. Devorah told me that he had not talked to people for a long time. There was a house *bachur* who attended to some of the routine household chores, but otherwise the house was still, with the quietness of a graveyard lying over it. I vowed to myself at that moment that I would do everything in my power to give my brother back his home.

Several people, including our friend Dovid Baranhor, tried to convince me that this burden was not mine. "You just came from Bergen-Belsen," Dovid said. "You're a young girl, and you have to take care of yourself. You have to start thinking about the future. This is not a job for you . . . you should at least take a rest first."

"This has nothing to do with my future," I told him. "Do you know what? If I could marry that man, I would — just to give him a home again, the way he was used to. But since I can't do that, I have to help him as much as I can, to make him happy. There's no one in the world who is more deserving than he is."

The very first thing I did was to collect the children and bring them home. The two younger boys, Moshe Leib and Yitzchak Yaakov (who are, respectively, the Munkatcher *Rebbe* and Dinover *Rebbe* of today) were brought home from *Yerushalayim*. They were about three and five years old then, and the baby girl, whom we retrieved from the children's home, was nearly a year old. I remember taking pictures of them when they were all together in the apartment. The house began to have the taste of a home again, with the ring of childish laughter and the thumping of small feet filling its lonely corners.

What I am perhaps proudest of in my care of those children is that I nursed them to health, beyond any sign of contagion of their mother's illness. They were also poorly nourished and looked pale and thin. We took them straight to the doctor for a thorough checkup when they came home. Two months later when I brought them in again, the doctor was amazed. He told me that their health had improved so much that he barely recognized them. I am sure that this had much less to do with any medical care than with the attention I gave them. It was a tremendous satisfaction to me to be able to nourish those children back to normalcy.

The baby, whose name was Yitte but whom we affectionately called Zuta, was the biggest handful of all five. She had had a rough start in life; during all her months in the orphanage, she had not been held or even wheeled in a carriage, and the first few times I took her out, she was petrified. When Devorah went walking with her baby, I used to take Zuta along. Every time we came to the edge of a curb and she felt the carriage dip, she would get hysterical. Who can imagine what kind of unique terror she must have felt; she had never received proper stimulation and was oversensitive to her new surroundings.

None of my efforts to comfort her in those early days were of any avail. She cried so much during our strolls that some of the neighbors began to go in to my brother to complain about me. "Who is that girl who is taking care of your child?" they would ask with wagging fingers. "What's going on out there? It sounds like she's beating the poor child to death!"

I thought to myself that some things never changed. The *Rebbe* was still the *Rebbe*, and — just as in Munkatch — the *chassidim* still looked upon him more or less as their property. Although the Munkatcher following in *Eretz Yisrael* was a small one, the *Rebbe* was still the center of attention, especially now that he had a younger sister who had just come from *Gehinnom*. These people were well meaning, but my brother knew enough to ignore their complaints.

Little by little, Zuta adjusted to ordinary life, and within a short time she was displaying the characteristic impishness of her age. It also pleased me very much to see her developing a healthy appetite after the poor treatment she had received in the orphanage. On Friday afternoons when I was cooking noodles for the chicken soup, she used to waddle over to the table when my back was turned, drag the bowl of noodles down onto the floor, and quietly polish them off before I had a chance to do anything about it. I also discovered that after I fed her breakfast in the morning, she would sometimes make the rounds of the neighbors in our building. "I'm hungry," she would announce. "Peska didn't give me any breakfast today."

With all five of my brother's children in Tel Aviv. Little Zuta is sitting on my lap.

"What?! You didn't have breakfast?" each of the neighbors would exclaim in turn, and they would immediately feed her. This clever little girl sometimes had several breakfasts in one morning, as well as much care and affection.

Slowly, we all began to settle into a comfortable home routine. I felt that I had started over again from scratch about ten times in the past few years, taking a few pieces of raw material and trying to fashion a sense of normalcy from them. But none of those beginnings seemed as precious as this one: the launching of a young family into a life of Jewishness, in a world at peace.

By this time I had the house organized and was able to relax a little. I began to get in contact with several of my relatives in Israel, particularly my father's daughter Esther, whom I went to visit in *Yerushalayim* several times. Esther was now well into middle age, and I often used to think in wonderment of how many years — how many worlds — had passed since the day I had gone sledding with her and her two young children in Siedlice: the day of my father's death.

I was very thankful that I had the opportunity to see Esther during that year, for our reacquaintance was tragically short. The last time I visited her, she was not feeling well. As I walked down the curved stone steps of her apartment on my way out, she called after me, "Peska, wait . . . I want to give you something — a gift to remember me by." She went inside and came out a moment later with a beautiful silver brooch, a work of the well-known jewelry designer Betzalel. A week later, Esther passed away unexpectedly. The brooch is the only thing I have left to remember her by, and it is a gift I still cherish very much.

I had been with my brother for only a few months when people began coming around with prospective *shidduchim* for me. I was almost twenty-five years old, and my relatives in *Eretz Yisrael* were all hoping to cure me of my unmarried state. My father's sister, *Rebbetzin* Chava Kalish, who was the B'nei Braker *Rebbetzin*, even got involved and set me up with the much-sought-after son of a very rich, well-known family; but somehow nothing went.

Yaakov Yitzchak and Moshe Leib Rabinowitz, the Dinover and Munkatcher Rebbe of today, in Tel Aviv.

Reb Boruch had begun to receive people again. Among the visitors who frequented our house on *Motzaei Shabbos* was a young *bachur* named Chaim Yerucham Klein. Chaim Yerucham also happened to be a first cousin to Volvy Friedman. He once mentioned to me that Volvy's wife and child had been deported from Salish during the war and had died in a concentration camp.

Thereafter, whenever I was around on *Motzaei Shabbos*, Chaim Yerucham would come over to me quietly and make mention of Volvy. Even though I now knew that Volvy's wife was dead, these remarks always made me very uncomfortable. Somehow, although Volvy still continued to graze the surface of my consciousness, I didn't feel it was appropriate for me to be thinking about him.

"Why do you keep talking like this?" I asked Chaim Yerucham. "It's not my business to think about him."

"You're wrong," he would reply with a knowing look. "You *should* think about Volvy."

"I don't know anything about him. I don't even know his address — and I wouldn't know how to find out."

This picture of me was taken in Tel Aviv.

"I'll find out," he said, and right after Shabbos he brought me Volvy's address in the Displaced Persons camp he was running in Bregenz, Austria.

I put the address in my pocket and did not do anything about it for several weeks. Something about the whole matter just did not seem proper. Even if it turned out that there was something substantial in the match, it seemed very inappropriate for me to take the initiative. But one day, when my sister and I were out walking with the children, some compelling urge seized me.

"Listen," I said, "let's go to the post office."

"What do you want in the post office?" Devorah asked.

"You know English, and I would like you to do me a favor."

I said no more to my curious sister until we were inside the building. Then I pulled the scrap of paper with Volvy's address out of my pocket.

"I would like you to send a telegram for me. Here's the address — send it to Mr. William Friedman, and it should say: 'Glad to hear you are alive. Perhaps our paths will cross. Peska.'"

Devorah looked at me as though I had just broken out in some strange, exotic rash. She was so dumbfounded she couldn't even speak. To tell the truth, I was a little shocked myself, but I reasoned that I had nothing to lose. The *Ribono Shel Olam* had guided my footsteps so carefully until now; He had supported every one of my instincts, logical or not, and I did not think He would lead me astray. But first I had to assure my horrified sister that I was still in possession of my wits.

"You don't know Volvy," I told her. "I've been going out with all these *bachurim* here, and they're very nice, but I am not much interested in them. Volvy's wife has been dead for a few years. If there were a possibility that something could come of this, I think I could be happy."

Chapter Nineteen / 239

Devorah found her voice. "You're crazy," was all she said.

"Maybe I *am* crazy, but this is how I feel."

Two weeks went by, and no reply came; three weeks went by. I was beginning to regret my brazenness when a letter from Volvy finally arrived at the end of the month. He had apparently done a great deal of deliberating before replying and had chosen his words carefully.

He indicated that he was not the *bachur* he had once been, that he was no longer a free man in the ordinary sense. He had lost his wife and child, which made him less than desirable as a first-choice *shidduch*. I, on the other hand, was a very eligible young woman from an excellent family, and he did not want to stand in the way of my making a suitable match. Volvy concluded by saying that years had gone by and the mountains had grown tall between us. Who knew if we would understand each other as we once had?

The children came home from school just as I finished reading the letter. I gave them lunch, and then I asked the woman who helped us out if she would take them for a walk. For the next few hours I was in the house by myself, and I sat down and thought hard about how to answer the letter. I had read mixed feelings between the lines that Volvy had written: a mature practicality that advised caution, and yet at the same time a barely repressed interest.

When I had searched my heart thoroughly and gathered my thoughts, I took out a pen and paper. I told Volvy that I didn't think we should make any decisions until we had seen each other, and that if he agreed, I could ask my brother-in-law, Jacob Landau, to send him a certificate to come to Israel.

After that letter, some sort of intangible barrier must have mellowed across the many miles that separated us, and we began to correspond more normally, more in the comfortable vein of the past. Volvy wrote that he could not come to Israel now. He had gotten involved with Agudas Yisrael and was about to leave to America with the first overseas European relief delegation. Volvy was away for six months. During that time he worked with Mike

A painting of Reb Naftoli Friedman, Volvy's father. At this time he was no longer alive.

My future mother-in-law, Leah Friedman, a"h.

Tress, the president of Zeirei Agudath Israel in the United States and legendary Holocaust rescue activist, to publicize the needs of the European refugees and to collect *tashmishei kedushah* to bring back to them.

Volvy was also heavily involved in several refugee camps, one of which was in Boulee, outside of Paris. He wrote that he could arrange to send me a visa to America via France, and that he would meet me in Paris when his American tour was finished. I decided to go.

I was very torn about leaving my brother's children, but Devorah encouraged me to make the trip. Six months earlier I had been a brash young sender of telegrams in her eyes, but now I stood before her an adult, a woman on the threshold of enormous change. She said to me, "If your heart tells you that this is your destiny, you have no right to deprive yourself of it. You're young — it's only a matter of going and coming for you to see for yourself if this is what you want."

My brother's reaction was much more reserved. He did not

want to suffer another loss in his household, to have his family disrupted once more and left without the guiding hand of a woman, but neither could he hold me back. He saw that my heart was across the waters, and he held his peace.

My uncle,
Reb Shlomo Ackerman, zt"l.

Volvy had a number of relatives who had come through Cyprus after the war and were now living in Israel. They were Munkatcher *chassidim* and knew my brother well. Volvy's father was no longer alive, but his stepmother, Leah Friedman, used to come to our house for *Yom Tov*. She was extremely happy when we told her about my plans, and it pleased me very much to have her approval. I remember how she looked at me with kind eyes and said softly, "Be a good wife to him."

There was one other relative of Volvy's in Israel at that time for whose kindness I am still grateful. His name was Reb Shlomo Ackerman, my mother-in-law's brother. Reb Shlomo was then in his sixties, a soft-spoken man with gentle blue eyes who loved people unconditionally. He had lost his wife and seven or eight children to Hitler, and yet he remained a shoulder to the world. He could talk to anyone — young or old, *frum* or not *frum* — with sincere interest and make each one feel that he or she was the most important person in the world. The refugees had come flocking to him in the D. P. camps for advice, a smile, or a good word, and in spite of his own sorrow he was still playing father to anybody who needed one. Reb Shlomo, too, was pleased by the idea of a match between his nephew and me, and I cherished his approval. I felt that I was leaving Israel with the backing of a double blessing.

There were two very poignant moments that remain in my memory about my departure from *Eretz Yisrael*. The first was the wrenching talk I had with my brother's children. My heart was broken over them; I felt that I was abandoning them to the four winds. When I had first arrived in Israel, the two older boys had often woken up in the middle of the night, asking for their mother. Who had taken her away? they wanted to know. Whose fault was it that she was not here? Well-meaning but naive answers had come their way from family and friends: "She'll come, don't worry — she'll come." But she never did come, and the boys were very bitter about the deception.

Now they were about to be left alone again, and I didn't know how to soften the blow. I gathered them tightly around me and said, "Children, I hired a wonderful governess for you. She will come and take care of you now, because I must go out and make my way in life. I didn't want it to happen this way . . . I didn't want to leave, but that's how it turned out; and I promise that I will try my utmost to come back to you."

Chaim, who was then seven years old and drifting in a private world of pain, muttered to himself, "They always promise to come back, but they never do," and his words pierced my soul.

The second moment that is so vivid in my mind is the talk I had with my aunt Chava Kalish, the B'nei Braker *Rebbetzin*, right before I departed for Chaifa. We were standing on the corner of Feierberg and Shenkin in Tel Aviv, and she said to me, "Peska, *fohr gezunterheit* — go in good health. But just remember: if it turns out that the *bachur* is not for you, don't be ashamed to come back — and I will have excellent *shidduchim* waiting for you here!"

Volvy's stepmother and Uncle Shlomo accompanied me to Chaifa to meet my boat. They stood on the dock at five o'clock in the morning, waving to me as the ship backed away from the shore. I had been in *Eretz Yisrael* a year and two weeks. Now it was time to go forward again — only forward.

Chapter Twenty

Volvy Friedman had reached Paris by a long and circuitous route, one much more painful than mine. I am still not sure how many concentration camps he went through, nor where he found the stamina to involve himself so heavily in relief work before his own wounds were healed.

The last camp Volvy was sent to was Bergen-Belsen. He arrived there at the very end of the war, after I had already left with my group for Switzerland. One day he was walking across the compound, dragging a pair of shoes by the laces because he did not have the strength to carry them. He weighed only forty kilograms then, about eighty-eight pounds. Ruchie Friedman, a girl from Salish who was working in the kitchen, saw him pass by. She recognized him from her hometown, where he had lived when he was first married, and ran out to see him. The two Friedman families, although not related, had once been very close.

"Don't worry," she said to him quickly. "I'll help you out." She began to slip him extra food scraps from the kitchen, no

Captain Monnheit.

doubt keeping him from the edge of a slow death.

On April 12, 1945, Bergen-Belsen was liberated. As in many other camps, large numbers of liberated Jews suddenly found themselves with no place to live; many wandered from town to town in search of relatives, in search of any familiar face from the past.

Ruchie, Volvy, and two of Volvy's cousins, the sisters Raizy and Simi Ackerman, formed a group. They were taken to a Displaced Persons camp in Zaltzvedl, Germany, and from there they went to Austria together. Volvy got in touch with a Jewish captain in the French army named Monnheit, who helped him to establish a D. P. center in Bregenz. Survivors who knew either Volvy or Ruchie heard about the camp by word of mouth and were soon pouring into Bregenz. Volvy also began to trace many members of his large family, including his uncle Reb Shlomo Ackerman, and arranged to bring them to Austria as well. These were the initiation rites of what was to become a tireless and immensely successful relief squad. Volvy was at the helm, supervising and providing ideas; Uncle Shlomo acted as surrogate father; and Ruchie Friedman played the role of mother, cooking and caring for dozens of young girls left orphaned by the war.

One of the very first weddings to take place after the Holocaust was celebrated in the Bregenz D. P. camp. Volvy's brother Yerucham became engaged to another member of the group named Rochel Rosa. Ruchie Friedman stepped into the shoes of the mother once again, promising the couple that she would make all the arrangements. She began with the *t'naim*, which all the refugees in Bregenz attended as a family. The

Chapter Twenty / 245

wedding was planned for Sunday, December 25, 1945.

There was no *mikveh* in Bregenz, so Rochel — Rachu, as we called her — decided to travel back to Zaltzvedl with a few of her cousins. Europe was still in a state of upheaval then, with a transportation system that operated chaotically. When Rachu and her escorts finally arrived in Zaltzvedl at the beginning of the week, they learned that the *mikveh* would not open until Thursday. With no other option, they were forced to wait — and then to wait again, for the next train back to Austria was not leaving until Saturday night.

After Shabbos they headed home, but their luck did not improve. The train stopped suddenly in the middle of nowhere, about ten miles from Bregenz. It was now Christmas day and there was not a buggy or car to be hired, even for money. Rachu and her cousins started to walk. The wedding was scheduled for one in the afternoon, but they did not return until four or five o'clock, and the *chasunah* had to be postponed until the evening.

Yeruchem and Rachu were fortunate. They had been given the opportunity to show the *Ribono Shel Olam* that they had not abandoned Him, *chas v'shalom*, after the war, that the Jewish nation had gathered together the last few cinders of its charred soul and was holding on to them gingerly. Blessed to share their *simchah* with their fellow survivors, the Friedmans began their new life together in sanctity. They were among the first couples to lift the heads of the Jewish people out of the debris of Europe and to begin building a new generation.

When the Bregenz camp was dissolved, Captain Monnheit arranged passage for the majority of the refugees to Paris, where there was already an organized *hatzalah* effort under the auspices of Agudath Israel. Paris now became a major transfer point for survivors who were hoping to go either to Israel or to America. Volvy and his two teammates quickly went to work again and set up another D. P. camp, taking along Yeruchem and Rachu and many other Friedman relatives. With the help of Mr. Matthew Miller, a lawyer who was president of the Agudah in France, and

Yeruchem and Rachu's wedding in the Bregenz D.P. camp.

another man named Mr. Berret, they were able to purchase a beautiful but neglected old estate in Boulee, a small town outside of Paris. Once again the word went out, and refugees from all corners of the continent began to appear on the quiet, tree-lined walkways of the Boulee camp, knitting together for comfort and courage. Eventually Volvy brought most of them into Paris, where they awaited visas to other destinations.

It was during this period of Volvy's relief work that our correspondence began. It warmed my heart to hear that his time was almost completely dedicated now to the welfare of others. His efforts were soon to touch me in a very personal way — for in one of his letters he wrote that he had found my brother Leiby and was bringing him to Paris. For me, this was one of the most profound miracles of the war's conclusion. My brother had been missing for more than five years, and we had given him up for dead.

Leiby had gone to learn in the Mir while we were still living in Warsaw. After the war broke out, he disappeared into the maelstrom of the Russian invasion of Lithuania and Latvia, and we did not hear from him again. Now, in Volvy's letters, I learned the truth — that Leiby had spent those five years of the war in a Russian prison. He had survived in jail by pretending to be deaf, mute, and retarded, and had passed the time by teaching himself how to make hats. The day after a bird flew through the window of his cell and settled briefly on his head, he was released in a prisoner exchange and returned to Warsaw to look for us.

No one was there. The Warsaw ghetto had been reduced to rubble, burned to the ground during the 1943 uprising. Devorah and I were gone; my mother and sister Chavcia were dead. Yankel had come home from Russia in 1943, very disenchanted with life under the Communist regime, only to find himself on the threshold of the uprising. He became a leader of one of the fighting units and died in the rebellion, but I did not find out about this until I was already living in America. Leiby had come from prison only to meet with another dead end. He now had nothing to his name except Devorah's address in Israel, which he had memorized long ago. He wrote to tell her that he was alive, and in the meantime he supported himself by making hats.

After a time he left Poland with the help of the Vaad Hatzalah and went to Prague, which is where Volvy discovered him. Even today I do not know the full extent of my husband's rescue activities during and after the Holocaust. It seemed to me that he had friends or connections in virtually every country in Europe. Through this elaborate network of contacts, Volvy learned that my brother had been released from prison and was now in Prague. He got in touch with a friend in Vienna named Dr. Kolmar, and asked him to arrange Leiby's passage to Paris.

And that's how it came to be that there were two people waiting for me when I arrived in France — my husband-to-be and my brother, both rare gifts rescued from a treasured past.

On *Erev* Rosh Hashanah of 1946, Volvy traveled from Paris to the port town of Cherbourg to meet my ship. He waited and waited, and when the ship did not come in, he hurried back to his rooming house to prepare for *Yom Tov*. He had been asked to *daven* for the *amud* in a local *minyan*, and he couldn't stay any longer.

My ship did not dock until the following morning. I was completely beside myself. I thought I had been through everything —

but arriving in a strange country in the middle of *Yom Tov*, with no one to greet me and no directions, was something I had never expected. I left all my things on board and disembarked, carrying only the slip of paper on which I had scribbled the address of Volvy's rooming house.

I didn't know a word of French or English, so I did the only thing I could do: I showed that little scrap of paper to every person I passed on the street who looked halfway decent, praying that they would point me in the right direction. I walked all the way to the boarding house in that haphazard manner — going a block or two, stopping the next pedestrian, and then backtracking. I can't report my first impressions of the city, because I didn't have any. I was vaguely aware that it was a warm, sunny day outside, but my eyes were glued to the street signs. I still think of it as a marvelous accident that I found my way to the right place. I breathed a second sigh of relief later that day when officials from the ship delivered my luggage. Thank goodness, I found everything intact.

The boarding house looked more like a large cottage, set back from the road and surrounded by a provincial garden. Volvy was still in *shul* when I arrived, so I sat down and waited for him to come back. I didn't even have a *siddur* or *machzor* with me, having left everything on the ship. I thanked Hashem silently for bringing me to the right address and asked His forgiveness for not having *davened* properly on Rosh Hashanah.

At about four in the afternoon, I heard voices in the hallway — not one, but two: "Is she here yet? Do you think she's here?" I thought I recognized the second voice, but I wasn't sure. I knew that Leiby was in Paris, but I hadn't expected him to come to Cherbourg to meet me.

I opened the door, and there stood the two of them — all of a sudden, after so many years of distance and toil and sorrow. Here was Volvy — the same familiar face, greeting me once again at a time when I was alone and in strange surroundings, reinvoking the pattern of the past; here was my brother, alive from the world of the dead. I didn't know whom I should be gladder to see! All three of us were speechless. It was a moment of unreality, and yet at the same time so natural; we were together, as we should be.

We sat down to the simple *Yom Tov* meal Volvy had prepared. As we ate, I glanced furtively at my brother from time to time. Ever since hearing about his release, I had been very concerned about him, but I saw that my worries were groundless. He had been living with Volvy's brother and sister-in-law, who had fed him and built up his strength, and he was wearing new clothes. The only difference was that he was unusually silent. Leiby had always been a quiet, soft-spoken person, but now he seemed to speak even less; his vocabulary was somewhat limited because he had not talked for so many years in prison, but he would recover the faculty as time went on. Otherwise, thank G-d, he was fine.

Volvy, too, seemed just as I remembered him, though perhaps his face had a firmer set. I looked around that little table and was overwhelmed with gratitude. Volvy and my brother and I, though awkward and shy on the brink of our reentry into the world, were together in safety and in good health, and we stood with hopeful hearts in the doorway of the New Year.

Over the next few days Volvy and I became acquainted again. We were both much more comfortable because my brother was there, acting as an informal chaperon. The two of us ate and took walks together and talked. It did not take very long for us to see that the old connection was still there, and it seemed clear that we would soon become engaged.

After Rosh Hashanah, we returned to Paris. Volvy had rooms in a hotel on Lafayette Street, where several of his relatives were also staying. Many of them had come recently from Boulee, and he was largely supporting them through various business ventures that he had started in Paris. Meeting Volvy's family set the butterflies loose in my stomach. They were a very close-knit clan, and I was walking into the circle a complete outsider, but I tried to find a niche for myself. My brother moved out of Yeruchem and Rachu's apartment and came to stay in Volvy's room in the hotel so that he could be near me, which helped set me at ease.

Volvy, too, was very understanding of my discomfort and did all he could to make me feel at home. He took full responsibility for both my brother and me, paying for our rooms in the hotel and making sure that we had what we needed. Soon after we settled in, he bought a bolt of beige tweed fabric and had nearly identical coats made for the three of us. Soon we were walking jauntily in the streets, looking like the Three Musketeers and feeling almost lighthearted again. Such gestures made me feel more comfortable and took the edge off my sense of displacement.

The culture in Paris was very interesting, much more cosmopolitan than any city I had seen yet. The streets were full of an animated elegance, energetic but without the coarse hustle-bustle of Warsaw or Budapest. The city's artistic stone buildings rose glamorously at night over the waters of the Seine, and counts and princes could frequently be seen riding to the opera or theater. Just below the surface of this glittering pageant throbbed a strong undercurrent of anti-Semitism. The French could tell with one look who we were, and they made us feel unwelcome wherever we went.

In the Pletzel, the quarter where most of the Jews were living, a thriving subculture existed, as far from the stately sophistication of Paris proper as night from day. Here, numberless survivors sought each other out in the crowded buildings of the quarter's narrow alleyways, sharing food and solace, trying to piece together the broken shards of their lives. Volvy seemed to know everyone. His friends were collected from every end of the world and every station of life. He knew many of them from the refugee camps in which he had worked, and now they looked again for his strong arm and dependable advice.

I started out making Shabbos meals for the three of us on the small electric burner I had in the hotel. We were officially not allowed to cook in our rooms, but if we wanted to eat kosher food, there was no other choice. After a short time the word got out that "by Peska you can get a meal," and before I knew it, there were fifteen or sixteen people coming to eat every week. I made *cholent* for all of them on that same tiny burner, which was somehow always just big enough. Volvy's friends were interesting people and they accepted me very quickly — maybe because I could cook!

On Shabbos, my room in the hotel was filled with a band of people as mixed and disparate as the contents of the *cholent* itself. Old and young, they came from behind the barbed-wire fences of Hungary, Poland, Germany, Czechoslovakia — groups of mismatched people who represented the remnant of Jewish Europe and who clung to each other in the pain and joy of rebirth. Among them was a man named Shmuel Lerner, whose sister Tzivia later became my brother's wife. The guests squeezed themselves into the corners of the room, sometimes sitting on the floor or on the windowsills. Those who had no place to sit remained standing; we kept each other company, and we were comfortable enough.

Our meals were not extravagant, but neither were they meager. There was no reliable organized *kashrus* supervision in Paris yet, so we could not eat meat, but we had *challos* and cake from the kosher bakery, fish and sardines, and fresh foods from the outdoor markets. Thank G-d there was enough to eat. As refugees, we were on our own now; we received no help from the French government, but the war had turned us all into a very hardy lot. There was little now that could daunt us. We had seen Hell — the rest was a mild inconvenience. I had no refrigerator and my burner was no bigger than a plate, but I didn't think life could be better than it was.

Volvy and I had been informally engaged for about a month when his brother and sister-in-law treated us to a surprise engagement party. Their apartment was constantly bustling with people, so I did not think much of it when we came in one evening to find a crowd in the dining room. But something was different this time. The table was beautifully laid out with fruit, cake, and *schnapps*, and the people had a look of pleasant antici-

With my friend Magda Seidenfeld, in Paris.   *Yeruchem and Rachu.*

pation on their faces. Yeruchem and Rachu greeted us with a hearty *Mazel tov*. They had invited a *rav*, who wrote our *t'naim* for us that evening. When I saw the two *eidim* signing the paper, the reality was suddenly before me: the war was really over, and I was in Paris, and I was safe — and I was engaged to be married! I couldn't believe my good fortune.

Volvy and I wrote to my sister and brothers in *Eretz Yisrael* and told them the good news. We planned to be married in Paris at the beginning of January. I begged Reb Boruch to come for the wedding, hoping very much that he would be our *mesader kiddushin*.

I spent the next two months or so trying to put together the wedding myself. There was almost nothing to be gotten in Paris at that time. Stores were open but merchandise was scarce, as most of the goods had disappeared during the war years. The wife of one of Volvy's friends, a girl named Magda Seidenfeld who was familiar with the ins and outs of the city, told me about a place where I could purchase white fabric. With her help I sewed my own wedding gown. I also made myself a headpiece with tiny white doves on it, reminiscent of the doves that had adorned the bride's chair in my mother's wedding room in Warsaw.

I thought of my mother often, grieved that she would not be able to walk me down the aisle. I prayed quietly that she would

Chapter Twenty / 253

> חדש טבת תש"ז פה פריס
> הננו מתכבדים להזמין את כבודו לבא על שמחת נשואין של
>
> הבתולה הכלה מרת   עב"ג החתן כמר
> **פסה ראבינאוויטש** תחי'   **זאב פריעדמאנן-קאהאן** ני"
> בת הרב הגאון האדמו"ר   בן המנוח הנגיד והסיד
> מפרצי"ב זצוקלה"ה   ר' נפתלי פריעדמאן זצ"ל הי"ד
>
> שתתקיים אי"ה בשטו"מ ביום א' שמות תש"ז (5 יאנואר 1947)
> במעין רע'טא-אנט אינטערנאציאנאל Rue Roi DE SICILE 22
>
> בכבוד רב
>
> מצד הכלה   מצד החתן
> הרב ב"וך י. י. ראבינאוויטש   לאה פריעדמאנו
> האב"ד ור"מ דק"ק מונקאטש יצ"ו   זכרון מאיר—בני ברק
>
> Télégr. : FRIEDMAN, Otellafayette, PARIS

My wedding invitation

come and walk beside me in spirit. She had always liked Volvy, and I felt sure that she had given her blessing in heaven to the match; but even so, I had no idea how painful it would be to go to the *chupah* without her.

The wedding meal was patched together in bits and pieces from various sources. We were able to purchase baked goods, fresh fruit, and fish, and we made a herring salad ourselves. My brother-in-law Jacob Landau had a cousin in Paris by the name of Hertzberg, a refugee who was a winemaker by profession, and he made a batch of wine especially for us. Then we heard of a man named Wagshal who owned a small hall in the Pletzel. It wasn't exactly a hall in the modern sense; it was simply a room in a dilapidated old apartment building that was available for functions, but we were very glad to have it. We rented it together with another couple, Binyomin Oestreicher and his *kallah* Faigie, both of whom were marrying for the second time. The Oestreichers were to have their *chupah* at three o'clock in the afternoon; ours would be at seven, and we would have the meal together. The date was set for January 5, 1947.

One of the happiest moments of my life was when my brother

arrived from *Eretz Yisrael* for the wedding. It was the most wonderful wedding gift I could have received, a reprieve from my sudden plunge into the unknown. After leaving Reb Boruch and his family in Tel Aviv, braced for the prospect of a permanent separation, I had been granted a few extra weeks with the person who had received me with love from the clutches of the war and to whom I owed so much.

I did everything I could to make my brother comfortable. I wanted to feed him decently and bought two chickens and a goose at considerable cost, for meat was a delicacy in postwar Europe. We hired a *shochet* to come up to my room at the hotel and slaughter them on the spot, but this left us in a sticky spot. Because of the regulations against cooking in the rooms, we could not afford to have the remainders of three dead birds found in our garbage cans! Cleverly, we asked a number of friends to come up to the room with newspapers, and we sent everybody home with a "package." When the hotel boy came around to empty our wastebaskets, there wasn't a scrap of evidence left, and I had the satisfaction of providing my brother with several respectable meals after his long and tiring journey.

The day of the *chasunah* was a leaden winter day, raining and misty. I remember slogging on foot through the mud from Lafayette Street to the Pletzel together with the Biale *Rebbetzin*, praying that my *mazel* would be better than the weather.

Before the *badecking*, I was sitting in the reception room in my homemade wedding gown when I suddenly began to shake. A rush of panic vibrated through my system; I realized with a startling intensity that I had no idea at all what I was walking into. I know that this is not an uncommon feeling for a young bride, but I was not an ordinary bride. I had chosen my new life without parents, without even the security of convention — for Volvy had already lost a wife and child, and on paper our match was less than desirable. My rational judgment had never dictated too many things to me, but rather my instinct and a sense of blind trust in G-d and in people. That instinct had not led me astray before, but now it suddenly seemed undefined and uncertain.

When Reb Boruch came in to give me a *berachah*, I burst into tears. I never cried during all the years of the war as I cried then. A film flashed rapidly before my mind's eye: I saw and felt vividly the love of my father, who should have been in Reb Boruch's place; the caring of my mother; the closeness of my siblings. My feelings were a stream of every color and shade in the rainbow, a combination of thankfulness to Hashem *Yisbarach* for the presence of my two brothers, prayer for the future, and fright. I never regretted my decision, but I was scared to death.

The Biale Rebbe, my unterfierer.

I didn't want Reb Boruch to leave the room. My soul clung to him with a desperate hold, for I knew that when he walked out, my past would be gone and I would be left to fend for myself. And he blessed me and left; and I was on my own . . . going forward.

When I went out to the *chupah*, my eyes were red and my face swollen, but I didn't care. I had expressed myself from the heart, and that was all that mattered. My *unterfierers* were the Biale *Rebbe* and his wife. The *Rebbe* was the son of Chavale Rabinowitz, the aunt who had died of typhoid fever in our house in the Warsaw ghetto seven years earlier. The *Rebbetzin* had given me a great deal of emotional support and advice before the wedding, and I was glad that my own blood relatives were able to accompany me down the aisle.

Somehow I knew that my mother was there beside me too, her grip firm on my arm, her gaze steady and moist. I was only now beginning to understand how much she had loved me. I knew that she was sending me her blessing from the other world,

At my wedding. From left: Zissy Friedman, a friend whom I met in Paris; two officials from the Slovakian embassy; Binyomin and Faigie Oestreicher; me and my husband. Leiby is standing in the back.

and I promised her in my heart that I would try my best to be true to her teachings.

The *chupah* took place in the courtyard of the building, under the wintry January sky. As I stepped outside, I looked up and saw dozens and dozens of people crowded together on the balcony that ran around the second floor of the building. There were even more people in the streets, masses of people as far as the eye could see. It took me a moment to realize that they had come to my wedding — scores of people whom I had never set eyes on in my life. Ours was one of the first Jewish weddings to be held in Paris after the war, and it looked as though every single person in town who still retained his Jewish identity was there.

At least seven hundred people attended the reception that evening — some invited, most not. There were even two officials there from the Slovakian embassy, whom Volvy had met through his relief work. People told me afterward that they would not have missed the wedding for anything. For many, it thawed out the numbness in their hearts and reawakened yearnings they had thought they would never feel again. It was an announcement that life could — and would — go on.

There were no flowers at my wedding and no smorgasbord. We did not even have any music, for there was no one to play it. There were only hopeful faces and good wishes and sincerity — and on these we built our union.

I stood under the *chupah* surrounded by that swelling throng of well-wishers — Mrs. Volvy Friedman, several lifetimes away from my home in Siedlice, on the edge of an unshaped future —nervous, determined, and very, very happy.

My husband and me before we left Paris.

Chapter Twenty-One

Volvy and I stayed in Paris for less than a month after our wedding, part of the time at the hotel and part of the time at Yeruchem and Rachu's apartment. I had had a feeling ever since leaving Israel that my husband's destiny lay in America and that if we returned to European shores, it would be only to visit. When I left the continent, I cut the last fragile strand of connection to my old life, the last trace of the ever-present human dream that things will somehow return to the way they once were. My family was a unit now only in spirit, and I would begin my own without their closeness and support. The only reminder of the pleasures of my youth was my brother Leiby, who followed us to America a few months later with his *kallah*, Tzivia Lerner. He, too, no longer had a home in Europe.

We traveled across the ocean on a Pan American flight, with only the clothes on our backs and one or two small valises. We had accumulated many gifts during our weeks in Paris, but it was impossible to take everything along. Volvy knew a refugee couple with several children who were planning to come to

America by boat, and they agreed to take our boxes and hold them until we picked them up in New York.

We left Paris on January 31, 1947. The trip took about twelve hours, with one stop in Shannon, Ireland. As if to remind me that there was no safe nest waiting for me on either side of the Atlantic, the flight was awful. The small propeller plane knocked and bumped its way across the ocean, and I was sick the entire way.

I did not have any idea where we were going to stay when we arrived in New York — but my husband did. "We're going to Ruchie Friedman," he said simply. Ruchie, my husband's comrade and fellow relief worker, was now living with her siblings in East New York, a neighborhood which had become a haven for survivors. We showed up on the Friedmans' doorstep to stay for the night, and we stayed for half a year.

We never got our belongings back from the family who had brought them over on the ship. Volvy's friend said that he had no idea what had happened to the boxes, and that was the clearest answer we ever received from him. In those boxes were all our *drusha geshank*, including a silver *esrog* box that Devorah had given me, along with my entire trousseau. The only item of value I had taken with me on the plane were my *leichter*, a gift from Reb Boruch, and that is why I still have them today. I never saw my other things again.

But that was not the worst of our slippery start in our new country. Through various business ventures, my husband had accumulated a substantial sum of money in Paris. When he went to the bank in New York to redeem the money, he was told that the transferral papers he presented had been falsely drawn up. In other words, they were worthless.

"We know you're an honest man," the bank official told Volvy. "You just came to America, and we know you didn't steal these papers. But they are not authentic. You can leave them here and go free — but if you fight us, we'll have no choice but to turn you in. You could wind up in jail."

In an hour we were penniless. We did not even have a nickel

With my husband (left) and my brother Leiby in front of a butcher shop in East New York. We also sent this photo to my mother-in-law in Israel to show her that we were able to buy kosher meat in America.

to get on the train. We had less than nothing — nothing except each other and faith. We had been swindled twice: Hitler had taken six years of our lives, and those we trusted had taken our money. It took many months for us to regain a sound financial footing. But as I had learned in the past, an ending is never truly an ending; often it simply marks a new and difficult beginning. I was able to tell myself that as bleak as our situation was, I had seen worse, times when the tunnel in front of me was so narrow and filled with a blackness so thick that it was nearly impenetrable — times when I waited for a small bird to hop into the road in front of me and guide me to safety. G-d has many ways of sending His messengers to us, and He never lets us flounder for very long.

I also had one priceless asset whose power had not diminished over the years — my *berachah* from Reb Shayale Czechower, *zt"l*. Not long after our arrival in America, I learned that I was carrying twins. We were elated and worried at the same time, anxious not to wear out our hosts' welcome. When we were in a position to consider moving out of their home, we began to hunt for an apartment. We finally found one in Williamsburg that was suitable and within our budget, and we were just about to make the final settlement when the landlord remarked, "You know, I had a nice young couple living here, but she got pregnant, so I told them to move out . . . but I don't know. I like you. I'd like you to have the apartment."

I was already four months pregnant, and I didn't know if I should say something or not. We were desperate to have a place of our own, and this was the best we had seen so far. I held my tongue, and we moved in; but after a few days, I began to feel uncomfortable and decided it would cause worse trouble later if I did not lay all my cards on the table. I found an opportunity to mention to the owner that I was expecting.

"Never mind," he said with a wave of his hand, and that was that. I wish Reb Shayale were alive today so that I could thank him for all the wonderful benefits his *berachah* gave me over the years.

It was only after our arrival in America that I was finally able to fill in the last remaining gap in the chronicle of our family's wartime history.

Of all my siblings, five were fortunate enough to survive the scourge of Hitler: my brothers Boruch, Elazar, and Leiby, my sister Devorah, and myself. Chavcia had perished of illness; of Yankel, my brave and good-hearted oldest brother, we had heard nothing.

In 1947 I happened upon a book written in Hebrew called *Yoman Ghetto Warsaw*, by Dr. Hillel Zeidman, in which he described my brother's fate. It seems that Yankel had returned to the ghetto from Russia in 1943, only to find that my mother had passed away. There was no one left at home; he was alone. Seeking a purpose in his suddenly barren life, he had gotten heavily involved in the resistance effort, dedicating himself heart and soul to the defense of the ghetto Jews. During this time he was arrested in a roundup and deported to Majdanek, where he was given the job of loading the clothing of gas chamber victims onto wagons bound out of the concentration camp.

One day he decided to risk escape by climbing into one of the wagons and burying himself in the garments. The Nazis discovered during the roll call that day that one person was missing from the count and began a search. They approached the wagon where Yankel was hiding, thrust their bayonets into the pile of clothing — and missed. Thus, Yankel escaped and returned to the

Warsaw ghetto to continue his resistance work. During Pesach of 1943, when the uprising broke out, he was one of the first people to climb the wall of the ghetto with a grenade in hand, but he was killed immediately by a Nazi soldier.

Reading this account of my brother's final hours struck fresh blows to my heart. Although in some sense I was relieved to know with certainty what had happened to him, I was astonished by the force and depth of the pain. Over three years had gone by since I had left Germany. I did not know if the bruises would ever disappear completely, but I wondered if they would even fade . . .

When my children were born, I made a firm decision to lock the past out of my consciousness. I wanted my kids to grow up normally, laughing and playing, with no Hitler in sight; I did not want them to suffer the burden of the suffocating sadness that still clouded my heart. I knew, too, that the *Shechinah* would not follow me in sorrow and that I would not be able to establish a joyful home in the shadow of the Holocaust.

For all those years, I put it away. I tried to behave like an ordinary person, to focus on normal needs. It went so far that I actually began to forget the names of people I had known during the war. I remembered numbers, but not names; names were too personal. All of us, the *"greene,"* came to America with our loads on our backs, haunted by nightmares and longing for the sacred havens of our youth, but we tried to crush our memories in an effort to enter the mainstream. And we were in a rush. We wanted to establish ourselves quickly in a community, in a livelihood, in a home. We competed strongly in our urgent bids for a very, very ordinary existence.

I can't say our children didn't feel the aftershocks of our tragedy. Despite our most valiant efforts, the war had built an uncertainty and a tension into our souls that seemed to surface involuntarily, again and again. It hurt us that we could not accommodate our children with the ease that the Americans did, that we could not immediately give them the comfortable life that we wished for them, both financially and emotionally. But we tried our best to be happy around them and to shield them from our hurts. Although their consciousness of the Holocaust was raised by their environment and schooling as they were growing up and we had to promise them that we would tell them more about it "one day," I like to believe that we did not weigh them down unfairly with the intensity of our feelings. I hope that we were at least partially successful.

I think that even if we had wanted to talk about our pain in the early years, we would not have had the words to express it. We ourselves did not understand it. We were lacerated; the wounds were still festering, so open and raw that we didn't know where one pain ended and the next began. We could not subdivide our experiences coherently and view them in a rational way, to understand exactly how we had been affected and what our suffering meant to us as Jews. After the soreness had subsided a little, we were able to see the central threads of the Holocaust more clearly. And even though we still didn't understand them, there was more room in our hearts for acceptance and more of a willingness to continue living.

I thank G-d every day that I am still walking with my head up, that I did not fall a moral sacrifice to all the influences that crossed my path when I left my mother's house in the Warsaw ghetto. I don't claim this to my credit; I have no doubt that it is *z'chus avos*. As the years go by, I see more and more how true it is that one should listen to the *z'keinim*. I trusted my parents, but I didn't understand everything they said. Now I see that the wisdom of a *zakein* is more than a young person can possibly know.

It is my parents who have gone before me every step of my life, lighting the way over the obstacles ahead. I see their faces continually in front of me: my father's eyes, blue and smiling, and my mother's, direct and knowing. They brought out the best in their children; they gave me the inner security to face all the trials of my life and to remain standing upright. It is because of their guidance that I have been able to carry on my father's heritage and to fulfill my mother's requests. It is because of them that I am still going forward, thank G-d — only forward.

Afterword / A Friend's Tribute to Mr. Wolf Friedman ז״ל

by Joseph Friedenson

Much, though not enough, has been written about the Holocaust, but there is a related chapter of Jewish history that has barely been touched: the marvelous phenomenon of the survivors' vigorous rebirth.

This resurgence is truly unfathomable. Nearly all the liberated Jews left the camps famished and naked, physically and spiritually exhausted, orphaned of parents and bereft of siblings. Nevertheless, with the exception of the thousands who died soon after the War as a result of their privations in the camps, the great majority of the survivors recovered quickly. In the Displaced Persons camps or in the crowded apartments of various German cities, young Jews married and established new homes, and began living normal lives. Their accomplishments in many areas and their contributions to burgeoning Jewish life in Israel and the Diaspora are truly amazing.

Anyone who looks back to that period knows that the credit is due to a number of spiritual heroes from among the survivors. They were no better off than their fellow camp alumni, but they found the strength not only to renew themselves, but to encourage others to begin a new existence as human beings — and especially as Jews.

Without question, one of those chosen few was R' Wolf Friedman, husband of the author of this book, who emerged in the United States as one of the finest personalities in the Orthodox community. He was acknowledged as a model Torah layman — one who loved Torah, honored Torah, and supported Torah study and institutions — who pursued opportunities to help others and who possessed boundless personal virtue. Mainly, however, he earned respect for his activism. For over thirty years, from the moment he set foot on American soil, he served the community with loyalty and dedication. He was active in Agudath Israel and in any number of projects for the benefit of the Torah community. He maintained this devotion to his very last breath, even in the two pain-filled years of his final illness.

Much of this can be ascribed to his lineage and education. He came from a fervent chassidic family that was proud of its many prominent rabbis and outstanding scholars. His father, R' Naftali Friedman, was close to the Munkaczer Rebbe, the *Minchas Elazar*. The family of his grandfather, R' Chaim, the renowned rabbi of Dombrad, was famous throughout Hungary for its scholars and authors. His grandfather, R' Leibush Ackerman, one of the most prominent disciples of Munkacz, was known throughout the country as R' Leibush Strobitchier, proprietor of a large mill that provided a livelihood for the entire *shtetl*. In his youth, Wolf Friedman studied in several well-known Hungarian and Slovakian yeshivos, among them Selesz, Riskeve — where he was ordained at the age of 17 by the Riskever Rav — and Pressburg. He was one of the few young *b'nai Torah* from Hungary who studied in the yeshivos of Mir and Lublin.

From the start of World War II, he distinguished himself as a rescue activist. When Nazi-allied Hungary began deporting many Jews to slave-labor camps, he freed many prisoners by forging passports and he helped support the families of deportees. In the end, R' Wolf himself fell into the hands of the Nazis and endured terrible suffering in a concentration camp for the last several months of the war. Even there, in the vale of tears, he was outstanding for kindness to his fellow prisoners.

I remember the Melaveh Malkah at R' Wolf's *sh'loshim*, where Rabbi Shlomo Fishoff, a distinguished scholar from pre-War Pressburg, recalled him from the notorious concentration camp Finfteichen, in Germany. R' Wolf gave strength and encouragement to his suffering brethren and often shared his last morsel of bread and meager soup ration with others who were on the verge of death. Others who were with him in the camps related similar stories of his unselfish devotion to others.

One of the proudest chapters of his community service came immediately after the war. In the Jewish settlement of Bregens, Austria, he set up a kosher kitchen and revivified the religious life of the liberated survivors. He was especially involved in caring for orphaned youths and children, reigniting their enthusiasm for Judaism. Later on, he was similarly involved in the institutions of Agudath Israel and Vaad Hatzoloh in Paris, where young survivors were helped, both physically and spiritually.

Wolf Friedman Chairing Agudath Israel's 42nd dinner in 1964.
From L-R: Mr. Friedman (speaking), Rabbi Yaakov Kamenetzky, Rabbi Chaim Mordechai Katz, Rabbi Yaakov Yitzchak Ruderman, Rabbi Moshe Feinstein, Rabbi Moshe Horowitz, Rabbi Menachem Porush, Rabbi Moshe Sherer, Rabbi Gedaliah Schorr, Rabbi Chaim Krieger.

Mr. Friedman being presented with an award by Rabbi Moshe Feinstein at Agudath Israel's dinner in 1966 as Rabbi Yaakov Kamenetzky looks on.

As we see from the memoirs of his wife, Wolf Friedman was far from wealthy when he arrived in the United States, and he earned a livelihood only with great difficulty — but, nevertheless, he threw himself into community work, under the aegis of Agudath Israel. He helped organize the quickly growing branch in Crown Heights, and later became deeply involved in the national organization, where he was always among the first to take part in any new national or international initiative.

At the same time, he did not neglect his own Torah study. For twenty years, he and two friends, Mr. Chaim Hertz and Mr. Gavriel Fixler, had a daily *daf yomi* session during the commute to their offices. Mr. Friedman would review the Gemara over his morning coffee and, even though he was the driver — the *baal agalah*, as he called himself — he would lead the often heated discussions in the car, on the *daf*.

In the late '50's and early '60's, Wolf Friedman was one of the key leaders in strengthening the organization's fiscal standing. For many years, a small group of Agudah leaders met in his home every Sunday; those meetings were instrumental in planning its phenomenal growth and expansion. For many years, despite the pressures of his own business, he served the Agudah as Chairman of the Finance Commission and as National Treasurer, and was active on all fronts. He was one of the main organizers of the increasingly popular national conventions and of the Fifth and Sixth Knessiah Gedolahs in Jerusalem, where he was twice elected to the World Executive of the Agudah. At the Sixth Knessiah, he was also elected one of the treasurers of the World Agudath Israel.

However, his communal work was not limited to Agudath Israel. A broad array of institutions benefited from his wisdom and generosity. First among them was the village of New Square. He became close to the Skverer Rebbe זצ״ל in the '50's and for a long time held monthly parlor meetings in his home to help support the growth of the Rebbe's institutions. He became treasurer of New Square's building campaigns and took personal responsibility for its bonds. He was also one of the pillars of the Vielepoler Rebbe's congregation, K'hal Bnei Shlomo Zalman, where he delivered a regular Talmud shiur and served as the Rosh Hashanah-Yom Kippur *baal tefillah*.

Wolf Friedman's outstanding contributions to communities and organizations tended to overshadow his outstanding character. He was a loyal and generous friend. With his wife, he maintained a home that was always open to guests. Indeed, many of his closest friends first came to know him as beneficiaries of his hospitality. The Friedman home, like the Friedmans themselves, was a model for all Jews.

Wolf and Peska Friedman personified the heroism and commitment of the Jewish people, the virtues that kept our nation alive after its oppressors were defeated and forgotten. They personified the Jewish determination to go forward — always *"going forward"*!

This volume is part of
THE ARTSCROLL SERIES®
an ongoing project of
translations, commentaries and expositions
on Scripture, Mishnah, Talmud, Halachah,
liturgy, history and the classic Rabbinic writings;
and biographies, and thought.

For a brochure of current publications
visit your local Hebrew bookseller
or contact the publisher:

Mesorah Publications, ltd

4401 Second Avenue
Brooklyn, New York 11232
(718) 921-9000